J 6P $07.25

The Spirit and Purpose of Planning

The Built Environment Series includes:

Introduction to Transportation Planning *M. J. Bruton*
Introduction to Regional Planning *John Glasson*
Introduction to Town and Country Planning *John Ratcliffe*
Introduction to Town Planning Techniques *Margaret Roberts*
Citizens in Conflict *James Simmie*
The Dynamics of Urbanism *P. F. Smith*
The Future of Cities (*in association with the Open University Press*)

The Spirit and Purpose of Planning

Edited by
M. J. Bruton

Head of the
School of
Planning and
Landscape, City
of Birmingham
Polytechnic

HUTCHINSON OF LONDON

Hutchinson & Co (Publishers) Ltd
3 Fitzroy Square, London W1

London Melbourne Sydney Auckland
Wellington Johannesburg Cape Town
and agencies throughout the world

First published April 1974
© M. J. Bruton 1974

Set in Monotype Times
Printed and bound in Great Britain by
R J Acford Ltd, Industrial Estate,
Chichester, Sussex

ISBN 0 09 119960 3 (Cased)
         0 09 119961 1 (Paperback)

Contents

Preface

Although control over the physical layout and design of settlements was practised by the Greeks and Romans, Town Planning as a modern art and taught discipline is a relative newcomer. Its development in the late nineteenth century was stimulated by the aftermath of the Industrial Revolution and the efforts of social reformers. For almost three-quarters of a century the design and layout of settlement, and the control of land use, were practised in an attempt to overcome many of the social and economic problems manifest in both the built and physical environment.

More recently there has been a growing appreciation of the complex nature of these problems and an awareness that the control of land use and the design and layout of settlement cannot in isolation be expected to resolve these problems. This in turn has led to a questioning of the role and nature of Town Planning in modern society, and the development of new forms of planning such as Social Planning, Economic Planning, Transport Planning and Corporate Planning.

As a result of these developments and changes, the shape and purpose of planning as a whole has been obscured and questioned, with its many practitioners following paths which at times appear to be divergent. This book is offered as an introduction to the various forms of planning which are concerned to secure the improvement of social and physical conditions. It outlines the philosophy and purpose of planning, traces the development of planning thought and examines the scope and content of Physical, Social, Economic, Transport and Corporate Planning. Throughout, an emphasis is given to the inter-relationships between Physical Planning and the other forms of planning.

Although the book embodies contributions from several individuals, each section has been written with an agreed structure and objectives in mind. Through the selection of the contributors and the structuring of the book, an attempt has been made to secure a level of integration comparable with that which might have been achieved had the book been written by one person. Any shortcomings in this direction are my responsibility.

M. J. Bruton

1. Introduction: General Planning and Physical Planning

Michael J. Bruton

Whenever and wherever planning is discussed confusion is encountered as to the precise meaning of many of the terms used. At times it seems that planning means all things to all people, and in this situation lies an explanation for the apparent divergence of views amongst planners. The Concise Oxford Dictionary unhelpfully indicates that a plan is 'a drawing; a diagram made by projection on a flat surface especially one showing the relative position of parts of a building; a large-scale detailed map of a town or district; a table indicating times, places, etc. of intended proceedings, etc.; a scheme of arrangements; a project; a design; a way of proceeding'. More helpfully the same dictionary defines the verb to plan as 'to design, scheme, arrange beforehand (procedure etc.)'. Although the way in which these definitions are set out does not really clarify what planning is, nevertheless they do contain the essence of what planning is about, and point to what is a very basic confusion, i.e. the difference between what could be called general planning and physical planning. By implication general planning is seen as a procedure whereby one schemes or arranges beforehand, and as an activity this is undertaken to a greater or lesser extent by individuals (planning journeys, holidays, budgets) and corporate bodies (planning budgets, policies, etc.). Physical planning on the other hand is seen as referring to a physical design of something which already exists or might exist in the future and this sort of plan is a representation, in a geographical or spatial sense, of actual physical structures or elements. Now it is apparent that the majority of general plans have physical components, for instance an individual general plan to have a touring holiday on the continent would involve the mapping of the routes to be followed if the holiday is to be efficiently organised. Similarly a corporate local authority general plan to improve the health and welfare services could include a physical plan locating and designing health clinics. Depending on the nature of these general plans so the extent of the physical component will vary.

The characteristics of the general planning process implied in the ability to scheme or arrange beforehand are many and varied. For example, successfully to arrange beforehand one must be able to anticipate future events, and be capable of analysing and evaluating situations and circumstances, whilst an innovative ability is often essential if a satisfactory and acceptable plan or solution is to be derived. In these characteristics it is possible to distinguish a strong relationship between principles of management and the principles of planning, and indeed it could be argued that general planning is an aspect of the management process. Physical planning, on the other hand, is seen as representing physical structures in a geographical or spatial sense—a plan for a ship, or a dam, or a house, or a motorway is a physical plan. Yet these physical plans are related to, and are often integral elements of, other more general plans. The decision to construct a dam could well form part of a general plan to improve the supply of electricity to certain parts of the country. Equally it could form part of a general plan to increase the agricultural productivity of an area through irrigation. More likely it could form part of a general plan to achieve both objectives, i.e. the plan for a dam is a physical element within a general plan which has a series of different or multiple objectives.

Town Planning

The position of town planning (also frequently referred to as town and country planning, physical planning or spatial planning, territorial planning or urban and regional planning) within this loose framework of general and physical planning, is difficult to determine. To some people town planning refers to the Town Planning Movement, which had its origins in the social reforms of the nineteenth century. This movement eventually developed a practice and a profession of its own which had and has expression through the Royal Town Planning Institute. More recently town planning has developed (or is developing, depending on one's point of view) into a discipline in its own right. The movement, the profession and the discipline each have a different aspect of town planning and it is important that these aspects are clearly distinguished.

Town Planning Movement

Historically the Town Planning Movement was based on a comprehensive concern for improving social conditions in town and cities—through the medium of physical plans for town, country, and suburb the social reformers, like Robert Owen, Cadbury, and Ebenezer Howard, hoped to eradicate the social problems of overcrowding, poverty, ill-health, unemployment, and insanitary and inadequate living accommodation. Early practitioners in the movement, such as Geddes, developed this view. They saw that for town planning to be successful it must be concerned with the town as a whole including both the physical fabric and the life and activities contained within the town.

Town Planning—Practice and Profession

From these socially motivated beginnings the practice of town planning developed. In the early years it was moulded by the influence of the professions of architecture and engineering, although the legislation and statutory instruments introduced by successive governments have largely determined the practice of town planning. The aims of the first town planning act—The Housing, Town Planning, Etc. Act 1909—reflected the social concern of the Town Planning Movement, viz. 'to provide a domestic condition for the people in which their physical health, their morals, their character and their whole social condition can be improved',[1] but the Act failed to give any clear indication of what was involved in the practice of town planning. However, conferences organised by the Royal Institute of British Architects in 1910, and the Institution of Municipal and County Engineers in 1911, were formative in developing the design orientation of town planning practice, which rapidly came to be seen solely as a question of land use, layout, and physical design. Subsequent legislation tended to reinforce this design orientation. The Town Planning Institute was founded in 1914 and through its policy towards qualification for membership, tended to confirm the design emphasis of planning practice. For example, until 1931 admission to the Institute was obtained through a professional qualification in an allied architectural, engineering or surveying profession plus a post-professional qualification in town planning. In 1931 it became possible to obtain a town planning qualification without a prior professional training in an allied field although the emphasis was still on 'design'. Planning and related legislation passed since the Second World War emphasised the physical and spatial aspects of planning, by concerning itself primarily with questions of location and mobility, the design of new towns, new suburban estates, town expansion, and urban renewal. The definition of town planning which was put forward by the Town Planning Institute in 1967 reflects this emphasis, 'Town Planning is a process, involving a recurring cycle of operations, for preparing and controlling the implementation of plans for changing systems of land-use and settlement of varying scale',[2] although in more recent years the production of the PAG Report,[3] and the passing of the Town and Country Planning Act 1968, focussed the attention of practising planners on the problems of the town and its inhabitants as a whole, while recognising that the improvement and development of the physical fabric is an important element in this process.

Town Planning as a Discipline

Town planning as a discipline has emerged from the education policy of the Institute and the efforts of educationalists in universities and other colleges of higher education. The first examination syllabus of the Institute was issued in 1916, and the first examinations held in 1920. In the 1930s the Institute introduced the policy of 'recognising' certain town planning schools, and judged these schools against the yardstick of the Institute's final examinations. As a result the educational policy of the Institute has been fundamental in influencing the development of Town Planning as a discipline.

In the early years the teaching of town planning was dominated by the architectural and design professions, and the town planning schools were inevitably associated with schools of architecture. Architectural theory and teaching methods shaped the discipline, whilst all the early town planning courses were post-professional in timing. Although separate schools of planning, providing full-time undergraduate education, were set up in the immediate post-war years, it was not until the recommendations of the Schuster Report were accepted and implemented in the 1950s, that graduates from disciplines such as economics, geography and sociology, were admitted to the post-professional planning courses.[4] This influx of new blood to the profession, allied with a growing awareness that other significant aspects of planning, e.g. transport planning, economic development planning, were being developed outside the profession and practice of town planning, led to a conflict within the profession.

On the one hand it was felt that town planning as a discipline needed to expand its area of interest beyond the physical plan dealing with location and land use, to develop new planning knowledge, and produce new kinds of planners. On the other hand it was felt that town planning should confine itself to physical, spatial, and land use planning.

The upshot of this conflict resulted in the Town Planning Institute, and hence the recognised schools of planning, opting for the production of a 'generalist' planner with an extended but limited responsibility for the whole range of what could be loosely called environmental planning, encompassing issues of location, movement and the use of land as a resource, and the design and implementation of physical proposals such as new towns, urban renewal and rehabilitation. It is generally held amongst many town planners that this development has enabled town planning to establish itself as a discipline in its own right.

At the same time, however, there has been an attempt by some planners and other professionals to develop a planning system which reflects the social concern of the Town Planning Movement and attempts to cope with the problems endemic in the physical fabric of our towns and cities. In effect these critics are making the point that something more than a physical plan dealing with location, mobility and use of land is required to cope with the problems encountered in our towns and cities. Rather they are arguing that what is needed is a 'general' type of plan which deals with broad issues such as population, housing, employment, and transport; which concerns itself with social, educational, health and welfare policies. Out of this general plan, more specific physical/location plans will be produced to deal with physical problems as and when particular aspects of these policies need to be implemented in a locational or design way.

The Nature of Planning Problems

Most problems facing towns and cities in this country are related to four main issues—population, housing, employment and movement. Indeed it can be claimed that increases in population, the rate of that increase, and changes in the distribution of that population, are the root cause of many of the problems facing planners. At this moment in time approximately 50 per cent of the population of Great Britain live in the seven conurbations (in and around London, Birmingham, Liverpool, Manchester, Leeds—Bradford, Newcastle and Glasgow). A further 30 per cent (approximately) live in other towns. Thus the greater part of the total population of this country is urban, and consequently urban problems affect and influence approximately 80 per cent of the total population. In 1947 the population of Great Britain was 48 million; by 1971 it had increased to 54 million—an increase of 12·5 per cent. Thus in 25 years an additional 6 million people have had to be accommodated in this country, although it would be far from true to claim that all the needs of this additional population, such as schools, houses, shops, and factories, have been met in new accommodation, as a proportion of this additional need has been met by intensifying the use of existing buildings. In many cases this has led to problems of overcrowding, and the utilisation of accommodation of poor quality.

Although the total population in Great Britain has grown in this period, certain of the more remote parts of the country have suffered a decline in population, e.g. the Scottish Highlands, Wales, the South West, the North of England. Indeed it is estimated that between 1951 and 1961 some 300 000 people left the North of England and Wales for the towns and cities whilst in the same period the population of the South-East of England increased by almost 500 000. More recently the changing balance of population distribution has been further affected by the influx of migrants from the Commonwealth countries, the majority of whom have settled in the larger towns and cities. Such developments have placed inordinate pressures on the existing supply of jobs, accommodation, and facilities for movement, with the result that a myriad of problems within these areas has been intensified.

In the field of housing these pressures have led to a situation where the supply of housing accommodation is insufficient to meet the demand; where overcrowding in insanitary and inadequate accommodation is the order of the day for certain sections of the population; where lack of choice, high rents, an absence of accommodation to rent, and the establishment of areas with inadequate ancillary services such as schools, health and welfare facilities is commonplace.

In employment, the response to changing technology in certain manufacturing and comparatively high paying industries is that firms are moving out of parts of the large towns and cities and creating local areas of unemployment. This tends to reduce the range of employment opportunities available to the poorly educated manual worker, who is also disadvantaged by the increase of employment opportunities in the service section where 'white collar' (and generally better paid) positions are not available to him. The alternatives—either to accept a comparatively poorly paid menial service job, or commute to find a better paid job in manufacturing—tend to result in a reduction in the income or standard of living of the persons thus affected, so much so that in many instances poverty and low wages compound the problems already faced in the field of inadequate and insufficient housing. The problem is exacerbated by the 'flight' to the suburbs of those who can afford it, leaving behind the poor, and local authority tenants living in high density estates.

On the transport front the difficulties associated with moving around our towns and cities are readily apparent and publicised—congestion, delay, accidents, inaccessibility and comparatively high costs affect all sections of the community. However, it is inevitably the poorly paid who are worst affected in that either an appropriate means of transport is not available to cater for the type of journeys required, or the cost of making those journeys by an appropriate means of transport is prohibitive. Poor accessibility restricts freedom of choice on the part of the people affected, and the resultant frustrations can have unforeseen repercussions.

Although it is possible to categorise urban problems under the broad headings of population, employment, housing and movement, to do so runs the risk of obscuring what is perhaps the most significant aspect of urban problems—that is, their inter-related nature. Problems of one sort—inadequate housing, and educational facilities—tend to be reinforced by other types of problems—local unemployment due to firms moving out of the area, and a consequent reduction in income for many. This in turn can be compounded by problems of yet another type, for example, the elimination or reduction of level of service of public transport serving the area, reducing accessibility to other parts of the city, and hence reducing the levels of choice of the area. These problems inter-connect one with the other, and over time increase in magnitude and intensity.

Yet these problems are not new—they are essentially the same problems which faced the nineteenth century social reformers, and which motivated the Town Planning Movement to attempt to eradicate overcrowding, poverty, ill-heath, and insanitary living conditions through the medium of physical plans and developments. Despite 64 years of statutory planning controls, however, a satisfactory solution to these problems is only marginally nearer than it was in the nineteenth century, although it can be argued that in absolute terms these problems are far less severe than they were.

Town Planning in Great Britain since 1947

The Town and Country Planning Act of 1947 instituted a new era in comprehensive land planning in this country. Both this and other associated legislation were based on the findings of three important commissions which were presented in the Barlow,[5] Scott,[6] and Uthwatt[7] Reports respectively. The Barlow Report deals with factors affecting the location and distribution of employment and population; the Scott Report deals with issues concerning rural land use, whilst the Uthwatt Report was concerned with the financial implications of imposing planning controls. The earlier legislation concerned with planning (the Acts of 1909, 1919, 1925, 1932, 1943 and 1944) were really belated attempts to control and rectify problems which were already in existence.

They were largely optional Acts with the result that if they were implemented at all it was invariably in a half-hearted way. The 1947 Act by comparison was compulsory and required Local Planning Authorities to prepare development plans for their areas, which defined patterns of future land use. Government approval was required for these plans, and most forms of development required permission from the local planning authority before construction or implementation could take place. Other important legislation was associated with the 1947 Act, the most significant of which are listed here.

1. Distribution of Industry Act 1945. The main aim of this was to encourage new industrial development to establish in development areas, i.e. those parts of the country suffering the worst effects of unemployment and declining industry.

2. New Towns Act 1946, which set up the machinery for the implementation of the new towns proposed as part of the 'regional' plans for places like London and Glasgow.

3. National Parks and Access to the Countryside Act 1945, which allowed the designation of National Parks, areas of an outstanding natural beauty, and nature reserves and improved public access to the countryside.

4. Town Development Act 1952, which enabled agreements to be made between different local authorities whereby development (housing in the main) might take place in one area to ease the problems existing in another area.

The development plans required by the 1947 Act had to delineate, among other things, those areas intended for the main urban uses (residential, industrial, business, schools etc.); the principal traffic routes; areas set aside for the working of surface minerals; green belts; reservoirs, water supply, and sewage disposal; and where trees and woodland were to be preserved. This type of plan was essentially a 'land plan' concerned with policies of location, movement and the use of land as a resource—its objective in the broadest possible sense an extension of the 1943 Act objective, viz. 'to secure consistency and continuity in the framing and execution of a National Policy with respect to the use and development of land.'[8]

Although the 1947 Act plan was a land plan, nevertheless it had other limited and unstated social and economic objectives. Perhaps the most apposite assessment of the objectives of the entire post-1947 planning legislation comes from Professor Buchanan's interpretation of the policies developed and implemented by successive governments since 1947. These can be summarised as:

(a) 'Ensuring equality of opportunity, prosperity and standards throughout the whole country . . .

(b) Getting the urban areas into shape . . .

(c) Ensuring a sufficient and economical transport system for people and goods.

15

(d) Conserving the nation's natural resources . . .

(e) Conserving the nation's heritage . . .'[9]

Given these objectives it can be argued that in some areas the activities resulting from the post-1947 'town planning' legislation have produced some notable achievements. The New Towns, built to re-house and employ people from slum areas of the large cities, and to provide the ancillary educational, welfare, and leisure services so essential to the enjoyment of life, have been described as 'one of the most notable social undertakings of the century in world terms'.[10]

The worst excesses of urban sprawl and ribbon development have been avoided; some order has been brought to the exploitation of mineral resources; and the country's natural resources and heritage are at least well-documented, and, to a limited extent, protected through designated National Parks and Areas of Outstanding Natural Beauty.

In the field of housing the results have been mixed—1 million slum dwellings have been cleared, but 7·4 million slum dwellings remain (i.e. 40 per cent of the country's total housing stock). The price of land rather than human and social need has dictated urban housing policies with the result that in the inner city areas the majority of the inhabitants live in high-density Local Authority housing. Those who can afford it move to the suburbs in the private housing sector; those who cannot afford to move, and cannot obtain local authority housing, rent in near slum conditions. Central area redevelopment has been pursued with vigour in many towns and cities; and has provided safer, cleaner, and tidier shopping, working and recreational facilities. However the quality of the detailed design, and building finishes, often fails to match the quality of the original concept.

On the traffic side no real progress has been made in resolving urban problems. The approach adopted is haphazard, and fails to integrate transport policy with the social and economic needs of the community. This failing is compounded by a marked reluctance on the part of central government to match the level of investment of money in the private motor vehicle by individuals, with an equivalent investment in elements of the transport infra-structure such as railways, public transport and motorways. But perhaps the most significant failing since 1947 has been the inability to produce a satisfactory integration of land-use planning and social and economic policies. In the absence of clearly defined social and economic objectives the 'general' planning framework within which town planning needs to operate in the physical sense, is missing.

There have been various attempts to allocate national economic resources between regions, e.g. Distribution of Industry Act 1945, which gave the Board of Trade power to control the location of industry. More recently the setting up of the Regional Economic Planning Councils in 1965 has resulted in the production of regional studies which can be used by both Central Government, as a guide in administering economic policies, and by Local Government as a context within which town planning might take place. However, the absence of a clearly defined 'national plan' or set of policies ensures that these studies lack coherence and some credibility. On the social front research into urban social problems has more or less established the need for a framework within which social policy planning can be implemented, with a view to resolving or ameliorating the many social problems associated with poor jobs, low pay and poor housing. At the moment social planning is not formally practised, although in many Local Authorities the Social Services Department and/or the Town Planning Department are attempting to develop it. In the absence of clearly defined social plans and policies it is difficult to practise town planning in the physical sense without impinging on social problems in such a way that their resolution is made more complex.

In parallel with the growing awareness of the need for coherent and credible social and economic plans and policies at the national, regional and more local levels, transport planning developed as a skill or profession in its own right. In an attempt to cope with the problems of movement and congestion a sophisticated method of planning for transport was evolved in the period between the mid 1950s and the later 1960s. This method is based on the assumption that all movement was a function of the land (or activity) which occurred at the origin and destination ends of each journey. It utilises sophisticated modelling and forecasting techniques based on scientific method and systems analysis, and is more concerned with the overall characteristics of the transport system than the design of specific transport facilities. Although a vast body of knowledge was rapidly built up on this subject it developed almost

17

entirely separately from the town planning profession with the result that only in more recent years have the full implications of transport planning policies for town planning been realised.

The Emerging Planning Process

The institutions responsible for providing a town planning service are currently undergoing extensive reform. At central government level perhaps the most recent significant change in organisation and administration was the creation of the department of the Environment in 1970. This Department, under the control of one minister, now combines the functions of the former Ministry of Housing and Local Government, the Ministry of Transport and the Ministry of Public Buildings and Works. Thus, in theory, three formerly separate ministries, which were responsible for different aspects of the town planning process, are now better co-ordinated. At Local Government level, the Local Government Act 1972 will result in a major revision of territorial boundaries in local government, and a major redistribution of work between the new authorities. When the re-organisation is completed in 1974 a two-tier system of local government will operate uniformly across the country in the form of Counties and Districts.

The County areas in the major conurbations, known as 'Metropolitan Counties', will be responsible for land use and transportation planning and management, and for some aspects of environmental and recreational management. The 'Metropolitan Districts' will be responsible for education, personal social services, libraries, local plan making and the control of development. In other less populous parts of the country, the responsibility for land use and transport planning will be linked with education and personal social services at the County level, whilst the 'Districts' will be responsible for local plan making, the control of development, and most aspects of environmental and recreational management. At the same time as this new organisational structure has been developing, a considerable amount of work has been carried out with a view to determining the most appropriate internal organisational structure for the new authorities. Some authorities made an early start on their internal restructuring, and leant heavily on established business management techniques and consultants in doing so. The Maud Committee reported on management in local government in 1967 and made certain recommendations about Committee and departmental structure, and the responsibilities of councillors and officers.[11] The combined effect of this report, the Mallaby report on staffing in local government,[12] the Bains report on management guidelines for the new local authorities[13] and the introduction of management methods from business has brought about many changes in local government organisation in the last six years and some clear trends are emerging, e.g. the new organisational structures are reducing the number of committees dealing with the authorities' business; formerly separate departments are being grouped according to policy areas; officers are being given clearly authorised executive powers; whilst perhaps the most common trend has been the creation of a policy committee to deal with the formulation of high level policy matters in a corporate way.

Corporate Policy planning (or management) can be described as 'the creation of an administrative system which ensures that all activities of an organisation are directed to the achievement of the main objectives of that organisation and that each activity is separately evaluated for its effectiveness',[14] and within a local authority the body responsible for corporate planning generally aims to produce plans and policies relating to the three major resources of that authority—money, manpower, and land and buildings. The way in which this corporate planning process is being introduced varies from authority to authority. In some cases there is a separate corporate planning unit with the component elements of the corporate plan being 'fed-in' from the traditional local authority departments. In other cases the existing planning department, or the financial department, has become responsible for the production of the corporate plan, whilst other authorities have given a joint responsibility. Whichever way a corporate plan is produced it has great significance for the traditional town planning process—corporate plans are concerned with the allocation of available resources, and hence must act as a constraint on the planning and implementation of physical planning proposals; they are concerned with the inter-related nature of many social, economic and physical problems thus providing the essential framework within which the physical planning process can operate.

Changes in legislation in the planning and related fields have accompanied this reform of administration and organisation. The

Transport Act 1968 has created a system of Passenger Transport Areas, Executives and Authorities, with a view to assisting the integration of rail and bus services. The Local Authority (Social Services) Act 1970 adopted the main recommendations of the Seebohm Committee and has led to the creation of separate departments of social services within local authorities. But perhaps the most significant legislation passed in recent years is the Town and Country Planning Acts of 1968 and 1971, which introduced new development planning procedures. Under this legislation the old style (1947 Act) development plan, is replaced by a series of different plans each having a specific purpose and form.

For example: 1. Structure Plans are seen as policy statements on strategic issues such as economic, social and physical systems of the areas under consideration, insofar as these issues are subject to physical control or influence.

2. Local Plans are intended to deal with more detailed proposals within the context of the Structure Plan, and can take the form of a District Plan, where factors in a local planning issue need to be examined in a comprehensive way; or a Subject Plan where specific problems can be tackled outside of a timetable, or the territorial expression of other plans; or an Action Area Plan, whereby the local authority can plan in a comprehensive way for development, redevelopment, or renewal which it intends to implement within a short period of time.

The principal aim of this Act is to allow the development of large scale, long-term spatial policies as well as ensuring that physical development planning and implementation is carried out. There is, however, one major difficulty—the Act makes no provision for the inclusion in the Structure Plan of local authority proposals which are not physically based. Indeed it is important to realise that a Structure Plan, as defined by the 1968 and 1971 legislation, is no more than a policy plan for the physical area of the local authority. It is not a policy plan for the community inhabiting that local authority area.

Conclusions

Town Planning had its origins in the work of the nineteenth-century social reformers. Early developments in the legislation, the profession and practice of town planning gave an emphasis to the questions of location, design and layout, which was eventually given absolute priority through the 1947 Town Planning Act.

The period between 1945 and 1972 saw considerable activity and expenditure in the field of town planning, but the achievements in terms of solving the many and complex problems of urban areas were limited. This is understandable given that it was forced to operate in a context where social and economic policies were not clearly defined, and where definite national and regional plans were absent. During this period developments in the field of social, economic and transport planning began to impinge on town planning, whilst the introduction of legislative and organisational reforms in central and local government provided a framework within which the function and structure of town planning could be re-assessed, modified and developed to help cope with the complex problems facing today's society. The acceptance of corporate planning as the major tool in the policy making of local authorities, allied with the introduction of a new form of development planning through the 1968 and 1971 Acts, has given rise to a situation where the purpose of town planning must be defined, its relationships with social, economic and transport planning determined, and integration of these aspects of planning with the machinery of corporate planning, achieved.

It is against this background that the following chapters examine the content and scope of physical, economic, social, transport and corporate planning. At the same time an attempt is made to assess the inter-relationship between physical and the other forms of planning.

References

1 Parliamentary debates on the Housing, Town Planning etc. Bill, House of Commons Debates, vol. 188 (May 1908).

2 *Progress report on membership policy—revised scheme for the final examination* (Town Planning Institute, May 1967).

3 Report of the Planning Advisory Group on the production of development plans (HMSO, 1964).

4 *The qualifications of planners* (Schuster Report) (HMSO).

5 *The distribution of the industrial population* (Barlow Report), (HMSO, 1940).
6 *Land utilisation in rural areas* (Scott Report), (HMSO, 1943).
7 *Compensation and betterment* (Uthwatt Report) (HMSO, 1942).
8 Town and Country Planning Act 1943 (HMSO).
9 C. D. Buchanan, *The State of Britain* (Faber and Faber, 1972).
10 *ibid.*
11 *Management of local government* (Maud Committee) (HMSO, 1967).
12 *The staffing of local government* (Mallaby Committee) (HMSO, 1967).
13 *Local government in England: government proposals for re-organisation* (Bains Report), Dept. of Environment (HMSO, 1972).
14 F. J. C. Amos, *The development of the planning process*, RTPI Annual Conference (May 1971).

2. Philosophy and Purpose of Planning

Edgar A. Rose

Viewpoints

My contribution is very much a personal statement of belief. Although the approach takes account of the evolution of planning, the main thrust of my remarks is directed at some fundamental problems of planning. The emphasis is directed towards basic philosophy and social purpose in planning rather than methodological, organisational and institutional aspects. The activity we call planning covers a vast and growing spectrum of social action. It covers a multitude of sins. Problems of definition abound. But the mode and potential of planning as an approach to solving many contemporary problems is the underlying theme in all subsequent discussion. If justification for planning be needed, then it may be provided on both scientific and normative grounds. 'Self-direction' is the objective of planning which is 'an activity by which man in society endeavours to gain mastery over himself and to shape his collective future consciously by power of his reason'.[1]

Two beliefs deserve to be stated explicitly at the outset. First, the humanist belief that man has only his own intellectual, moral and social resources with which to face his problems and that human life can be made worthwhile and sufficient in itself. Second, the belief, so eloquently expressed by Rachel Carson[2] that we in this generation must come to terms with nature; that we are challenged as never before to prove our maturity and mastery not of nature but ourselves.

In any consideration of the philosophy and purpose of planning, it is axiomatic that questions of valuation and belief predominate. We view our world through normative lenses. The values which we hold, be they political, moral or ethical, our position in society and the understanding which we have of that position, influence and permeate our being, our thinking and doing, our individual and collective consciousness. In short, the notion of a value-free social science is a snare and delusion. Nevertheless, such a view cannot absolve us from the need to adopt a scientific and rational approach, nor can we deceive ourselves that the invention and development of scientific methodology and the application of relatively new powerful analytical tools will not transform our ways of thinking and doing.

There are other sources of confusion. Over-specialisation, fragmentation and compartmentalisation of knowledge in higher education, combined with rapid technological advance, will exacerbate growing social problems which look like being difficult to solve in the time available. Technology, in all its forms, is the dynamo within our society and it is essential that it is understood as a philosophy involving value judgements as well as a social technology of growing importance, requiring such breadth of treatment.

In both *The Commonsense of Science* and *Science and Human Values*, Professor J. Bronowski demonstrates the outlook of science as a facet of our western culture on the one hand and the essence of the creative process on the other. His passionate humanitarianism and belief in the need to develop an ethic for science is no more than the general case of the particular role argued here for aspects of planning. Despite the power of organised science and technology, an important—and in the planning field perhaps the main—body of knowledge available in understanding any social situation will probably be the accumulated, traditional, intuitive knowledge, which we describe variously as common sense, or more particularly as planning principles, rationales, standards, etc. For example, we have accumulated a remarkably sophisticated understanding and pattern of expectation of how people will behave in different situations which are not enshrined in any formal theory. Although the social sciences have a great deal to offer us, their theories 'must be used as adjuncts to our main body of informal knowledge, rather than as something to stand in its stead'.[3] Similarly, it could be argued that a specialist in planning, whether urban economist or urban designer, who approaches practical problems in the field believing that the main analytical tools were the theories he had learnt, would be less effective than most non-specialists.

Such a view of reality is not universally shared. It must be admitted that to discuss planning and philosophy raises profound questions about the relationship between the human sciences and philosophy generally. The ideological divide is seen at its sharpest in those writings which share a common ahumanistic, ahistorical and aphilosophical attitude. Such views represent the methodological denial of any historical dimension to social facts and avoid the necessity of subjecting our contemporary technocratic and consumer-orientated society to any systematic social criticism. Typically, it is argued that the social sciences may come to play a role akin to the physical sciences; our organised capitalist society may now be regarded as a social order endowed with regulative mechanisms, sufficiently refined and developed to deprive both the technological power of transforming nature as well as relations between men of any capacity to effect change in the basic values governing human behaviour in society; the problem of values would no longer be raised to a level sufficiently intense to act effectively on an individual's behaviour.[4]

This is not the approach adopted here. A critique of contemporary society is indispensable for reasons which will become plain. This is not an historicist view, intended to lead back to the past or indeed to question the considerable achievements of our industrial state—its high standard of living, advances in health, education, leisure and regulative mechanisms or forms of planning that allow society to avoid catastrophes like the 1926 slump—no one is suggesting a return to the pre-industrial society of the Middle Ages. But recognition of achievements should not blind us to the dangers which face us in the coming decades. All of us, including social scientists have to ask whether the evolutionary direction in which we appear to be moving is acceptable; spontaneous tendencies suggest increasingly technocratic structures and a way of life that is far removed from the ideal of a political and economic democracy. Worldwide political and social developments, including trends in the United Kingdom might suggest the necessity or virtue of a self-regulating approach towards economic and social institutions which would permit above all a significant extension of political and economic democracy, and its corollary, more individual responsibility for the collective decisions which govern our lives.

It has become a truism to suggest that we need to adopt an interdisciplinary approach to problems of environment and planning. The extent of our problems and concerns demands a sharing of knowledge and skills on a scale hitherto not appreciated and with results as yet difficult to anticipate. We need to draw on all the available evidence that can be brought to bear. The definition of subjects or sciences are identified not so much by the phenomena they study as by the integrating concepts and processes that they stress. Subjects must be defined by the types of evidence they are willing to consider.

Planning may be thought of not as a discipline in the nineteenth-century sense of that term, but as a core area within a field of study, an area of overlap and convergence in respect of real world problems. It is not so much a well-defined subject on the basis of the facts it deals with as it is an area of inquiry in which, for example (like urban geography) the inquiry is spatial and the area urban, and in which (like urban economics and sociology) the inquiry is non-spatial and the area urban.[5] Urban geography, urban history, urban sociology overlap one another and with other cognate sciences. Urban design overlaps to a lesser degree of the micro-scale of the urban field. Increasingly environmental physics, social psychology, and aspects of perception are seen as relevant extensions of the field, especially at the micro- or local planning scale. The development of further clearly identified areas within the field may be illustrated by the current vogue of transportation studies, spatially oriented and linking systems engineering, behavioural science, transportation economics, land planning and management methods. The study of urban institutions, government and the law relating to the field, are increasingly viewed in a cultural context and as essential components of any study syllabuses.

Planning is a multi-dimensional activity and ought to be integrative, embracing social, economic, political, psychological, anthropological and technological factors. The universe within which we structure the tasks of integrative planning comprises *man, society, nature and technology.*[6] Perhaps the most interesting and hopeful trend is that our evolving social processes place less relevance and reliance on technology as an approach to environmental planning and design and more on the design of social systems, organisational structures and institutions.

Planners are concerned with the future. So are most of us in one way or another. But it is intrinsic to the purposes and methods of planning that they are concerned with human 'betterment' and 'improvement'. It is evident that both questions of theory and practice arouse controversy and there is little that is exact or 'pure' about the field of study. However, like other professionals, the planner engages in activity in which he believes. At best he is concerned to understand what preferences are held by those for whom he is ostensibly planning. At worst he may adopt a position of spurious neutrality. The conventional wisdom is that he *ought* to be concerned with the social and other benefits which planning skills may increasingly help to bring to a world in which the majority remain hungry and poorly housed.

Students of urban society want to know how cities function. They seek to understand and explain the process of change. So do planners, who are often rightly criticised for intervening on the urban stage when they have little idea of the consequences and ramifications of their actions. This is only another way of saying that we need better explanations or theories of the effects of interactions between components of the urban system. There is justification for the view that planners and planning should concentrate on some of the more pressing issues and problems which face contemporary society. We need to be able to predict the more important consequences of change, whether political, social, economic or technological.

As the late Catherine Bauer Wurster expressed it, 'the "would-be movers and shakers", the urban critics and reformers, require bold hypotheses which lead toward viable concepts of the big alternatives which can be refined and tested by scientific research on the one hand, and simplified for general understanding and public decision on the other'.[7]

We are finding the process of adapting our urban regions, our cities and towns extremely difficult. Throughout the developed world increasing attention is being given to the problems of environment, the more effective allocation, distribution and management of resources for regional and urban development, to social change and the nature of planning itself.

To summarise, the essential features of the kind of planning envisaged are:

(a) Integrating in approach and multidisciplinary in character.

(b) Normative and self-directing; concerned with choice, preference and goals.

(c) Adaptive to change—continuously modifying ends and means, preferences and goals.

27

(d) Democratic and participatory.

(e) Based on adequate information and consideration of alternative courses of action.[8]

Ecological Perspectives

'Social institutions face growing difficulties as a result of an ever increasing complexity which arises directly and indirectly from the development and assimilation of technology. Many of the most serious conflicts facing mankind result from the interaction of social, economic, technological, political and psychological forces and can no longer be solved by fractional approaches from individual disciplines. The time is past when economic growth can be promoted without consideration of social consequences and when technology can be allowed to develop without consideration of the social prerequisites of change or the social consequences of such change. Diagnosis is often faulty and remedies proposed often merely suppress symptoms rather than attack the basic cause.'

Bellagio Declaration on Planning.[9]

I have quoted from the Bellagio declaration at some length, both because it reflects concern which we have already alluded to, and because it omits to emphasise that planning for posterity must be based on a full understanding of the interaction of human activities and natural forces, and of the ability of nature to sustain herself. Human Ecology is the science which seeks to elucidate the principles governing the interaction of the natural processes of land, water and all living things with mankind. Conservation involves the application of these scientific principles and a policy of trusteeship. Conservationist policies for countryside and nature generally demand planning of a specialist kind. All human activities have to be considered and the factors of supply and demand are critical to the process.

Dr Hugh Fraser Darling in the 1969 Reith Lectures spelt out the dangers which are growing year by year as we continue to ignore the relations of living organisms to their surroundings. We continue to act as if we have a social and biological existence outside of nature and can afford the luxury of blind faith in the virtues of science to solve all and any problems which mankind is responsible for creating;

not least those relating to urbanisation, wastage of natural resources and the pollution of land, air and water.

Professor Norbert Weiner anticipated the moral dilemmas which advances in science would bring.[10] Perhaps we are now more aware that cybernetics—the study of communications and control in living organisms or machines—poses moral and ethical problems not dissimilar to those which theology once did. It was Patrick Geddes who pointed out that hell and heaven 'are the necessary stereoscopic device of the social thinker as much as of his predecessor, the theologian'.[11]

The mode of planning challenges the hitherto-accepted notion that in purely technical terms we may assume a 'natural' superiority for the market. If the wretched freedoms of the slums are the counterpart of the individualism of the makers of horse-drawn carriages, as J. K. Galbraith has suggested, then the unquestioning belief in the magical powers of science to solve all problems is as Victorian an idea as unbridled individualism and *laissez faire* economic doctrine.[12] Science as a category of knowledge is neutral; its future development and uses are part of the social process.

The management of life-sustaining systems will need drastic improvement in step with our understanding of the processes involved. Without such measures, illumined by social responsibility and respect for individual choice, the *quality* of life, the natural and man-made environment, will suffer further erosion. Nothing less than our heritage is at stake.[13]

Increasingly, informed observers are adopting a broad ecological approach to the environment of man which seeks to demonstrate that the problems of both the developed countries and the underdeveloped Third World, the mounting evidence of environmental deterioration, hunger, resource depletion, and war are closely interacting systems which, together, constitute a challenge without precedent in human history. We are being forced to make decisions in the face of uncertainty. Data is not always available, rarely is it reliable. Our understanding of the complexities of ecological systems and human behaviour is still fragmentary. But on the worldwide scale who doubts any longer that we face massive problems of overpopulation with resulting demands on food, resources and the environment?

Some observers present a bleaker and more nightmarish picture of spaceship earth than others.[14] But the message is not so significantly different as may appear at first sight. The future is departing radically from the past and old remedies are both inappropriate and irrelevant. In such circumstances we need to exercise our creative imaginations, envisioning what might be. Perhaps the shadow of nuclear annihilation and latterly the ecological prophecies of doom have brought home more forcibly than hitherto the notion that trend is not destiny, that the possibilities for the future are not foreclosed. Planning in such circumstances is called upon to explore new possibilities. In short, scenarios for alternative possible futures are valuable; they not only free the imagination, they expose the fallacies and limitations of what we believe might be—'a vision of the kind of spaceship earth that ought to be and the kind of crew that should man her'.[15]

If, as H. G. Wells observed with prophetic insight, human history becomes more and more a race between education and catastrophe, strategies for survival will become essential; inevitable to some, impossibly utopian to others. Yet is there no connection between the cholera epidemic in Italy—which rages as I write—and the neglect of Venice, from which city I recently returned? Is there no connection between the absence of any credible land-planning system and the unbridled corruption and speculation that disgraces the story of postwar planning in the eternal city?[16] Is there any doubt about the desirability of translating some dreams into plans of action; planning as action within the context of a *co-ordinated*, dynamic policy framework which would guide decision making? Such intervention assumes both ends and means for planning which do not yet exist; which are not yet on the political agenda of most nation states.

Elsewhere, I have underlined the need to develop worthwhile education in environmental studies, an essential attribute of which would be the development of a new ethic of knowledge or philosophy of technology. We need to cultivate a more profound understanding of the relationship of men in society towards the natural environment. The professional must aspire to become an agent of social change, not the mindless servant of an insensitive bureaucracy.

There is some doubt about whether the odds are heavily against *Homo sapiens* in this battle for survival. Will mankind choose the battleground, anticipate the nature of the combat in time to forge the necessary weapons for victory? The environmentalist lobby is growing and is gaining adherents all over the world. The scientific community has joined the debate; survival is the goal and the means for achieving this end vary—population control, political pressure, massive campaigns to improve environment, calls for concerted international action, international conferences, and so on ...

The philosophical and scientific standpoint which I adopt is that there can be no technological panacea for the complex of problems making up the population-food-energy-environment crisis, although technology properly applied in such areas as pollution abatement, communications, and fertility control could provide massive assistance. The basic solutions involve dramatic and rapid changes in *human attitudes*, especially those relating to reproductive behaviour, economic growth, technology, the environment and conflict resolution. It remains to be seen whether the need for new attitudes and calls for a new ethic for knowing and living, concepts and ideas intrinsic to the ecological standpoint, will be heeded in a world of narrowly practical men where power and often outmoded ideology hold sway. It should be borne in mind that planning techniques have invariably followed behind the events they were supposed to control and direct; they were strictly remedial in character.

The task can be stated in theoretical terms thus; if man is part of the biosphere and does not exist outside its physical and biological constraints, then a sociology which is aware of the ecological problems leads to a theory of man in nature as well as society—a theory that is capable of being tested by scientific method, is capable of correction, is probabilistic, and takes account of the dimension of time and the dynamics of change and chance.[17]

How to deal with man's environmental crisis requires policy formation illuminated by good theory, and as we have already indicated, collective wisdom and common sense. Few informed commentators would argue that modern man can voluntarily abandon the technoscientific culture of which he forms such an integral part, even if this were really desirable. The rejection of science-based technology or its uncritical acceptance offers no solutions. The evidence suggests that the only practicable policy would be to control the uses of science and technology towards ecologically wise ends.

This essay is about ends as well as means, substance as well as procedure, product as well as process. As such it aims at making a case for 'planning' of various kinds. Before proceeding to examine

31

what we mean by planning, we should note that once the notion of 'wise ends' is accepted, it implies an acceptance of an 'edited culture' in which the future shape of society would be socially planned and guided in accordance with appropriate criteria.

A fundamental task for society, therefore, is to determine what the culture is to be. In this process, scientific knowledge although indispensable is only one category of knowledge. 'Social, ethical and aesthetic values, subject to scientific analysis of their implications, would afford more significant criteria for cultural "editing" than relying primarily upon science or the humanities for guidance.'

The difficulty with this argument is who tells us how we 'edit' our culture. It was Raymond Williams who pointed out the planners' dilemma, namely, the essentially unplannable nature of culture. Perhaps this is the function of politics, policy making and planning. What appears indisputable is that the philosophical basis for the ecological attitude implies an ethic, or in the words of Rene Dubos, a 'theology of the earth'.

How far is it possible to affirm that as 'ecological science' develops, it will develop a capacity for reliable prediction? It might be argued that the ideological attitudes which accompany ecological statements need far more explicit articulation. It is a truism that further study in the human sciences and philosophy is required. But we may see both value and hope in exploring a new world view or paradigm within which our problems may more successfully be resolved. Perhaps this will lead to an ideology more effective than any we have experienced to date, corresponding to the emergence of a new world science. We will have to wait and see, since it is in the nature of all visionary propositions that they are not readily verifiable by methods we recognise as scientific. The ecological attitude, however defined, is a normative response, though we may recognise that it arises in part from our growing scientific and technological knowledge.

The Scope and Meaning of Planning

Planning, like science or branches of scientific activity, has a number of aspects which may be considered from different viewpoints; likewise it is linked with other social activities; it is still in many ways a craft seeking to improve its practice by the application of theory which has originated in other and older areas of study; we have neither a general theory nor special theories *of* planning, though we utilise theory *for* planning. Generally, we are aware of its tactical components or special applications; urban and regional planning, business planning, social planning, management science, systems analysis, corporate planning and so on. Planning certainly admits no sharp boundary between knowledge and use.

As planning develops through time and space, any definition can only express more or less inadequately one of the aspects, often a minor one, that it has had at some period of its development. The question what is *the purpose and meaning of planning*—receives quite different answers at different times and from different sorts of people. Einstein once said much the same about science. Nevertheless, if we want to understand what planning is we could do worse than consider its growing functions and examine its institutionalised role in this country or abroad, its methodology, its cumulative tradition of knowledge, its relationship to the economy, its cultural influence, and its interaction with society.

Important aspects of the activity we describe as planning are not necessarily scientific. Like science, it is not concerned with theory or thought alone, but with the thought continually carried into practice. It is both a philosophy and a technique and, therefore, cannot be studied separately from technique. The implications of this view in the educational and vocational context are of considerable significance.

It was the late Professor D. Bernal who wrote that the problem of planning in the widest sense demands a solution of an equation with many variables representing different ways of expending human effort so as to give the maximum human opportunity for action and the best biological and sociological environment for humanity.

How far are we justified in seeking an understanding of these wider problems? Is it seriously possible to restrict our concerns to the use of land? Is it meaningful to regard the physical planner's skill as his synoptic integrating view of systems of land-use and settlement and the factors affecting them? Is it correct to describe town planning as a process, involving a recurring cycle of operations, for preparing and controlling the implementation of plans for changing systems of land-use and settlement of varying scale?

33

Such questions are relevant because this is just the view that has been taken by the Royal Town Planning Institute until very recently.[18]

Definitions may have their limitations, but they are indispensable in trying to understand what 'planning' is, and subsequently to distinguish planning activities of very disparate kinds. Perhaps the basic distinction to establish initially is between generic or general planning and physical planning, if only because historically physical planning emerged in professional form as a conscious public activity first and consequently has tended to become artificially separated from other kinds of planning that have emerged in the meantime. Such a distinction may also be justified to describe current practice, but it is a characteristically fragmented and limited distinction reflecting a fragmented view of environment and culture generally.

In addition to definitions, and not quite the same thing, we will also find meanings given to 'planning' of assistance. But definitions and meanings abound in ambiguity. The problem of 'ubiquity' will not be resolved by writing about it. I prefer to emphasise planning's many-sided aspects, implications and problems; terminology in the planning field does not excel in precision, primarily I suspect because the application of terms to very different cultures, ways of doing and behaving, as well as thinking, of itself generates ambiguity.

The general meaning given to planning suggests that planning is a mental preparation for action. In the words of Benton MacKaye— 'Every deliberate action . . . must be conceived and rehearsed in the realm of thought before it can take place in the physical. It must be *created* before it can be done.'[19] Thinking before doing can apply to almost every action. I recently returned from an extensive tour of European countries, 'planned' in advance. I am now working on this essay and other professional work according to a timetable—or 'plan'. Some eventualities I had not anticipated—like my car hitting a large rock lying in the middle of the road. This was a contingency for which I had no plan; an event for which I had made inadequate preparation. The point is that we plan in general terms all the time. These plans depend on statements of probability about situations which are reasonably familiar to us. Moreover, the objective of such a plan is relatively simple.

The more difficult general planning problems arise in contexts which are highly complex and when our knowledge of the situation(s) is so limited that we can place little confidence in anticipating future response. Our statements of probability may convince no one, least of all ourselves. Whilst we may conclude that planning is a recognised intellectual procedure and that both society and individuals plan, it remains a fact that the trends and tendencies that influence and determine the general planning process are not well understood, whilst the purposes of such planning are various and controversial. This distinction between simple and complex planning adds yet another dimension to our discussion.

But for the moment let us turn from the generic to a particular form of planning, which is usually termed town or physical, but which might more usefully be called spatial planning. If the general meaning of the verb to plan is ambiguous, either referring to making a plan 'plan of (ground, existing building); design (building to be constructed, etc.)' or 'scheme, arrange beforehand', the term 'town planning', first heard in the early years of this century is more precisely, if inadequately, defined in the Oxford Illustrated Dictionary as:

Construction of plans for regulation of growth and extension of town, so as to secure best conditions of housing and traffic, situation of public buildings and open spaces, etc.

I would set out the traditional concerns or objectives of town and country planning as:

(a) The use of land to the best advantage.

(b) The maximum improvement in physical conditions that can be obtained within the limits of available resources, in accordance with human needs and priorities.

(c) Surroundings of quality and beauty that will inspire and enrich human existence at home, at work and at leisure.

(d) The conservation of natural resources and beauty and the worthwhile historical and architectural endeavours of man.

Implicit in the notion of physical planning is the concept of a hierarchy of plans at different spatial scales. Arguably, and partly because of its origins, physical planning has been least practised and understood at both regional and national scale. Nevertheless, the Town and Country Planning Act 1943, still operative today, confers upon the appropriate Minister responsibility for

securing consistency and continuity in the framing and execution of a

35

national policy with respect to the use and development of land throughout England and Wales.

More recently the Development Plans manual[20] advises that development plans must be prepared and examined in the light of national and regional policies. It also suggested that the structure plans required under more recent planning legislation 'must take their place in national and regional strategies' and that because 'a considerable part of their content will have regional and national significance they will have to relate, therefore, to wider strategic frameworks at these levels'.

The relationships of folk-work-place, invented by Patrick Geddes and the objective of regional planning and planned decentralised growth—what has been defined as 'the cultivation of habitability'[21] have remained, for the most part, on tomorrow's agenda, sub-ordinated to the prevailing ideas on land ownership and its use and abuse, awaiting major reforms in the character and structure of government; equally important awaiting an understanding of forms of organisation planning that go beyond utilitarian and utopian formulations expressed in terms of urban design and individually separate works of architecture. Physical planning schemes have tended to pay scant regard to the ecological, economic, social and political processes which together make up the environment of man.

If we have emphasised the historical origins of planning, it has been to illustrate its limitations and contradictions. Its practice has been limited by the social system and the roles accorded its practitioners. Geddes was perhaps the first to comprehend this fully. He conceived no ideal plans or utopias, but retained synoptic vision. He saw a role for science as well as art in managing and improving both town and country. He anticipated the birth of a new approach to the region, and the unity of thought and action. He thought of the world as a total entity rather than as elements, each the object of self-contained study. The pre-occupation of Geddes, Mumford and the ecological school have already been obliquely referred to. They emphasised the organic nature of growth, a revived sense of life in contrast to the mechanistic ideas which have tended to dominate western thought since the seventeenth century.

In the past the geographical approach has been predominant. The anti-urban ideology has emphasised the need for new towns and planned physical decentralisation. General planning was preceded by physical planning—in terms of physical space with control of land as a central objective. More recently we have heard pleas for a combined geographical and sociological perspective and the need to combine the sociological imagination and the geographical imagination.[22] In practice, the distinction between the spatial and non-spatial is conceptual rather than real. When we are concerned with spatial form and social process, we are dealing with different aspects of the same thing. In brief, if there is an important interface between the socio-economic and the physical planning approaches they should be regarded as complementary.[23] Equally, many general plans may obviously have physical components. Physical plans are imaginary constructs which represent physical objects, and both their external and internal relationships in space. Such distinctions are of great importance to our understanding.[24]

If the emphasis of contemporary planning practice appears somewhat restricted to the analysis of spatial structure, urban form and land-use patterns, the synthesising and co-ordinating role of general planning is much broader, and embraces concepts of long-range forecasting and the management and guidance of urban systems—including changes in systems. Physical or spatial planning, in part concerned with the short-term decision-making that is required to implement the components of plans, is seen increasingly as only part of a larger process of planning and social change. While increasingly the methods of the social sciences may be utilised to better inform the decision process, planning practice retains its interpretative, artistic and cultural functions, aspiring to reflect and shape the ideas and values of the age. The complementary modes of science and art are brought to bear. The general social tradition of science fuses with the specific, unique and individual act of creation.

The urban or regional planner works within a general tradition which is empirically derived and which utilises elements of theory and technique which are now becoming, despite their heterogeneous origins, fused with contemporary practice. Nevertheless, each scheme embraces decisions of individual choice, artistic preference, specific and unique qualities pertaining to place or culture. We cannot test or calculate all our answers, but this does not invalidate the need for recommendations and action. We do not yet know how to predict or effectively anticipate and plan for cultural change; culture, whilst it is being lived, cannot be known completely; there are no ready-made formulae, no certainties, only probabilities. Political and social policy decisions which must inform, and be informed by, long range forecasting and planning, and within which physical planning schemes find their context, present similar philosophical dilemmas. As the American scientist-philosopher Abraham Caplan suggests:

the perspective remains that of middle range skills, middle range research; neither a full formalised theory, calculable only by machine, nor brilliant aperçus each a separate stroke of planning genius.[25]

In my view, the search for a *separate* theory of planning is misguided. The Scientific Revolution is providing a wide range of theoretical concepts and techniques that can now rarely be effectively circumscribed by, or restricted to, one specific subject, discipline or field of study. General systems theory, the bridging role of operations research and management science, illustrates this point admirably.

If we are to reconcile the spectacular development and importance of general and special kinds of planning with the spatial/physical planning embodied in contemporary urban and regional planning practice, we need to distinguish carefully between the planning legislation that exists and the extent to which there is any 'useful' planning. Perhaps this is why social critics have emphasised the institutional and bureaucratic aspects of town planning in attempting to assess its impact and role in contemporary society.

Historically, town planning was accorded a restricted social role and the nature of the art was largely dictated and influenced by its architectural and engineering design origins; its field of operations was limited to a series of clearly defined and relatively straightforward objectives of little fundamental importance. Such a limited and myopic view of planning is fast disappearing.

It is a relatively recent phenomenon to see the process of effective synthesis between economic, social and spatial aspects being explicitly directed towards operational ends. This is precisely why the focus on philosophy and purpose, on the goals of planning, preoccupies so many professionals as well as people generally, at the present time. The outcome of this dialogue will profoundly affect the quality of our urban society.

Education for planning today is not only concerned with concepts of urban form, but with spatial problems of the British economy, with poverty and race, community organisation and the politics of involvement, with the role of institutions in urban change.[26] Education for planning is being profoundly influenced by the new methods of acquiring and processing information. Professional roles are changing rapidly and educational objectives are being revised. Professor M. Webber believes it is now inaccurate to label contemporary professionals with names we have inherited. The best of them are no longer economists or operational researchers or city planners. 'Rather they are men with specialised roles, confronting specific tasks with thoughtways and methods that originated in a wide spectrum of professional fields.'[27]

At the risk of repetition, it is evident that any productive educational or professional strategy which seeks to define and solve problems in the environmental field will require interdisciplinary collaboration at all levels. It is not criticism of the idea of professionalism to suggest that its purposes may need redefinition.[28]

Origins and Ideology

The cornerstones of British physical/spatial land-use planning policies have been and remain dependent upon concepts of density, built form, green belt, and overspill to new towns. National policies relevant to redevelopment and other aspects of land-use and spatial planning have always had regard to the conventional wisdoms enshrined in these four complementary sets of rationales for planning. They reflect the origins and character of the town planning movement.

The limitations inherent in such rationales are becoming better understood. If Donald Foley identified three ideological strands in British planning it seems fairly clear that ideological preconceptions generally hindered and retarded the efforts to extend the scope and character of British planning.[29]

The critical evaluation of planning policies, the systematic exploration of the *process* of planning have not been features which have distinguished British planning practice or research.

It is a truism to refer to a lack of research tradition in British town planning. The production of books on new towns, for example, has become almost an intellectual cottage industry, whilst the process of renewing the obsolete inner areas of housing around the core of many of our cities has received considerably less notice and (to date) little of it critical in its orientation to the subject.

But the situation is changing to the extent that social theory and the methods of the social sciences are applied to the tasks in hand. It has been said that what distinguishes the historian from the other social scientists is not that he writes about the past, but that he considers things in process of development. 'History' and 'sociology' are not concerned with different objects, they are different ways of looking at the same object.[30]

If planners have been reluctant to examine the tenets of their faith, social scientists have shown no such diffidence. The objective role within our society of the public planner has become an area for critical study. Sociological analysis of the process of planning, as well as its products, is seen as an important contribution to social policy formation in the environmental field.

Utopian Origins

If attention is to be given to the products and processes of British planning, its origins must be understood. We are interested in the process of development through time. Modern town planning sprang from the fusion of two streams of thought, responses to the dirt and grime, and the mushrooming towns of the Industrial Revolution. The town and country planning movement emerged from two different worlds, far removed in time and space: its origins are increasingly well documented,[31] the one embracing ideal cities and finite visible utopias, heavenly and earthly Jerusalems, perfectly formed works of art; the other composed of documents, manifestos, pamphlets and blueprints for new social orders. The dreams of visionaries finally merged with the philanthropists and those practical administrators of the nineteenth century, and decisively influenced the direction in which society has travelled. The futuristic cities were largely social reformers and socialists, Children of the Enlightenment.[32]

The visual representation of the heavenly Jerusalem was typically archaic; the vision of the mind's eye was represented in terms which could be understood by the audience to whom it was directed; in the architectural vocabulary and syntax of the time, in historicist form. The past is ransacked not for its own sake, but for models of what the future may be. The illustrations to More's *Utopia* are trite and conventional compared with the prophetic power of the social imagery. The search for the ideal city in design terms, even the preoccupation with pattern and urban form in our own day, has been regarded—quite erroneously—as an architectural question; a subject for research by art historians.[33] However, the physical bias and architectural origins of town and country planning may also reflect the separate culture of the humanist and the natural scientist; the intellectual division between verbal and visual culture.[34] In this sense the verbal and analytical was forward-looking, progressive and scientific, the visual encapsulated within the classic heritage and reinterpreted to fit the static platonic world of Renaissance man, a world from which it is arguably difficult to rescue the imagination and ideological posturings of too many architects and engineers. The world of the Beaux Arts lives on in our collective imagery and little of substance has replaced it.

If the gulf between the visual and social, visual and verbal is one point of departure or basis of comparison, then the ideological and the technical adds a further dimension. The former stems from social theoreticians such as Owen, Cabet and Saint-Simon, who sought to restructure society in accordance with a comprehensive vision; the latter, from the work of such men as Hausmann and Bazalgette, who attempted to tackle each problem separately because they neither conceived of their world in terms of interaction nor in the process of development. They had no overall vision of the town as a single organism. They had no synoptic view, unlike the visionaries.[35]

It must be appreciated that the piecemeal social engineering of engineer or administrator represents an approach, which contains implicit social values rooted in ideology, no less relevant than the categorical imperatives of the writings of an Owen or Marx. Technological change spanned ideology; ideas which served change and those who sought to direct it in particular directions; ideas which resisted change or which painted a Pre-Raphaelite world of romantic wonder. The history of planning thought and planning practice suggests a dialectical relationship between these two approaches; they are inextricably linked. We need to understand both traditions and the culture from which they derive, if only because the fusion of these approaches provided the conditions for the genesis of town and country planning.[36]

If technology and social structure were conveniently overlooked by most inventors of utopias, whether social or visual, a wide variety of underlying ideological assumptions were certainly made. Engel's polemic against utopian socialism reflects the nineteenth-century ideological background and still retains a contemporary flavour, appropriate for a Marxist classic still in good currency today.[37] It is also worth reminding ourselves that social utopias have hardly ever considered elements of the physical environment. Frederick Engels was contemptuous of the holistic utopian schemes which were worked out in detail. Thought divorced from action was foreign to his beliefs and 'new social systems were foredoomed as utopian; the more completely they were worked out in detail, the more they could not avoid drifting off into pure phantasies.'[38]

It may be that if we search through contemporary science fiction we will begin to see reflected some of man's present concerns for his physical environment. Until now, they are concerns which encapsulate nuclear disaster and the ecological limitations of the paradigm of spaceship earth. It remains an interesting feature of science fiction writing and indeed scenarios for the future that they are not able to delineate with any real confidence or sociological conviction the social relations of their future states. The visions are culture bound.

Changes in social practice, indeed the supreme invention of local government, were the adaptive responses to pressing ecological and social problems which threatened the very basis of industrial society. Social inventions mediated technological changes, begetting further inventions in the process. The great Reform Acts of the nineteenth century were one side of the coin, the Public Health Acts the other; social inventions the purpose of which were to assist the government, regulation and management of a predominantly urban society. Technical and administrative methods were needed. The process itself was one of social systems in action, the regulation provided was political in essence. Part of this legal and administrative super-structure was to become concerned with the use of land to meet the needs of urban growth. The utopian rhetoric and woolly thinking which attended the passage through Parliament of the first Town

Planning Act, the Burns Act of 1909, tended to disguise the very limited and practical powers which it contained.

In 1913 the Town Planning Institute was founded which was to become the centre and sounding board for wider and more far-reaching concepts of physical planning. The tension between the advocates of more profound change and reform, whether couched in visual or social terms, and those who would seek modest regulation and minimum intervention has remained a feature of the planning scene, part of the dialectic of change itself.

Reducing the city to some visual order was and remains a powerful doctrine, the rationale for concepts of amenity incorporated in forms of social control. When allied to social concern it has on occasion led to a crude belief in the power of physical arrangements of buildings to cure all social ills, a belief that has come to be known as 'physical determinism'.

With the advantage of hindsight we may recognise that the new towns and cities which have been planned were the erstwhile dreams of men like Ebenezer Howard and other 'utopians'. The weakness of their utopian vision was the finite and static conceptualisation of the utopia; their understanding of the social system was erroneous rather than the method of thought which was essentially inventive and imaginative.

Nevertheless, Lewis Mumford points to Ebenezer Howard's ability to envisage and distinguish that which is general and exemplary from that which is particular, aesthetic and unique.

In framing his new programme, Howard had stuck to essentials, and had not tried to give the architectural and planning details the stamp of his own imagination. He had come forth, not with a new plan for the city—he carefully refrained from confusing the essential issues with any visual image whatever—but with a new programme for the balanced organisation and contained growth of cities, in a general process that could take care of an indefinite increase in the national population. Howard expressed his diagnosis and his programme by means of a series of clarifying diagrams; but even the scheme that pictures the arrangement of the physical parts of the city was carefully labelled 'A Diagram Only'. His idea of the balanced community lent itself to a variety of urban forms, from that of his utopian predecessor, Charles Fourier to that of Le Corbusier: . . . and more than once, often in the guise of refuting Howard or demolishing the garden city idea, the principles of balance and functional completeness

43

which Howard enunciated have been re-invested or re-stated without such assignment of credit to Howard as he himself always made to his precursors.[39]

Utopias and science fictions, the scenarios for the future that have so captured the public imagination, should not all be regarded as escape routes from today's reality. They need not all be interpreted literally as static documents and blueprints. In the face of threats of ecological disaster, utopian thinking presents an intellectual challenge and raises the question of what we may become, if we correctly understand the environment within which we live, the limitations of living within nature and the limitations of being part of that nature. Possible futures demand a consideration of alternative courses of action, alternative trajectories through time and space, potentially desirable ends or objectives which may be tested in the light of experience and reason. In this context planning may be considered as an ends-means continuum if it is to be an effective social instrument of change and choice. As the American planner Martin Meyerson has expressed it, one man's utopia is another man's tomorrow.[40]

Sir Colin Buchanan rightly argues that physical surroundings count.

If you will accept my view that the ordinary family is better off in a warm, dry, sunny and reasonably quiet house than in a cold, damp, gloomy, rat-ridden tenement on a main road, then perhaps you will accept my extension of the principle to include physical surroundings *in toto*, and you will accept that shabby, dirty, dreary, inconvenient towns, and a soiled and neglected countryside are severe drags on human contentment.[41]

Dimensions of Change

Philip M. Hauser tells us that since 1650, world population has grown six-fold; estimated at about 500 million in the mid-seventeenth century, it exceeded 3000 million in 1964. Population living in places of 5000 or more inhabitants, approximately 3 per cent in 1800, had reached 30 per cent by 1960; about one-third of the earth's population lived in cities and towns. By the turn of the century, more than half the world's population could be living in urbanised areas of 100 000 or more. As Lewis Mumford has said, the city was once, symbolically, a world: today the world has become, in many practical aspects, a city. Urbanised societies represent a new and fundamental step in mankind's social evolution; all industrial nations are now highly urbanised, and throughout the world the process is accelerating.

The world's population increases by about 60 million each year. The major problem faced by planners everywhere is that this growing concentration of population in urbanised areas is in danger of outstripping structures. Karl Sax of the Bassey Institution at Harvard notes that, at the present growth rate, a population of 100 billion would be reached in two hundred years and 3000 billion in less than five hundred years. Nevertheless, if the nations of the world desalted ocean water, irrigated all the deserts, built plastic domes for farming in the Arctic and underground caverns for hydroponic farming and even developed food synthetically, enough food could probably be produced to feed hundreds of billions of people.

But even if population growth in Britain is not on such a scale as in other parts of the world, we know that by the year 2000 there could be an additional 10 million people. This represents the equivalent of something in the order of 100 new towns, each with a population of 100 000. Growth in the South-East is equivalent to providing a new town as large as Bristol or Coventry every few years.[42]

An increase of population in the order of 10 million would bring changes of great magnitude to the natural and man-made environment. Population growth will need to be planned if the benefits which science and technology could bring are to be realised. The way in which population control systems work and the issues of social policy are resolved may well depend on much more fundamental changes in our cultural patterns of behaviour. It is not a utopian dream to envisage that planning of a higher order and *quality* could provide forms of social intercourse and settlement form, as yet not fully comprehended.

There is growing recognition that this country is now part of an increasingly urbanised area embracing Belgium, the Ruhr and indeed Europe. The proposed channel tunnel or Maplin City, port and airport, are relevant at the national, regional and local planning level, whilst the economic, political and social implications of development on this scale are of even greater importance. We are seeing the emergence of *policy planning at the strategic level* as an absolutely essential prerequisite to the *physical* planning of cities and towns and their hinterlands.

The nature of industrial production, rising living standards, consumer needs, the motor car and motorway, increased mobility and leisure are transforming social life and the structure and form of our cities. Over the last decade the new dimensions of time and space have become evident. Public transport has begun to experience acute financial problems, the effect of increasing motorisation and mobility, new patterns of journey to work or to shop. The growth in service employment, the mushroom growth of offices in our city centres exerted pressures on an antiquated road system and it became clear that the concentration and congestion of our metropolitan centres was a characteristic and a function of the activities carried out there; the result of intensive development without a corresponding transportation infrastructure, including car parking and restraint, policies generally related to highway capacities, realistic investment programmes and programming over time.

There are obvious and not so obvious locational arrangements of uses and activities which have an important bearing upon the qualities of urban living. The core of the city is the intelligence centre and hub of the contemporary world. Professor Florence Sargent has graphically analysed for us the advantages and disadvantages of metropolitan life in several important papers.[43] We want propinquity and privacy, concentration without congestion; the choice and opportunity to meet men and women with the most esoteric interests. The planner's responsibility is to manipulate the economic, social and political processes, guiding land-use patterns that will effectively increase accessibility and enlarge the range of opportunity for productive and diverse relationships that are latent in the modern city.

Sir Colin Buchanan's team in 'Traffic in Towns' revealed our contemporary dilemma which we show little sign of resolving; it brought a new awareness of the vital relationship between traffic, transportation and planning; the danger to environment inherent in the unrestricted use of the private motor vehicle as the dominant mode of journeying to work; the prohibitive costs in conserving existing environment if the growth and usage of the motor car increases. The Report of the Layfield Inquiry into the Greater London

Development Plan and the reactions of Government generally suggests a profound change in public attitudes.[44]

It is evident that commuting operates at metropolitan scale. Technological changes in transportation are going to have a dynamic effect on patterns of land-use, the intensity of activity on land and in buildings: the need for effective co-ordination has never been greater. Likewise, the role which social policies play in respect of the use of transport in relation to planning at all levels has assumed critical dimensions; social policies have an important bearing on the extent to which we utilise new inventions and make them operational.

The development of cost-benefit analysis, balanced transportation systems and the very expensive land-use transportation studies have revealed the advantages and pitfalls of adopting complex mathematical models and integrated techniques.

The achievements of physical/spatial planning, like many things about our national life, are most appreciated and understood abroad. The plans of a quarter of a century ago may be 'old hat', but translated into town and communities, they demonstrated the opportunities and value inherent in organising the physical environment; providing the framework within which some of the finest and most enlightened comprehensive central area and housing development has taken place.

Nowhere have new towns been built in such substantial numbers as a matter of policy as in Britain. The New Towns Construction Programme was launched with the designation of Stevenage in 1946. By the end of 1972, some 30 new towns have been designated in Britain. Some of these are virtually complete, in others building is well advanced and a number are only at the planning stage.

The proposed structure and form of settlements which have been designed over the last decade and, in particular, the South Hampshire Study, the planning proposals for the new town of Milton Keynes, or the plan for the Central Lancashire New Town, indicate that planners are now thinking in regional terms and are very conscious of the need for flexibility. The self-contained and finite master plan concept is now replaced by a series of principles or guide lines which give maximum freedom of choice, communication and association; each phase of development is capable of functioning efficiently without necessarily becoming dependent on further growth. Opportunities are provided for subsequent changes in the location of functional elements of the urban system; in other words, current physical planning, insofar as it is pre-occupied with urban form and structure, seeks to avoid rigidity and attempts to simulate organic processes of development. The planner no longer arrogates to himself the task of determining the way in which people will subsequently seek to clothe the skeleton with flesh; there is room for subsequent revision and decision-making at a later stage in the process of growth.

In the years following the Second World War, national economic policies reflected in the physical planning of town and country did not anticipate the propensity for continued growth of Greater London in the wider context of the South-East, or the West Midlands, for example. Far too little account was taken of the economic forces making for growth. In particular, the fatally magnetic attraction of Cobbett's great 'Wen' was repeatedly under-estimated.

Population forecasts and intelligence data for planning generally have been inaccurate. The number of cars on our roads exceeded estimates and it has now been appreciated that the Welfare State has not removed poverty. Green Belt policy and the failure to make sufficient land available for residential 'overspill'—the number of new towns and the speed of development and town expansion was not sufficient—increased congestion, and helped to force up land prices, undermining physical planning policies with serious results in both the more prosperous and less fortunate regions.

But with the advantage of hindsight, the continued failure to deal with compensation and betterment has not only encouraged land speculation, it has made effective and purposeful planning increasingly difficult to achieve.

People become mobile when they buy a car; they continue to put as much distance between the Bull Ring or Piccadilly Circus and their homes as they can afford. The poorest sections of our population in the inner areas are the least mobile and could soon find themselves with less and less job opportunities. The polarisation between home and work could increase. The urban poor, the uneducated and the social outcasts could be confined to ghettos in the inner city not of their own making. The nature of service employment in the core of central London and other great cities will become progressively more skilled and will increasingly make use of automated data processing;

there will only be a limited demand for unskilled jobs in the core and this could shrink dramatically over the next twenty years.

People are living longer and we need to integrate the requirements of the aged, handicapped and the sick with those of the wider community. Large-scale public or private housing development needs much more careful consideration from a social point of view than hitherto. Evidence is accumulating which indicates the need for a thorough reassessment of housing policy directed towards enlarging choice and consumer preference, greater social mixing and forms of assistance to those who need it most.

The need for houses and accommodation is most acute in the big cities and especially London; attempts to interpret statistics to show that the problem is disappearing or is no longer very serious are misguided. The situation is getting worse.

One thing appears fairly certain; the number of people to be housed or re-housed by the turn of the century is unlikely to be less than 25 million; it might well be higher. Studies carried out at the National Institute of Economic and Social Research suggest that by the end of the century, the very most that is likely to be achieved would be the replacement of pre-1940 dwellings. It has been suggested that we are only likely to be able to replace pre-1970 dwellings if the resources required per unit can be halved. This seems to be a good example of the *constraints* which have to be considered and reconciled with the notion of providing increased choice and higher standards.

The accumulating evidence of increasing social differentiation and pluralism of publics emphasises that whilst they seek a life style that offers the most orderly life, they demand the privilege of being allowed the maximum of possible disorder, and the real problems of the future will most likely be concerned with equality and choice. We will hear more of the demand that things should be allowed to 'happen'; for a greater permissiveness. Standardised physical solutions, arbitrary objectives reflecting professional arrogance, hasty decisions and inadequate consultations will be challenged strongly by publics anxious to assert their new found power; to participate.

The role and importance of voluntary organisations and pressure groups, civic societies, conservation groups, students against pollution, and sectional interests of every conceivable kind, is growing

49

apace and the encouraging interest in conservation, indicates that public opinion is a force to be reckoned with.

We should encourage communities and organisations of a voluntary nature to play an increasing role in deciding priorities and extending choice. This could provide an extra dimension to political democracy; it might also conceivably help promote appropriate economic growth, extend social harmony and create a more equal society. *Most important of all remains the need for a more regional framework, for an effective system of strategic and local planning.*

Planning in Transition

Whilst the 1968 Town and Country Planning Act, the Transport Act, the Countryside Act, the Civic Amenities Act and the Skeffington Report indicate the speed and volume of legislation, local government reform is essential if the 1968 Town and Country Planning Act is to fulfil the hopes placed in it; the structure policy plans and local plans, the wide variety of sub-regional plans, will be effective to the extent that there will be a new political structure with powerful executive authorities to *implement* the plans. Central government practice will need to adapt to meet the need for efficiency and establish a more effective decision making hierarchy.

There are surely three levels of planning; the provincial economic resource allocation and policy level which is largely aspatial, concerned with broad economic and locational decisions; the strategic primarily physical, concerned with spatial structure; and the district or local level.

The essential working relationship between economic resource planning and regional and urban planning is still far from clear. The need to provide an appropriate spatial scale within which strategic planning may take place is left largely unresolved by local government reorganisation. Apart from the metropolitan areas in England which will undoubtedly have problems arising from the distribution of planning powers as between the County and District level, all the evidence suggests that authorities will be making structure plans for areas which are much smaller than the province or the economic region. Although it may appear that we are a little nearer to that elusive recognition of regional fact, without a more effective role at metropolitan or provincial level, so-called strategic planning will have its difficulties, especially as population growth and urban development continue to be no respecters of boundaries.

The need to co-ordinate national economic growth and its physical expression in the regions is one of the most intractable problems. Although it is obvious that centralised economic planning cannot be considered in any sense as a blueprint or end-state plan, it is both necessary and possible to effect a much greater degree of co-ordination between economic growth, regional resource allocation and strategies of settlement location.

The resolution of regional issues or central city financial problems depends increasingly on central government. As the American historian Oscar Handlin remarks, 'the great cities do not control themselves, they are subordinate to the State and its policies'.[45] Physical planning, not being divorced from the social system, operates within these constraints and whilst the extent to which government interferes with the free working of the economy may be debated, it is evident that planning seen as a co-ordinated and rational approach to securing explicit objectives is unavoidably and inherently a political activity. Scientific analysis and sophisticated models may allow us to measure efficiency with greater rigour but the re-allocation of costs and benefits is a matter of political decision.

Investment in the public sector has been increasing and planning now also seeks to be more responsive to the needs of the private sector; government has limited resources for public expenditure and authorities are encouraged to seek to utilise private initiative, capital and expertise; it is argued that consumer preference, in housing for example, can be met largely by the market.

National governments are becoming increasingly involved in measures of economic planning. The United States, OECD, many international and national agencies, are concerned in economic development programmes which are interrelated with specific programmes of physical development. The experience of the post war years has shown that economic factors have profound implications on the distribution of employment and population; on the success or otherwise of physical planning proposals.

The relationship between the national economy and regional planning is critical. Important though the functions of plan making and management may be, a realistic *economic* context for the making and implementation of plans is even more necessary.

The timescales of economic and physical planning are very different. Economic planning is short term and easily blown off course by the vagaries of the international monetary system, the changing climate of world trade, or by unforeseen political events (for example, the Middle East War, the escalation in fuel and world commodity prices, since this essay was written). Decisions on atomic power stations, power and pipe lines, motorways, transportation, airports, major factory complexes, national and regional facilities for exhibitions, the arts and recreation, and many other examples . . . not forgetting new cities and towns, demand large scale and continuing investment. The co-ordination and sequential phasing of economic decisions and the implementation of physical planning is still a relatively unsophisticated activity. We require improved co-ordination between economic investment programmes and the physical implementation of a wide range of schemes at regional and city scales. Likewise, we need integrated decision making between government departments and a much more vigorous approach towards co-ordinating social as well as economic and physical planning goals and objectives.

Future Directions

Physical spatial planning has undergone some dramatic changes of emphasis. There is now no finite or static conception of an optimum or ideal environment; ideas of urban settlement are no longer concerned with a social or physical ideal state; rather with understanding the process of change. New models and concepts, greater understanding of the interaction between economic, social and physical processes, ways of structuring settlement growth are of critical importance for progress in this field of planning.

The land planning system has exerted a positive influence when it has been used effectively to secure appropriate objectives. Perhaps the outstanding weakness, when we look back, was the inadequate provision at the regional level for effective co-ordination of the activities of the different planning and highway authorities. The institutional framework was ill-equipped to tackle the problems of urban change whilst there were critical failures in the information required to inform decisions. The political dimension of decision-making was barely understood. People were supposed to believe that decisions in 'the public interest' were non-controversial, merely technical decisions of no political consequence.

The 1968 Town and Country Planning Act promised a more flexible framework for land planning which, given effective local government reorganisation, could allow the content, form and method of policy plan making to be reformulated in practice with the object of strategic and local planning playing a central role.

The concept of strategic and local planning implies an effective hierarchy of decision making and an understanding by the newly established authorities of the need to regard planning as a continuous process; likewise, policy planning at the strategic level will need to integrate more effectively than hitherto the diverse 'plans'—a better word would be programmes—of departments or groupings of departments (education, health, housing and other services); budgeting and management techniques must become effective instruments in programme evaluation, in responding to perceived policy needs and implementation, in reducing lead and lag times. Land and spatial planning, not being divorced from the social system, operates within these constraints and must be recognised as a genus of planning that has a much more limited and circumscribed role than is often recognised.

Nevertheless, the inadequacies of old or new systems need not blind us to the successes of public planning. Although we have fought what sometimes appears to be a losing battle with the motor car or with unseen economic forces and pressures, the physical environment would have been much more adversely affected by a 'free for all'. The criticisms that the system was not flexible enough at one end and not comprehensive enough at the other has given rise to the concept of 'strategic' and 'local' planning as activities within a continuous process, capable of being considered at various scales in space and time.

The major lesson we have learned is that we need many different kinds of planning and planning agencies. Statutory land planning may be a vital element, but it remains only one element in any effective organisational planning system. Until this is more widely understood we shall make little progress.[46]

It seems likely that the integration of various central government departments to produce the Department of the Environment, the adoption of corporate forms of organisation by that Department, the Greater London Council and other organisations are the shape of things to come.

If we have distinguished between generic and physical/spatial planning, it has been with the object of recognising their separate, if related and interacting, development. But this distinction is an oversimplification and 'general' planning itself may be subdivided into a growing number of specialised areas. Planning is concerned with resource allocation, programmes and projects, co-ordination and guidance, and conflict resolution. The difficulties that arise are finding the most effective instruments or methods for dealing with the problems locating and allocating these planning functions at the right level in the decision-making hierarchy, and ensuring that the necessary institutional/organisational framework exists or is created/designed/invented.

We are beginning to design networks which will be adequate for our defined needs. In such a context 'planning' closely approximates to a goal directed, decision making process where there is systematic provision and improvement of information and data for decision making for predicting consequences for the future of alternative courses of action taken in the present, and consequences for present action of alternative goals in the future.[47]

The notion of organisational or corporate planning corresponds and responds to the complex environment in which we live today:

Adaptation is the crux of planning, although it is not its ostensible object . . . The real object of corporate planning is the continuous adaptation of the enterprise towards continuing survival.

This is all a very different approach to traditional comprehensive planning which was characterised by a long-range ideal end state for urban development in the framework of a synoptic master plan. Policy planning aims to deal with pressing urban problems, for example, by influencing, guiding and extending communications and dialogue on the means and ends of public decision making. It is becoming evident that systems experts and planners, whether in government or university have a new social role combining political and technical dimensions, a role that cannot be separated from judgments of value, and issues that are inherently political.

The first plans prepared under the new system have been submitted to the Secretary of State and Examinations in Public are timetabled for the end of 1973. The Layfield Report on the Greater London Development Plan devoted an important chapter to structure planning that deserves close study[48] and raised three issues of general importance for structure planning:

(a) the problems which planning for uncertainty, confidentiality, and blight pose for government.

(b) the extent to which transportation, housing and to a lesser degree, perhaps, employment—as well as unemployment—have become highly charged political issues.

(c) the relevance of national and regional policies, or the absence of such policies.

The structure planning process could well be used to promote new, or modify existing, regional and national planning policies. Where the process is distinguished from the outset by technical competence, good publicity and effective participation by representative groups and individuals, a planning authority has the opportunity to draw attention to a range of problems such as pollution, water resources, housing, social welfare and to advocate various policies and actions, all of which may be beyond the powers of the statutory submission. At a time when there is much talk of the need for community action and grass roots political activity on environmental matters, it is interesting to speculate on the changes which may be brought about indirectly by campaigns on issues which lie outside the powers of planning legislation entirely, but which nevertheless have important spatial and locational implications relating to and including the use of land.

It follows that an understanding of the legitimate scope and powers of a structure plan is essential to any discussion on the future of the planning system in the UK. The statutory plan and its essential components as defined by regulations is contrasted by a number of commentators with a dynamic generic planning process which is progressively tending to embrace a widening area of concern.

Such a distinction may be valid, but it is confusing. Many adherents of a broader view of the planning process saw the new system as a golden opportunity to extend the role and content of the Development Plan. Paradoxically, this may well inhibit the evolution of more effective and adaptive mechanisms. On the limited evidence available to date, it seems erroneous to suppose that the statutory system will extend its areas of concern very much wider than the 1947 Development Plan system which it replaced. Indeed, unless the problem of land speculation and compensation and betterment is tackled effectively, the implementation of many plans at both strategic and local level will be highly problematical. There are vocal and insistent demands to redefine ends and adopt appropriate organisational means to achieve them. The social front of planning has become part of the political foreground in response to critical urban problems. How far the redistribution of the good things in life can be brought about by specific spatial and locational policies is difficult to establish with precision. It may be that social action and fiscal measures would be more effective and less costly in some contexts but not in others. The substantive scope of ongoing policy planning in any authority extends beyond land planning, but this is no reason or justification to interpret the structure plan as *the* vehicle for what is in effect organisation or corporate planning.

Moreover to go well beyond the bounds of physical planning is to risk many problems and administrative confusions. It certainly vitiates the objectives of the Planning Advisory Group (HMSO, 1965). The statutory local and administrative constraints have to be recognised and the complexities of effective collaboration between authorities is a *sine qua non* of the successful production of structure plans and the structure plan process. It is particularly acute at this point in time following local government reorganisation both between and within authorities.

At this point in time it is difficult to evaluate the extent to which structure plans are being prepared in a coherent relationship one with another, or are interpreting regional strategies in a similar way. The movement of jobs and services, commuting across administrative boundaries, are critical issues with important political, social and economic implications. There is little evidence which suggests that it is becoming easier to *implement* strategies that cut across arbitrary administrative and political boundaries. If anything the evidence is in the other direction. It is important also to appreciate that while administrative procedures need to be clearly understood, effective and expeditious, they will not resolve conflicts of interest, real or imagined, between authorities or different levels of government.

If structure plans are to be effective strategic policy instruments, they will need to be highly selective, concentrating on broad principles and strategic issues, responding to national and regional policy, as well as providing a context for design planning and control at the local level. 'Broad-brush' planning is not only an administrative convenience—it is made necessary by the speed of change and the limits of effective prediction. The Greater London Development Plan Inquiry highlighted this over and over again.

The lessons are fairly clear:

(a) The power and ability of plans and our planning system to bring about desirable changes is much more limited than is generally realised. Major housing questions of strategic importance, whether in London or the West Midlands are, in practice, matters for central government rather than the structure plan; it is a question of where the power and responsibility lies.

(b) The danger of exaggerating the extent to which policies may alter trends in population or employment needs to be recognised.

(c) The danger of adopting unrealistic timescales within which to bring about changes in trends in the short and medium term needs to be recognised. Similarly, long-term possibilities are subject to still higher levels of uncertainty.

(d) We have to accept that the information available in a form which is useful, for example, to monitor change, and in particular, to measure and evaluate the effects of various policies, is extremely limited.

The levels of uncertainty in exploring alternative ranges of figures requires articulation. If we are considering alternatives and different components of a plan, we should avoid adopting on the one hand a spurious technical neutrality, or pretend that it is impossible to adopt a relatively objective stance in considering normative factors such as housing standards or slum clearance. We have to accept that uncertainty, complex problems of values and valuation, as well as political decision, are involved in the calculus. The implications of such a stance towards information, to facts and values

57

derived from facts, for the political process and people generally, are enormous. Such a process of de-mystification could transform the role of the professional and make his advice both more credible and acceptable. Such an approach requires a greater emphasis on the evidential basis of planning proposals and respect and encouragement for relevant research findings. Above all strategic objectives should be clear and unambiguous providing the general policy framework within which subordinate, if interacting, policies for implementation and development can be formulated and applied.

The public through their organisations have shown their ability to argue the merits of alternative strategies and policies. Choice and alternatives are possible. The future is not determined by esoteric methodologies and techniques, nor by the selective applications of particular technologies. If the emphasis has shifted to the political process, it is because administrative and bureaucratic approaches have proved inadequate to the tasks facing our cities and society generally.

Two conclusions may be drawn. Firstly, whilst the structure plan process may embrace rather more than an old style land-use plan, how much more is not easy to ascertain. However, from a conceptual viewpoint, it is helpful to view the structure plan as one of a number of public policy plans, but perhaps one of a special kind, occupying a pivotal position that gives synoptic, spatial, locational expression and interpretation to all or most of the other plans and policies of the Authority. Equally, the structure plan also may be viewed as the spatial and locational expression of a corporate plan *where one exists.*

Secondly, if the planning system faces formidable procedural and methodological problems in the foreseeable future, the substantive problems appear even more intractable, a point of view sometimes overlooked by procedural critics, management consultants, and those over pre-occupied with a rational model of man and market. If these two conclusions are generally valid, it follows that present arrangements may change substantially. We may see the development of very different fiscal and social policies to alleviate the growing financial burden of central cities, very different social technologies to deal with social malaise, overcrowding and homelessness. The physical and spatial implications of such changes may be considerable.

Renewed interest in an indicative national physical plan on the lines of the Dutch model, growing emphasis on regional and sub-regional planning scales, underlines what is rapidly becoming a major political issue, namely the failure of central Government to consider its own planning and resource allocation functions in any coherent or public way. This is not a new point. It goes back to Geddes' time. But the issue of regional policy in the EEC highlights the importance it assumes in the Council of Europe. The way in which decisions are being made about the third London Airport, the channel tunnel, and transport generally, should be giving concern to many government advisors. Corporate planning, more effective organisation and integration is now of growing importance in Whitehall. The inescapable conclusion is that greater attention must be given to national policies, to the regional context and, in particular, to economic and social analysis.

The structure planning process provides, or should provide, spatial and locational guidelines, investment options, in response to such analysis. It should provide positive policies for the redistribution of population within a region, the location and development of major sub-centres, the priorities and standards for residential development in various areas, clear guidelines for conservation and environment; the strategic plan must secure consistency, adequate tests, criteria, guidelines and standards to secure the environmental and other objectives it seeks to achieve; at the heart of the structure plan process is the task to ensure effective communications planning. Integrated transportation and land use activity policies reflecting economic investment, social behaviour and activity patterns are probably the major components of the structure plan, they are certainly the key issues for debate and political decision. *The structure plan in this context is a special strategic variety of land plan.*

To Summarise:

One of the problems which emerges from this review and indeed from the literature on planning is the lack of clarity as to the nature and role of objectives. This confusion is worse confounded when the statutory structure planning process is studied from the point of view of its appropriate areas of concern as well as its procedures.

There is lack of clarity on the extent to which structure plans will fulfil a strategic planning role and in turn this is bound up with the relationship between such statutory plans and policies/plans for the sub-regional, regional and national levels.

The geographical areas for plan making may become increasingly unrealistic politically and socially.

Reorganised two-tier government and the introduction of organisation planning brings in its wake new problems of organisation and co-ordination.

We may hopefully expect greater integration at the national level of government. New opportunities for improving the hierarchy of plans and planning may occur.

Nevertheless, the regional context is important and the absence of more effective regional policy plans remains a source of weakness and confusion.

If more effective regional and sub-regional policies, constituting more generalised plans, are to evolve, then a more limited and realistic role may emerge for the structure plan as the physical and spatial and locational expression of wider more generalised policies. To that extent it will reflect and interpret financial, human, material and land resources in so far as they are relevant for its more restricted and modest purposes, namely the provision of an appropriate context for the co-ordination of physical design plans and control policies. As such, a more modest role is advocated for the structure planning process. Statutory structure plans would be less ambitious. They would be considered and approved in stages. They would not promise what they cannot hope to do. The corollary is that *more detailed local planning and design* would take on a greater and more considered role within local government. Such developments would require the Royal Town Planning Institute to re-define more carefully what its appropriate professional sphere of interest is and what consequential changes are likely to be necessary in its educational and other policies.

Corporate planning procedures may take some years to become established. *In the meantime, the structure plan process may well have to do service for the policies of an authority.* Moreover, the process may continue in a wider context which is ill-defined and unsatisfactory. If so, then the relationships of the structure plan process to other forms of planning and organisation will be critical so far as land, spatial and locational policies are concerned. *The extent to which the structure plan/process is coherent and credible in practice is, therefore, influenced, if not determined by the state of other forms of planning and the ongoing processes so far as national, regional and sub-regional levels are concerned.*

It is the aims of town and country planning that are being questioned. Practitioners should play a part in the growing debate as to the distribution of resources and facilities in urban society. They should be prepared to make informed comment on the social system, recognising that the *instrumental* role of physical planning is objectively restricted. If physical planners had a clearer grasp of social theory, they would be blamed less for society's failures. They would not regard such failures as necessarily all to be laid at their door.

Conclusion

I believe that the planner aspires to take sides, for example, where ecological ethics are relevant. If it is necessary to advocate smaller newspapers to preserve the culture of our forests then so be it. We are concerned with the ethics which relate man to the land and the animals and plants which grow out of it. Regional planning is concerned with ecological balance between man and nature. It implies concern for more than remedial action to safeguard biological and social life. The idea of civilisation and cities is perhaps the most important of all ideas; it requires long-term thinking and concern for the form of settlement pattern that harmonises with nature. The countryside is not what is left over between urban areas; this is both an erroneous and suicidal view. We have it in our power to restructure our physical and social life and maintain that equilibrium with nature. This is not a rustic or romantic, anti-city view, but the result of what we know about the effects which man is having on the natural world about him. Planning with social purpose should result in a better and more habitable environment for man, and the creation of populated regions, cultivated and developed in accordance with their economic and biological potentialities and their capacity to meet the demands and pressures generated by the pattern of settlement.

This suggests the need to recognise that the economic doctrines and the utilitarian ethic of the nineteenth century, is making way for the rationale which accepts that the era of cybernetics, leisure and different social attitudes to employment, may not be too far away. This demands a higher quality of planning which goes beyond the maximising of economic resources or cost-benefit techniques.

There seems little doubt that an international and national policy on population is required which seeks to stabilise populations. This would make it easier to ensure that the process of urbanisation takes place in a co-ordinated way; that human and natural resources are synthesised so as to ensure their use to maximum effect.

I think planners must hope and *believe* that there is a unifying theme in human affairs. The great historian, Thomas Macaulay, visiting the Great Exhibition of 1851 said he experienced the same feeling of awe as he had first felt on entering St Peter's in Rome, the same sense of wonder when confronted by two marvellous triumphs of the human spirit. He spoke of man's progress—material and spiritual. In his *Essay on Bacon*[49] Macaulay expresses his faith in the view of history as progress:

It has lengthened life; it has mitigated pain; it has extinguished diseases; it has increased the fertility of the soil . . . it has spanned great rivers and estuaries with bridges of form unknown to our fathers . . . it has multiplied the power of the human muscles; it has accelerated motion; it has annihilated distance . . . these are but a part of its fruits, and of its first fruits. For it is a philosophy which never rests, which has never attained, which is never perfect. Its law is progress. A point which yesterday was invisible is its goal today, and will be its starting-post tomorrow.

As Sir Peter Medawar has written[50] to deride the hope of progress is indeed the ultimate fatuity.

Nevertheless, the era of blind faith in progress is at an end. It is possible that the technological power released in an overcrowded world may overload any guidance system we devise for its control.

If planners and social scientists are to play a rational and effective role in society, perhaps they need to adopt a strategy that is more modest in its hopes for the perfectability of mankind and more conscious to the dangers which face us here and now.

Scientific knowledge may provide fundamental advances in scientific theory, but it cannot provide all the answers for the formulation of social policy. If we make this point clear the charge that the scientific mode of thought is a fundamental threat to humane values will no longer receive credence. The corollary is the need to disabuse some people of the idea that the adoption of advanced technology is automatically beneficial.

Public service and social responsibility are concepts with meaning; they are exercised by professional men and women with high moral and ethical standards, within a highly developed institutional framework which extends far beyond the limits of planning activity. We are heirs to the practical and pragmatic decision-makers who built our great industrial cities. But our urban and regional planning must be concerned with more than management and programme budgeting; its purposes seek to provide a framework within which we may lead fuller and more productive lives. The role of the art and science of planning and its application to society should help to clarify our public values, define our policy options and assist the politicians and policy makers to legislate wisely so that, as Bacon said, human life can be enriched by new discoveries and powers. I believe that urban and regional planning will be judged by its results. It will be most successful in a climate of coherent economic planning where the political and social goals are clear and may be realistically approached within the resources available. Above all, it requires a world and a culture that accepts the self-discipline and responsibility which planning demands in an open society.

References

1 J. Friedmann, Planning as a vocation, *Plan Canada*, vol. 6, No. 3/4 (1966).
2 Rachel Carson, *Silent Spring* (Hamish Hamilton, 1962).
3 R. G. Wilkinson, *Poverty and Progress* (Methuen, 1973).
4 Lucien Goldmann, *The Human Sciences and Philosophy* (Cape, 1969).
5 Yeates and Garner, *The North American City* (Harper and Row, 1971).
6 E. Jantsch, *Perspectives of Planning* (OECD, Paris, 1969).
7 Catherine B. Wurster, Introduction in *Explorations into Urban Structure* (University of Pennsylvania, 1964).
8 Jantsch (1969), *op. cit.*
9 Jantsch (1969), *op. cit.*
10 N. Weiner, *The Human Use of Human Beings* (Sphere, 1950).
11 P. Geddes, *Cities in Evolution* (Benn, 1968. First published 1915).
12 J. K. Galbraith, *The New Industrial State* (Signet, 1967).
13 R. Arvill, *Man and Environment* (Penguin, 1967).

14 See P. Ehrlich and A. Ehrlich, *Issues in Human Ecology* (W. H. Freeman, San Francisco, 1970).

15 *ibid.*

16 Fried, *Planning the Eternal City* (Yale, 1973).

17 L. K. Caldwell, *Environment and Administration, The Politics of Ecology, in Environment, Resources, Pollution and Society,* ed Murdoch Sinauer (1971).

18 R. Kantorowich, Education for planning; *Journal of Royal Town Planning Institute* (May 1967).

19 Quoted by A. Glikson in *Regional Planning and Development* (Leiden, 1955).

20 Development plans—a manual on form and content (HMSO, 1970).

21 Benton MacKaye, *The New Exploration* (NY, 1928).

22 See, for example, Murray Stewart, *The City* (Penguin, 1972).

23 'Social Processes and Spatial Form: an Analysis of the Conceptual Problems of Urban Planning,' *Papers and Proceedings of Regional Science Association,* pp. 47–69, vol. 25.

24 Peter Hall, *Theory and Practice of Regional Planning* (Pemberton, 1970).

25 Quoted by J. W. Dyckman, *Journal of American Institute of Planners* (Sept., 1969).

26 See Education for Planning, in *Progress in Planning,* vol. 1, Part 1 (Pergamon, 1973).

27 'The New Urban Planning in America', *Journal of Royal Town Planning Institute* (Jan. 1968).

28 *Town Planners and their future; A Further Discussion Paper* (The Royal Town Planning Institute, August 1973).

29 D. Foley, British Town Planning: One Ideology or Three. *British Journal of Sociology,* **2,** 1960.

30 E. H. Carr, *What is History* (Penguin, 1953).

31 L. Benevolo, *The Origins of Modern Town Planning* (Routledge and Kegan Paul, 1967).

32 C. E. Schorske, The Idea of the City in Human Thought, in *The Historian and the City* (M.I.T. and Harvard University Press, 1963).

33 H. Rosenau, *The Ideal City in its Architectural Evolution.* (Studio Vista, 1972).

34 M. Meyerson, *Utopian Traditions and the Planning of Cities* (Daedalus, Winter 1961).

35 Benevolo, *op. cit.*

36 W. Ashworth, *The Genesis of British Town Planning* (Routledge and Kegan Paul, 1954).

37 See G. Vickers, *Value Systems and the Social Process* (Penguin, 1968).

38 See W. Petersen, Some Meanings of Planning, *American Institute of Planners Journal* (May 1965).

39 L. Mumford, *The City in History* (Penguin, 1961).
40 Meyerson, *op. cit.*
41 C. D. Buchanan, *The State of Britain* (Faber and Faber, 1972).
42 J. R. James, *A Strategic View of Planning, RIBA Journal* (October 1967).
43 Florence Sargent, Economic Efficiency in the Metropolis in *The Metropolis in Modern Life* (Columbia University Press, 1955).
44 See Edgar A. Rose, Critical Questions, *Municipal Engineering Supplement* (May 25, 1973).
45 Oscar Handlin in *The Historian and the City, op. cit.*
46 Buchanan (1972), *op. cit.*
47 Stafford Beer, The aborting corporate plan, *Perspectives in Planning* (OECD, Paris, 1969).
48 Report of the Committee of Inquiry into the Greater London Development Plan (Layfield Committee Report) (HMSO, 1973).
49 Quoted by J. H. Plumb, *The Historian's Dilemma, Crisis in the Humanities* (Penguin, 1964).
50 *The Listener* (2 October 1969).

3. The Development of Planning Thought

Gordon E. Cherry

The factors which have contributed to the development of planning thought are numerous and complex; moreover they have been intertwined over time and woven into the fabric of our social, economic and political history. It would be spurious therefore to attempt to isolate contributory influences and place them in water-tight compartments. Planning had no simple origins, nor has its evolution been determined in any specific way; the best we can suggest is that in the context of broad social and political movements over the last two centuries in particular, cumulative ideas about planning have been successfully transmitted from one period to another.

It is possible to outline a convenient checklist for considering the many issues involved in the development of planning thought in Britain. This chapter offers such a framework. Five headings might be considered:

1. Inherited traditions.
2. Victorian urban management.
3. Reaction to the 'state of our cities'.
4. Centralist bureaucracy.
5. Changes in contemporary approaches to planning.

The contribution of the first category, inherited traditions, extends back until at least Renaissance Britain; the remaining categories follow largely in chronological sequence from about 1820 to the present day. Essentially, therefore, the framework is that of the last 150 years, a century and a half of social and political change consequent upon the industrial and economic transformations of this country. Planning as we know it today is essentially a feature and product of our modern industrial society, although there is a distinct throwback to the contribution of far earlier years.

Inherited Traditions

Two main features of Renaissance and post-Renaissance Britain contributed materially to the development of planning ideas in the nineteenth and twentieth centuries. One related to the compulsive social vision of ideal communities and the other to the idea of architectural order and formal spatial arrangement. Both these are concepts to which there has been a frequent return and to that extent they may be regarded as repetitive themes in our planning history.

The first might be said to begin with Thomas More's *Utopia* (1516) which, in a fictional narrative, presented a postulate of an ideal commonwealth, as a contrast to the turbulent situation of the time. A feature of Renaissance literature was the literary retreat to far-off mythical islands or lands in which quite different communities were described; More's narrator discovered and visited the country of Utopia and described its rigidly structured society and government. There were many subsequent variations on this theme. Francis Bacon's *New Atlantis* (1627) had a basis of scientific perfection and James Harrington's *Oceana* (1656) was a proposal for a new political constitution. Jonathan Swift's satire, *Gulliver's Travels* (1726) was another description of an ideal State, in Part Two, 'A Voyage to Brobdingnag'. From More's work, particularly, there built up a model of utopia where the central characteristics showed common features. The ideal state was homocentric rather than theocentric; in the new humanist tradition the concern was man and his organisation in community. Socially the emphasis was collectivist, on the group rather than on the individual or family life. Economically, the ideal was centralisation and collective control rather than individual effort. From the point of view of government, benevolent dictatorships were favoured.

The influence of the utopian tradition was strong right through the nineteenth century, and many of the precepts for an ordered, hard-working, abstemious community are to be found in More and similar writers. The activities of Robert Owen at New Lanark offer an obvious link. He reconstructed the organisation of a cotton manufacturing village at the Falls of Clyde during the first two decades of the nineteenth century, seeking, as linked objectives, both an efficient factory and a disciplined community. As a social reformer he strove to alter the conditions under which the inhabitants lived and worked so that the very character and disposition of the people would be improved. His *New View of Society* (1813) outlined his philosophy on the formation of human character and in his *Report to the County of Lanark* (1820) he described his proposals for the special establishment of communities in agricultural villages.

The Owenite tradition, which attempted to put into practice many of the utopian ideas, was very strong throughout the century. Through the influence of the housing reformers, for example, the idea of environmental determinism was strongly maintained. The desire for communities of small, self-supporting units ran through the idea of both co-operative and anarchist colonies and can be seen in attempts to disperse urban population from London and the big cities to surrounding countryside areas. General William Booth, the Salvation Army leader, favoured farm colonies and we might see the same idea of flight from the big city in Howard's proposal for satellite towns. This repetitive theme is illustrated in more detail in G. E. Cherry's *Town Planning in its Social Context* (1970).

The other Renaissance element was that of architectural order, a characteristic strongly maintained in Britain from the seventeenth century onwards—indeed, from the time when in 1615 Inigo Jones was appointed Surveyor to the King. A new era of progressive architecture began which set two centuries of taste; his Palladian style became a norm to which classical architecture returned repeatedly. This represented a tradition of conscious improvement and enhancement of the urban scene, and when combined with the regular laying-out of estates in London and elsewhere, it might be said to reflect a conscious pursuit of the ideal city in architectural terms as well as from the social point of view.

Wren's plan for London was an exercise in grand manner design embracing all the approaches to Renaissance town planning: geometric unity, piazzas, triumphal avenues, and an overall setting of dignity for churches and public buildings. Wren's City was never built but the Renaissance influence of formal layout was illustrated and continued to be demonstrated. In London, for example, successive waves of estate development beginning with Covent Garden laid out by the Earl of Bedford in the 1630s, subsequently spreading westward after the Great Fire to St James Square (Earl of St Albans) and Bloomsbury (Earl of Southampton). In the eighteenth century this continued with the development of grand residential squares in west and north London. Outside London, the Woods (father and son) built Bath, and this and other spa towns incorporated the fashionable elements of circus, parade and geometric designs. In Edinburgh, Robert Craig's plan for the New Town had a simple unity of parallel streets and terminal squares.

The significance of these examples was that they constituted a strong appeal as a principle of urban improvement. The unified architectural schemes became models for those who in the nineteenth century were distressed by the poverty of design and the philistinism of industrial Britain. Occasionally, a practical scheme such as the development by Dobson and Grainger at Newcastle in the 1830s, or a theoretical treatise such as that by James Silk Buckingham in his proposal for a Model Town of 10 000 persons known as Victoria published in 1849 (*National Evils and Practical Remedies*), kept alive the ideas so that the tradition was never entirely lost. The development of planning thought owed a good deal to the concept of an orderly, dignified urban environment which the rampant individualism of the nineteenth century so frequently failed to attain.

Victorian Environmental Management

Prior to 1830 this country was remarkably free from State direction and control. In place of central administration, there was a loose framework of local, *ad hoc* bodies which sought to regulate the matters over which they had responsibility. They were the boroughs and the magistrates, guilds, vestries, commissioners and corporate bodies. The tasks of central government were seen as framing national policy in foreign and commercial affairs and generally supervising the maintenance of good government internally. The years around 1830 saw significant changes in outlook and paved the way for quite different approaches later in the century. The reasons for these developments are many and varied. It is not necessary to go very deeply into these but we should recognise at least that this was a period of great upheaval. It was the aftermath of two great social and political revolutions (America and France), social and economic transformations (agriculture and industry) and of foreign wars. A tide of new forces in political ideas permeated national affairs and it became a period of great inventiveness. A period of urban growth, population expansion, social distress, unrest and economic crisis made necessary a new apparatus of government, management, direction, control and intervention. Developments were evolutionary but after almost a century there emerged the social welfare state, central to which was the idea of planning. In this context, town planning as an exercise in land and environmental management, took shape as a movement in its own right.

The Reform Bill of 1832 and its sequel, the Municipal Reform Bill of 1835, mark an important early stage in this development. Much was immediately implied by the transference of power to new classes, but much was still unforeseen. Few could forecast in 1835 that the newly created municipalities would be the essential agents of urban development that in fact they became. In due time they lit and paved the streets, controlled the building of houses, were responsible for sanitation and health, engaged in the transport of men to and from work, provided libraries, parks and swimming baths, and educated our children.

Once the new trend had set in things moved quickly. For example, Sir Robert Peel's institution of the civilian police had applied only to the Metropolitan area in 1829. By 1856 every county and borough had to employ a police force, half local, half national, in its administration. Lord Althorp's Factory Act of 1833 set legal limits to the working hours of child labour, and its provisions were enforced by the appointment of factory inspectors. Lord Shaftesbury's Mines Act of 1842 and the Factory Act of 1847 were the next stages in promoting a far-spreading code of statutory regulations governing conditions and hours of industry. Concern over provision of playgrounds might be seen as starting with the appointment in 1833 of a Select Committee to consider the deficiency of 'Public Walks and Places of Exercise'. The Victorian Park movement gathered force, stimulated by voluntary bodies such as the Commons Preservation Society founded in 1865. In education the turning point was in 1870, when Gladstone's measure provided for Board Schools paid out of local rates. In the new system of universal primary education, the school attendance increased from 1·25 million in 1870 to 4·5 million in 1890. Public libraries, dating from 1850, became popular towards the end of the century.

With regard to health, the Public Health Act of 1848 followed

Chadwick's investigations and set up public health authorities with new powers. The Act of 1875 gave a public health service covering the whole country for the first time. In the meantime, there was control over burial grounds. In respect of housing, legislation in 1868 and 1875 gave limited powers to deal with insanitary housing, and in 1890 there was provision for local authorities to build dwellings for the working classes. Concerning power supply, the production of coal gas for public and private lighting began early in the century and municipal supply was slow to gather pace. But electrical generation began in the last quarter of the century, and private schemes were increasingly discouraged in favour of local authority control. Municipal transport also developed strongly.

This is a brief and selective review of developments that occurred in the half-century after 1830. Many details can be added from the rich canvas of social history. The point being made however is a simple but important one: the second half of the nineteenth century marked a fundamental point of departure in the way we regarded and dealt with our internal national problems. In many ways, these, in fact, might almost be equated with the urban situation because the problems were those of housing, health and environment. To this extent there was a reaction against the problems of unplanned development: rapid urbanisation, the huge and increasing size of London, and the loss of population from rural areas; and health, sanitation, housing and conditions of life and labour in the big cities. There was also a substantial shift in the political system. Over the years, municipal authority was transferred from co-operative oligarchies of Tory Lawyers, Churchmen and noblemen's agents to Dissenters, shopkeepers and middle-class citizens. Power and influence was gradually redistributed and widened, and the new franchise saw to it that corporate interests were more broadly based than was formerly the case. An understanding of these aspects of British social history in the last century, offers important pointers to the course of the development of planning in the twentieth century. The increasing readiness to intervene in urban affairs was made possible by the strength of local government and the powers they assumed. Recognition of the actual need to intervene was sharpened periodically when public attention was focused on particular problems.

Reaction to the State of Our Cities

In the 1890s the critical urban problem could be summarised as 'the state of our cities'. Descriptions of the physical and social environments bore many resemblances to those of today; as now, the protest literature of the time exposed the problems which so far had been inadequately tackled. The extent and severity of the problems obviously differed, but the *type* of urban problem was the same. It is the relative constancy of the scene which gives British planning, over the last 70 years, its many repetitive themes. The essential problem was housing, particularly housing for the working classes. The Royal Commission on the Housing of the Poor had reported in 1885 and great hopes were set by the Housing of the Working Classes Act of 1890, which gave extra powers to local authorities to close or clear unhealthy dwellings, and to build new dwellings for the working classes out of public funds. The complex linkages between overcrowding, high densities, ill health of slum dwellers, large families, unemployment, and low and irregular pay combined to provide a situation we would now describe as 'social deprivation in the inner city'. Inflammatory tracts like Andrew Mearns' *The Bitter Cry of Outcast London* (1883), followed by General William Booth's analysis of the 'submerged tenth' in his *In Darkest England and the Way Out* (1890) provided disconcerting evidence. This was amplified by the sober fact-finding of Charles Booth in seventeen volumes of *Life and Labour of the People in London* (1889 *et seq*) and of Seebohm Rowntree in *Poverty, a Study of town life* (1901) in a study of York. Marr's *Report on Housing Conditions in Manchester and Salford* (1904) was just one illustration of the wretched housing conditions in the North at the turn of the century. The census of 1901 gave ample evidence of overcrowding in towns throughout the whole country.

In comparison, suburban expansion was meeting the needs of a widening section of society: skilled artisans, clerks and shopkeepers. In London, in particular, the pace and scale of suburban growth was causing concern and the spectre of the big city put the problem on a new strategic level. At the turn of the century, London's population was 4·5 million, and there were ten more cities in Britain with populations greater than 250 000. In London, the outer ring was expanding at a dramatic rate. There were sanitary and building controls over this development, but the way in which land was laid out was uncoordinated and subject to no regulations. This led to increasing pressure for effective municipal control over the use and development of land; the 1909 Act was the first permissive forerunner.

The rise of the town planning movement occurred in this situational context. W. H. Lever, in a Christian business enterprise at Port Sunlight, showed what could be done in the way of an enlightened housing layout and provision of planned facilities, just as Titus Salt had done thirty years before at Saltaire. George Cadbury applied the principles of open estate design to Bournville and gave form to the cardinal requirements of the housing reformers: air, space and light. Ebenezer Howard's *Tomorrow: A Peaceful Path to Real Reform* (subsequently *Garden Cities of Tomorrow*, 1902) gave a strategic answer to the housing problem in a regional context through a concept of satellite development in garden cities of 30 000 people. Letchworth was an early response, and Earswick embraced the design principles at least, although not the strategic setting, for Rowntree at York. The garden city movement was in fact a package of policies designed to harmonise spatial development with meeting social and housing needs, and it was this idea that spread rapidly through Western Europe in particular during the early decades of the century.

Reaction against the housing, environmental and many social problems of British cities was linked with an important aesthetic and design movement which developed during the latter decades of the nineteenth century. It was supported by an idealistic vision of the future, as interpreted by William Morris, socialist poet and designer and sustained by a hostility towards the visual barbarism of the products of the Industrial Revolution. From Europe came new design innovations, centred on the work of Camillo Sitte and others; in Britain this was translated into a new interest of civic art, and Raymond Unwin in particular, as at Hampstead Garden Suburb, introduced new residential design concepts. His *Town Planning in Practice* (1909) was significantly sub-titled 'an introduction to the art of designing cities and suburbs'.

The early approach to town planning was essentially a rational, single-minded, conformist approach to urban problems: it implied and sought public control, decentralisation, and a loosening of urban form. Its first identifiable form was the product of a vigorous private lobby by reformers and propagandist bodies, which gradually became a consensus objective by all those who had views about our urban problems; in due time it was supported, albeit tentatively at first, by government through legislation. Essentially it was a policy devised by a minority, a dedicated interest group, on behalf of the majority. This may be regarded today as paternalism by the action of a middle-class interest group, broadly radical in politics and with a social conscience sharpened through Quaker tradition, evangelical Christianity or socialism. But at the time it was a typical response of Victorian society, whereby, in order to secure better working-class housing conditions, and to provide for a more contented labour force, the support of private lobbies and voluntary action was activated. The mobilisation of the efforts of government was slow and unsure. In the twentieth century this was to change as the planning ideas that had emerged were taken up by professional and technical interests, and the action of government superceded voluntary endeavour.

Centralist Bureaucracy

The inter-war years saw a strengthening of interventionist policies and a broadening of their application. The Housing and Town Planning Act of 1919 called upon local authorities to prepare immediate surveys of their housing needs and to submit plans to the Ministry of Health for dealing with them. New standards of working-class housing were laid down by the Tudor Walters Report of 1918, and these were adopted. The new geometric layouts of Council estates and their low densities enshrined the necessary principles of space, light and air. Later in the period, a slum clearance drive in the 1930s was the first comprehensive approach to dealing with the national scandal of unfit dwellings. In the same decade a positive attack on reducing overcrowding began and the 1936 Public Health Act defined overcrowding for the first time. Intervention in questions of housing and densities was, of course, assisting other forces which were strongly at work. A reduction in family size was having the effect anyway of reducing the statistics of overcrowding, but a substantial easing of densities was being recorded as new suburban areas spread outwards. Fresh air and gardens were the social dictates which planning policy encouraged. Although Welwyn was only the second (and last) garden city, the ideal still held out promise, as the Hundred New Towns Society of the 1930s advocated.

State involvement in economic management was made necessary through the unemployment crises of the 1920s and particularly the early 1930s. The pattern of regional prosperity changed abruptly after the First World War. London, a prewar unemployment black-spot, became a favoured area as the Home Counties generally proved a favourable location for vehicle manufacture and a host of new light industries supporting a growing consumer-oriented domestic market. In contrast, South Wales, the textile areas of the North, the coal mining areas of Scotland, the North-East and elsewhere, and the iron and steel and shipbuilding areas suffered a marked decline. Government groped towards the principles of a national economic policy: the setting up of an Industrial Transference Board in 1928 marked the earliest approach of encouraging labour to migrate to the more prosperous areas, but the Special Areas Act of 1934 saw the policy of aiding development in the regions themselves, by supporting the resuscitation of economic growth. The government-sponsored trading estate became the symbol of planned intervention.

Other aspects of national policies began to develop in a field which the town planning movement embraced. Government toyed with the idea of National Parks and the Addison Report of 1931 found in favour of them, but no action was taken. With regard to roads, a Ministry of Transport allocated investment to major schemes including by-passes, tunnels and bridges, and there was a national concern over measures concerning accident prevention. In the statutory planning process successive legislation extended the scope of planning; the 1932 Act may be regarded as the first national legislation, which brought virtually all land under planning control. As with the 1919 Act, the emphasis was on scheme preparation. In the rural areas increasing attention was being paid to the need for countryside protection and the reservation of land for public enjoyment. In the 1930s the London County Council took a major step forward in financing the reservation of open land surrounding London as a Green Belt, and followed this by a Green Belt Act in 1938.

A hardening of planning thought around the idea of centralist intervention took place in the 1930s and the war-time years brought this to a head. There seemed to be two separate strands to this

75

development. One was the reaction to the economic and social disorders of the inter-war period, whereby the solution, with increasing inevitability, seemed to lie in more government control and direction in accordance with national policies. The other was a reaction to political developments, notably the rise of totalitarian regimes in Europe. British democracy was increasingly seen as a vital bulwark against this menace and democratic planning was regarded as a basis of our national life. Both aspects led to one conclusion: planning was a matter for central government, to be made operational and effective through the medium of local government. An umbrella of new powers was called for and a new central machinery of government was demanded. This was to be the high water-mark of the centralist approach.

A trilogy of influential reports helped to ease the way, while the experience of the war years themselves helped substantially to swing public opinion behind the idea of national responsibility for planning. The Report of the Royal Commission on the Distribution of Industrial Population (the Barlow Report), published in 1940, advocated planning policies for decentralisation, not only of the big cities, but also on a regional scale to give more positive assistance to the depressed areas. A Minority Report (by Abercrombie) called for a central Ministry of Planning. This was to come quicker than observers might then have foreseen. A reconstructed machinery of government provided, in 1943, for a new Ministry of Town and Country Planning.

The Uthwatt Report on Compensation and Betterment (1942) raised the essential problem of control over land use; consideration of this question led ultimately to the financial provisions of the Town and Country Planning Act of 1947. But, in the meantime, the Scott Report on Rural Land Use (1943) had put forward a package of countryside policies including green belts and national parks, and had spoken confidently of an assumed central planning machine. Abercrombie's Plan for Greater London (1944) outlined a disarmingly simple strategy for regional dispersal: reduction of densities in the inner ring and the decentralisation of people and jobs to new centres including those beyond a green belt. A New Towns programme was foreshadowed and the Reith Reports of 1946 were followed immediately by the New Towns Act in the same year. Eight New Towns for London, as well as Towns in the North-East, South

Wales and Scotland were designated. But a national programme for industrial dispersal failed to materialise. The Location of Industry Act, 1945, was rushed through by the Caretaker Government and, although it provided the basis for a policy of 'Industrial Development Certificate' control over new factory floor space, it needed considerable subsequent amendment to give it any coherent shape. The Town and Country Planning Act (1947) decimated the number of planning authorities and provided for a new, compulsory, system of public control of land use. Recreation planning was not to be denied and the National Parks and Access to the Countryside Act (1949) enabled a National Parks programme to be worked through in the 1950s.

The statutory planning process, emanating from the 1947 Act, centred on the Development Plan, and local authorities assumed extensive new powers for control over land use. The essential feature of the system was 'end-state planning' as both national and local administrations worked towards future blueprint solutions. There was, moreover, a remarkable orthodoxy of opinion as to what the country needed and what should be done to rectify the inadequacies of the past. There was a certainty about the nature of the problems to be tackled. There was also unanimity for a short while at least about methods. This was the high water-mark of the centralist approach to planning. It was an exercise in State direction to secure ends which everyone agreed were right and proper and in the interests of the public as a whole. This was the day of the consensus.

This unquestioning state of affairs did not last for long, although the characteristic features of planning thought and practice remained well into the 1960s. The initiative was seen to lie properly with central government and what was right or wrong was seen to be a matter for central authority. Ministry publications, for example, advised on the layout of Roads in Built-up Areas, and Densities in Residential Areas. National strategies were laid down and were expected to be worked towards; urban population was to be redistributed, jobs encouraged in certain parts of the country as opposed to others, national landscape areas reserved, and so on. The local tail wagged occasionally, however, as when the traditional, engineer approach to city centre redevelopment thwarted the Ministry in their advocacy of pedestrian-oriented design. But usually the whole approach to planning was still a matter of following a centralist line of advocacy. Policies and practice were formulated at hierarchies of decision-making; planning was experienced by the general public as an operation determined by others.

Changes in Contemporary Approaches to Planning

During the last ten years in particular, the consensus that formerly surrounded planning has been eroded; gaps have arisen between authoritarian prescriptions and community needs, and a much greater variety in planning practice has arisen. The centralist philosophy is now seen as of less overriding importance, and new developments in planning thought have emerged. A number of factors have played their part in this movement.

In the first place the actual operation of planning in the post-war period revealed deficiencies. The co-ordinated comprehensive planning machine was seen to have limitations through its failure to deal with certain questions. Especially on the social side many problems slipped through the safety net of provision for all; too many casualties in the welfare state reflected the minority problems that were not being tackled. But, in addition, new larger problems were not being dealt with. The package of planning policies devised in the later 1940s were largely designed to meet the economic and social problems of the 1930s. The economic and social developments of the postwar period sometimes demanded new approaches which the collective orthodoxy failed or was slow to respond to.

Secondly, the operation of physical planning proved to be insensitive to a range of social problems. The policy of transferring people through slum clearance and new housing programmes into new areas, either at the periphery of existing towns, to New Towns, to expanded towns or to inner area redevelopment districts, proved a remarkably complex affair and demanded a high measure of understanding of social processes and management techniques if it was to be successful. Young and Willmott's *Family and Kinship in East London* (1957) advocated caution in wholesale clearance, and Harold Orlans' sociological study of *Stevenage* (1952) illustrated the political difficulties of New Town development. Moreover, there were other types of development projects which also impinged directly on people and their dwellings, such as new roads and land-use requirements of many kinds, and all these provided evidence of how the planning machine could ride roughshod over the interests of those directly affected. J. G. Davies has written emotively about *The Evangelical Bureaucrat* (1972) in a Newcastle setting; and Norman Dennis in *Public Participation and Planners' Blight* (1972) has described the situation in Millfield, Sunderland. More sedately, Jessop and Friend have described, from a Coventry case study (*Local Government and Strategic Choice*, 1969) the difficulties that exist at the point of confrontation between the community system and a governmental system. In all these cases, imperfections in the planning machine were revealed, suggesting the need for major modifications.

Another new factor was the realisation that planning was not the apolitical process that had been assumed. Planning had been universally regarded as outside politics, with a kind of technical wisdom all of its own. As such, it was ideally suited to the centralist philosophy whereby common sense, universally-applicable policies were dispensed. But with the new political and social science insight of the 1960s it was appreciated that the planning process, far from being above politics, was very much part of it. For example, one view of planning was that it was essentially a reallocative process whereby resources were redistributed throughout the community. Given the fact that society was seen to be inequitably structured in terms of the rewards and benefits particular groups received, planning was held to have a prominent role in the total process. Planning could not remain aloof: the policies undertaken in its name had both political origins and political consequences.

Associated with this realisation was the appreciation that our society was essentially pluralist, composed of a number of different interest groups, who did not necessarily share the consensus values ascribed to post-war planning. The erosion of consensus has indeed been one of the social characteristics of the last decade or more. The fact was that there was not simply one way of doing things, not just one course of action for the future, but a variety. A pluralist society implies that there are alternative solutions to a particular problem and these depend on the different assumptions and values held by the groups concerned, and the way that problem is perceived. For example, there is not just one (technical, common sense, above politics) approach to housing improvement or road programmes;

there are a number, and these vary according to the interests and perceptions of the affected parties.

Lastly, we should note the increasing desire of some groups to direct their own change rather than be governed by the prescriptions of the centralist authority. There are a number of community development experiments which have this objective. More widespread are the many developments in the field of public participation, and a marked change in the nature of planning is clearly in evidence. Advocacy planning, the idea of planning aid centres, and the mobilisation of grass roots activity generally in the planning process, not only add new safeguards to the central planning system but should be seen as essentially a different style of planning, one which is built-up from below rather than directed from above.

The development of planning thought is, therefore, now proceeding on a new course. At the turn of the century the critical problems concerned housing for the working classes; a few enlightened people saw how a co-ordinated programme of garden city development could effectively redistribute population from overcrowded cities. In the 1940s the strategic ideas about redistribution of both people and employment had become very firm and were central to the national planning programme of the time. The planning process was seen fundamentally as a centralist matter whereby policies were framed for and on behalf of the population as a whole, by an elitist political and technical hierarchy. Today the problems have shifted and the highlight is probably on the inner city and the forces which make for deprivation. We now realise that a bureaucratic planning machine needs considerable modification if these problems are to be tackled effectively, and there is greater emphasis on the micro-scale of political activity. We can no longer necessarily rely on that elitist hierarchy either to define or identify the problems, to prescribe remedies, or to suggest adequate methods of implementation. The argument now is that we should attempt to build-up from the grass roots rather than lead from above; the problems and methods have to be restated, and this needs the articulation of those most affected.

This modified approach to planning thought and practice might be described as incrementalism as opposed to end-state planning: a matter of making incremental advances with no surety about long-term goals, as opposed to decisive blueprints which determine successive stages of development because the objective, already defined, is inviolate. The Town and Country Planning Act 1968, and the new reliance on structure plans illustrates the shift of emphasis. The contrast between 1968 and 1947 (or at least 1932) is between planning with confidence and certainty towards a known end product, and planning for uncertainty, simply making most effective use of our existing resources and resisting dramatic interventions in the system to achieve some desired end. At the same time, however, we should not over-exaggerate the changes which have taken and are taking place. Even at its most paternal, centralist planning in this country was never totalitarian, and the local planning process, centred round the Development Plan, was considerably influenced by popular opinion in the rules of participation that then applied. Likewise, the freest form of locally generated planning, which many would advocate, can only operate in a framework where there are some known and accepted parameters of a central planning system. Perhaps all that we can say at the moment is that the democratic events of the last ten years have acted as a most valuable check on a centralist authority that was becoming out of step with popular opinion and requirements. It is very hard to look very far forward with certainty. Some see considerable changes taking place in grass roots politics, whereby new micro-units of political organisation are going to help to formalise the new, local, incrementalist, planning system. Others see these experiments as more transitory and anticipate a return to a new, reformed style of central planning some years hence.

These changes in outlook have been very much part of a substantial shift of allegiance by town planning from the land and development professions to the social sciences. Planning in this country as a profession developed under a parental umbrella of engineers, architects, surveyors and lawyers. It needed the Schuster Report, *Report of the Committee on the Qualifications of Planners* (1950), to give the impetus for the major break from this background to encourage wider inputs of skill and approach. The last twenty years have seen marked changes in membership composition and training of the profession, reflecting a new emphasis on the social content of planning rather than the physical and land use manifestations. It is true that from the first decade of the century Patrick Geddes, as a sociologist, contributed a good deal to planning thought and practice, particularly in his concern for an integrated approach to 'civics' and the simple rigour of his research method, 'survey, analysis and plan'. But this was not to be a mainstream in the evolution of planning, and the full influence of social science was reserved until later.

The consequence has been to shift an emphasis on land, buildings and design to a wider regard for the social environment. There has been a new upsurge in research method, particularly through quantitative techniques; the influence of geography has given new spatial dimensions and assisted in landscape interpretation; political science has given new insight into decision-making, and sociology into community structure and organisation. Over the last ten years the history of town planning is mirrored closely in the history of the social sciences. Experiments in public participation and community development are obvious illustrations, but perhaps the biggest influence on town planning has come through a 'systems' approach. J.B. McLoughlin's *Urban and Regional Planning* (1969) and George Chadwick's *A Systems View of Planning* (1972) sketch the implications. Planning is now seen as a cyclic process, becoming a matter not of land use design but the control of complex systems. The development of models to simulate the behaviour of these systems led to work on urban land use models, and provided a new technical armoury in the field of planning research. It is not too much to say that the future development of planning thought lies with contributions from the social sciences, at least in the short term.

We may conveniently conclude this section with an observation on changes in planning thought which takes us back to an earlier point. We have noted that modern town planning took shape in a period marked by disjointed attempts at aspects of urban government; in due time town planning was to achieve a measure of co-ordination. We are now going through a phase when considerable interest is being expressed in new possibilities of a comprehensive, well managed urban government. It is seen that although plan making in local authorities is undertaken in a range of different enterprises, nevertheless one single operational framework might be recognised: the idea of management by objectives is common both in town planning and many other government functions. Furthermore, if planning is correctly identified not only as plan-making, but as management of an on-going process as well, then town planning becomes not just the separate function in government that it has often been, but one of a number of control mechanisms which we require in order to intervene in, or guide, the complex system (cities, regions or whatever) which forms our terms of reference. In short, town planning takes its place amongst a number of management schema, not necessarily *primus inter pares*, but none the less offering some synoptic overview for urban government.

Concluding Observations

This chapter has concentrated on the British scene. The story in continental Europe or America is significantly different. Mel Scott's *American City Planning* (1959) traces the history of planning in the United States; G. E. Cherry's *The Evolution of British Town Planning* (1974) sketches the rather different history of the professional movement in this country. It is worth while making the point that despite the very great intellectual and other links between America and Britain in recent years, originally the greater relationship was with Europe. In Germany, particularly, the development of planning on the basis of municipal administration had made important strides well before the end of the century. Britain was much impressed by the German system of government and T. C. Horsfall's *The Example of Germany* (1904) was an influential publication in this country. Additionally, there was the influence of the new civic design movement led by Camillo Sitte, and English architects were keen to follow; Unwin certainly shared common approaches with him.

The essence, however, of this chapter's brief review is that the course of the development of planning thought has not been shaped in a vacuum. Nor will it; it will continue to be fashioned by a context of political and social attitudes. The scope and content of our planning system, its objectives and methods will reflect our style of democracy and its assumptions. From a reliance on voluntary reformist and propagandist efforts at the turn of the century, which were primarily reactive to a set of urban problems, we proceeded to a dependence on a largely centralist system, confident in its national planning strategy for a post-war, reconstructed Britain. Changes are now suggesting a popularist, incremental view of planning with an emphasis on information and power sharing. We must wait and see how far this latest approach will supplant others.

Certainly, today's contrast with the 1940's is striking. Then, confidence abounded, there was sureness about what needed to be done and how it should be achieved, and authority could be relied on to carry the day. But authority is now more muted and there is little conviction about our contemporary planning; a cocoon of scientific method all too often obliterates clarity of purpose. Regard for the historical development of planning suggests that this might be a passing phase, but it is not at all clear how the next will unfold.

The planning process may change, adapt and reorient, but there are constant factors in this situation. Admittedly, a number of repetitive themes relating to architecture, land and development, and social purpose hardly gives a unique identity, but planning has become a way of looking at environmental problems as much as a subject matter in its own right with fixed boundaries. With this driving force, innovation and experiment constantly seek new ground and new methods. Planning thought consequently continues to evolve, fed and stimulated by a rich technical and cultural background.

References

This chapter has reviewed a large subject field and even a provisional reading list is of formidable length. Other publications of the author, however, relate to the issues considered here and they contain the more important pointers to wider reading:

Leonard Hill, *Town Planning in its Social Context* (1970), see Chapter 1.
G. T. Foulis, *Urban Change and Planning* (1972).
The Evolution of British Town Planning (International Textbooks, 1974).

4. Physical Planning

Geoffrey R. Crook

Planning activity of any kind is concerned with change. Physical planning, as a distinctive form of planning, is essentially concerned with changes within the physical environment. The physical environment is taken to mean the land on which activities of living are based, the buildings which house these activities and the artifacts which are necessary for society to function. Physical planning, however, is not solely concerned with changes within the physical environment in themselves. This is mainly the province of those social scientists who are involved in the detection, analysis and explanation of the locational, social, economic and behavioural changes which are taking place within society. Rather, physical planning is concerned with the prevention, the control and the promotion of changes which have, which are and which might occur within the physical environment. Indeed, one of the distinctive characteristics of physical planning is that it is prescriptive rather than analytical in nature, although the success or failure of its solutions may well depend upon the adequacies of the analyses and explanations of the phenomena which underlie change.

In a highly urbanised, highly complex and rapidly changing society such as ours, the causes and effects of change are often difficult to detect, anticipate and comprehend.

This in some ways makes the need to try and plan more important and at the same time makes its operation more difficult and challenging. This chapter is primarily concerned with some of the issues which are intrinsic to the development and operation of physical planning in contemporary society. It seeks to examine some explanations of the nature and aims of physical planning; to examine the agencies responsible for physical planning; and to examine the means through which physical planning operates.

Change in the Physical Environment

In exploring the nature and aims of physical planning it might be helpful to start with a hypothetical example. Imagine a street of large Victorian houses fairly close to the centre of an industrial city. These houses, of course, were built to cater for the requirements of well-to-do families and their servants in the latter part of the nine-teenth century. Gradually, as the city grew in size, many of these families moved out to the new and more spacious suburbs being built on the outskirts of the city. They moved for a variety of reasons. Some, perhaps, because many of their friends and business colleagues had already done so; some because they thought that the city had become a noisy, dirty and unhealthy place; some because they wanted more spacious surroundings and anyway, travel by tram or the motor car had put the new suburbs in easy reach of most parts of the city to which they needed to go. Others stayed. Some perhaps because their network of friends centred around that part of the city; some because they felt they were too old to move and some perhaps because they could not afford to buy the new houses in the suburbs. At first there were other aspiring, well-to-do families to take the place of those who had left but as time went on they too moved out and the street began to change. Today the street looks rather different. At one end, the houses are dilapidated with unkempt gardens partly used as car parks. These houses have been converted into flats and bedsitters and are mainly occupied by students from the nearby university. Four of the original houses on one side of the street have gone altogether and have been replaced by some new three-storey flat blocks which are advertised as being 'highly desirable one bedroom flats. Suitable for young couples without children or large dogs.' At the end of the street adjacent to the city centre some of the houses have been converted into offices for a typing and secretarial agency, estate agents, solicitors and insurance brokers.

In a relatively short period of time it can be seen that this imaginary street has changed in a number of ways. Its visual appearance has changed with the redevelopment of some buildings, the conversion of gardens into car parks, the conversion of some houses into offices and a general air of neglect. The function of the street in relation to the fabric of the city as a whole has also changed. It is no longer a purely residential street containing a small number of relatively affluent familes—now it contains a large number of relatively poor small families and single persons together with other non-residential uses connected with the city centre. The intensity of the way the street is used has also changed—now there are very many more people using the buildings, many more activities and much more traffic.

Many of these changes would be apparent to an observer passing through the street. However, what he might see are visual and physical effects of change and it would be much more difficult for him to discern the underlying causes. He probably would not comprehend the interwoven matrix of changing fashions, cultural values and social relationships which together with economic forces and technological developments contributed to some of the original occupants and their predecessors leaving the street. Neither would he easily comprehend the dynamics of the housing market which made it profitable to convert some of the houses into small flats or bedsitters and to redevelop others. Additionally it would be difficult for him to assess the effects that the expansion of further education has had on the street and the operation of the economic forces within the city centre which made certain users seek premises on the periphery.

Also from the example it can be seen that these forces for change have led to processes by which the physical make-up of the street has been adapted to meet changing circumstances. Some buildings have been adapted to meet the requirements of new users, others have been adapted to meet increased intensities of utilisation and land has been adapted to accommodate changing methods of transportation. McLoughlin[1] provides a useful framework for the identification of changes relating to the adaptation of the physical environment to meet new conditions. The occupation of the flats by students, with their particular behavioural patterns, might influence other people living in the street to move out. Similarly, the movement of office users into the street might well influence other office users to seek premises there, and these might possibly be made available by the out movement of people caused by the in movement of students! Also, if other office users moved into the street from the city centre they would, of course, leave premises which could be used by some other office users seeking a city centre location which might in turn leave premises vacant elsewhere.

Systemic Change

It can be seen that there is a kind of chain of change—that changes occurring for one reason may well affect and generate other kinds of change. The example given only illustrates some limited changes within a street but if this idea is extended to cover a whole town, a city, a region or a nation then some of the complexities and the difficulties of understanding the nature of change and therefore the complexities and difficulties of guiding and controlling change can perhaps be understood. If a comprehensive view is taken of 'this ceaseless flow of change resulting from development relocation and change in the manner of use of spaces' the condition which it represents is usually described as systemic change 'since it is boundless and occupies the whole system of the physical environment'.[2]

The operation of physical planning is concerned with the guidance and control of systemic change within the physical environment. It is not, however, the sole means of guidance or control. Changes in the international monetary situation, world trading patterns, government, the availability of materials, the bank rate and mortgage rates for house buyers, for example, can exert profound influence over the nature of changes which take place and also the rate at which changes occur. These changes can be described as exogenous, i.e. although they might exert great influence over change in the systems encompassed by the physical environment they are outside these systems and outside of the direct control or influence of the operation of physical planning.

Referring back to the example of the street it was shown that many of the physical changes which took place were a consequence of exogenous influences, for example fashion, cultural patterns, social values and economic forces. Additionally many of these exogenous changes are also guided, controlled and arise from other forms of planning activity carried out by both public and private agencies. These could include, for example, economic planning concerned with the development of the national economy, social welfare planning or planning to expand educational provisions carried out by public agencies, and also the plans of the multinational corporations to expand production, to set up new premises, plans to exploit mineral resources and plans to innovate new technological developments primarily carried out by private agencies.

The nature of the interaction of these exogenous forces with the changes which take place within the physical environment illustrates a central problem in the operation of physical planning. The problem largely arises because physical planning, by attempting to control and guide change in the physical environment, intervenes in these more general processes of change.

The Aims of Physical Planning

In the operation of physical planning this interaction takes two forms. Firstly, the formulation of plans and policies which are meant to indicate those changes in the physical environment which are considered necessary and desirable and also those changes which should be prevented. Secondly, a system of controls to allow for those changes which are in accordance with the plans and policies and to prevent, those that are not, from taking place.

However, the formulation of plans and policies together with systems of control imply that intervention through these means is attempting to meet some specific aims and that the nature of these aims relate to the values and priorities of those who formulate them. In other words, what is the operation of physical planning attempting to achieve by intervening in processes of change within the physical environment?

In an analysis of physical planning in this country, Foley[3] has identified three general ideologies which have underlain the operation of physical planning. These ideologies can be taken to illustrate in general terms the main operational aims of physical planning. Foley identifies the idea that 'planning's main task is to reconcile competing claims for the use of limited land so as to provide a consistent, balanced and orderly arrangement of land uses'; that 'planning's central function is to provide a good (or better) physical environment; a physical environment of such good quality is essential for the promotion of a healthy and civilised life'; and finally that 'planning, as part of a broader social programme, is responsible for providing the physical basis for a better community life'.

The forms that these broad aims can take in the operation of physical planning can be illustrated by an examination of the aims and objectives of the Coventry, Solihull, Warwickshire Sub-regional Study[4] (the Coventry Study). This Sub-regional Study is of particular importance in that it was one of the first recent major planning studies to attempt to make explicit the aims and objectives which the plan was intended to achieve.

The aims expressed in the Coventry Study fall into two categories. The first consists of a number of very general goals which can be interpreted as wide statements of societal values and these indicate that the plan at some time in the future is intended to provide a better life for people by achieving 'balance and prosperity in the sub-regional economy and the greatest social welfare' and 'the best living and working environment throughout the sub-region' together with ensuring 'the greatest choice of opportunities'.

The second category consists of a number of specific aims by which the general objectives can be achieved. These aims closely reflect the operational aims of physical planning as stated by Foley. For example, there are a number of aims which are concerned with the resolution of land-use conflicts and making efficient use of land resources. These include aims to minimise the loss of good quality farm land; avoid the loss of workable mineral resources; and keep the cost of utilities and land-development services to a minimum. There are also aims which relate to the provision of a good environment essential for the promotion of a healthy and civilised life. These include the location of new housing areas in pleasant surroundings and the location of new development in areas which will not be adversely affected by atmospheric and noise pollution.

The largest single group of objectives coincide with the concern of physical planning in providing the framework for a better basis of community life. Such objectives include: locating new development so that there is the greatest possible choice of jobs available to all workers; increasing the potential range of shopping facilities available and providing the greatest possible accessibility to them for all residents; and providing sufficient roads and public transport to meet the future travel needs of the population.

Other objectives, specified by the Coventry Study, extend across either two or three of Foley's ideologies. Examples of these include: clearing obsolete and unfit dwellings; the rehabilitation of a large number of dwellings and the conservation of the remainder of the housing stock; providing sufficient land to accommodate the forecasts of future levels of population and employment at appropriate space standards and with all supporting services; and the conservation of areas of high landscape value and sites of architectural, historical or ecological significance.

This example is meant to illustrate a number of points. It is clear that many of the general and specific aims indicated in the Coventry Study cannot be achieved solely by the manipulation of the physical environment. A plan for an area may anticipate the expansion of employment to provide a large number of jobs at some time in the future. The plan may make the appropriate land allocations for them; incorporate transport provisions to cope with the journeys to work they might generate; and allocate land for new houses, schools, shops, open spaces and so on which will be needed for the people attracted to the area. However, the allocation of land, the building of roads, the provision of all of the services to support an expansion in employment cannot, in itself, ensure that this anticipated expansion will take place.

Equally, the allocation of sufficient land to build new houses in pleasant environments away from noise and atmospheric pollution, and near to shops, recreational and other facilities again does not ensure that people will necessarily lead happier or better lives.

Conversely, if insufficient land is allocated for housing and employment or if it is allocated in locations which are inaccessible or mean long, expensive journeys to work, to school or to shop then people may well be denied opportunities to which they are entitled. Additionally if beautiful areas of countryside or parts of towns are despoiled and valuable agricultural or mineral-bearing land used up indiscriminately then there is a loss to society as a whole which is irreplaceable.

Demands upon Land

Many trends and changes taking place within contemporary society imply increased demands upon land. Increasing population means more houses, hospitals and schools and jobs; increasing income means more mobility and more time for holidays and recreation; new automated methods of production and new technologies mean larger factories employing fewer people. Demands upon land have escalated over the past fifty years. A new primary school today occupies about twenty times the land area occupied fifty years ago. The land required for a new motorway is about six times as much as its equivalent of thirty years ago. Admittedly there are some shrinkages in demand (railways for example) but these are relatively insignificant compared to the total increases.

91

As any economist will point out, increasing demands upon scarce resources lead to an increased value of that resource. The value might be a monetary one or a societal one. Increased demand also means increased conflict between potential users—the civilised veneer of an auction often conceals very uncivilised feelings. Resolution of these conflicts implies sets of values and priorities. Is keeping good agricultural land more important than building factories or airports? Is building more houses more important than building more roads?

Obviously different people have different values and priorities in relation to these kinds of questions. Inevitably, the allocation of land for one use rather than another; the priorities in a plan which indicate that one area in a city will be improved before another; the demolition of houses with the consequent social problems this raises to make room for more roads to be used by other people; involve questions of judgement made upon the basis of values and priorities and as such bring the operation of physical planning into the arena of political choice. It must be stressed that in the operation of physical planning there are three sets of people involved. The technical officers who formulate plans and policies, the elected representatives who make judgments upon whether or not these plans and policies should be acted upon and the people who might be affected by the implementation of the plans and policies.

Agencies Responsible for Physical Planning

The nature and aims of physical planning cannot be divorced from the operation of physical planning in practice. This leads to the second major theme of this chapter, concerned with the agencies responsible for physical planning. The organisational aspects and the responsibilities of the agencies involved in physical planning are described fully by Cullingworth[5] and their development up to the 1950s by Ashworth.[6] The following comments are only meant to provide a summary of some of the major points which arise.

Local Government

Since the 1909 Housing and Town Planning Act[7] the responsibility for the preparation of physical plans and control over development has been vested in local government through the medium of central government. The powers given to local authorities and the delineation of which local authorities should receive powers has varied a great deal over time. The powers themselves have varied from permissive (the decision of whether or not plans should be prepared was up to each local authority) to obligatory. The 1947 Town and Country Planning Act[8] made it obligatory for plans to be prepared covering the whole country and instituted a consistent and comprehensive system of controls over development. The 1947 Planning Act also reduced the number of local planning authorities from 1441 to 145 and in the process, vested plan making powers in the hands of the larger local authorities namely County Councils and County Boroughs, although provision was made for the delegation of control powers to other local authorities in particular circumstances.

The 1968 Town and Country Planning Act which introduced major changes in the nature, form and content of plans did not depart from these general arrangements.

However in the operation of this act, a phased sequence of vesting local planning authorities with the power to produce the new form of plans was introduced. Currently, then, some local planning authorities have the powers and are producing new plans (structure plans) under the provisions of the 1968 Act, whilst others are still operating, as far as plan making procedures are concerned, under the provisions of the 1947 Act. Ultimately, it is intended that all the local planning authorities will be vested with the new powers. An exception to the general principle that planning powers are vested in local authorities are the New Towns. A separate Development Corporation, which is not a local authority, is set up by the Minister for each new town. The Development Corporations, under the New Towns Act of 1946,[9] have separate powers of formulating and implementing plans.

The 1968 Act was introduced prior to the reorganisation of local government[10] which is now taking place. The reorganisation has profound implications for the future operation of physical planning through local authorities. Briefly the new system now coming into force introduces a two-tier arrangement of plan-making functions. The new arrangement has at one level Metropolitan Counties, which largely encompass the areas of major conurbations, and County Councils which represent the amalgamation of previous

County Council areas less the areas incorporated into the Metropolitan Counties.

The second level consists of Districts within Metropolitan County and County Council areas. Planning powers are now to be divided between these two levels. The Metropolitan and County Councils will have the responsibility for the preparation of structure plans and the Districts will have the responsibility of preparing local plans which can cover all or part of their areas.

This situation is somewhat complicated in that some local planning authorities, for example, Coventry, Birmingham and Worcestershire, are preparing or have prepared structure plans under the provisions of the 1968 Act. These plans relate to their respective local authority boundaries as at 1973. Other authorities, for instance in the Manchester area, are preparing structure plans which cover the whole of the Metropolitan County area as it will be in 1974. The two-tier arrangement and division of planning powers is similar to the arrangements which have developed for the London area since the setting up of the Greater London Council. P. Self[11] has analysed some of the difficulties which can arise and some aspects of the Inquiry into the Greater London Development Plan indicate some lessons which can be learnt.[12]

Management in Local Government

The arrangements and responsibilities between the various departments within local authorities are also in many cases changing. It has increasingly become recognised particularly in the larger authorities that there is a need for arrangements to co-ordinate the activities of various departments and to co-ordinate the formulation of policies arising from these. For example a scheme to improve a street of older houses may well involve the work of the public health, town planning, architecture, housing, social services, highways and engineering departments. Co-ordination between their various activities is obviously essential if the scheme is to be successful. The traditional breakdown of local authorities into separate departments each one essentially concerned with its own activities which could well be out of step or even in conflict with those of other departments has obviously led to problems. In order to overcome the kinds of problems arising from this kind of situation and also to provide a more satisfactory basis for policy formulation, some authorities have adopted Corporate Management systems.

Central Government

At the level of central government, most of the responsibilities for physical planning are now encompassed by the activities of the Department of the Environment (DOE) under a Secretary of State.

The responsibilities of the DOE are widespread and cover 'the whole range of functions which affect people's living environment'.[13] Similarly, the powers of the Secretary of State in his duty of 'securing consistency and continuity in the framing of a national policy with respect to the use and development of land'[14] are also very wide. These powers, under the general control of Parliament, include the framing of general planning policies which are communicated to local authorities through circulars, memoranda etc. However, local authorities usually have the discretionary power to interpret these policy guidelines to meet their own particular circumstances. Local authorities also need the approval of the DOE for many of their activities connected with the preparation and implementation of planning proposals. Development plans and structure plans need the approval of the Secretary of State before they can become operative and the Secretary of State can make major modifications to these plans before giving his approval. The Secretary of State also has powers, on appeal, to modify or revoke decisions made by local planning authorities on planning applications. Allied to this he has powers to call in planning applications and determine them himself.

The DOE also has executive powers to prepare plans although these powers are seldom used. These powers allow the DOE to prepare development plans or structure plans for a local planning authority area if the local planning authority fails to produce a plan or if the Secretary of State is not satisfied with a plan which has been produced.

Regional Planning

The responsibility for the operation of regional planning agencies and for the preparation of regional plans and studies has only relatively recently come under the control of the DOE. This machinery was developed by the Labour Government in 1965 after the launching of the ill-fated and short-lived National Plan[15] for economic growth. The Labour Government, through the then Department of Economic Affairs, set up a number of Regional Economic Councils and Boards. There are now ten of these, eight in England and one each for Scotland and Wales. The terms of reference of the Councils defined their functions as being

to assist in the development of planning in their regions in the context of the national plan and with a view to making the best use of the regions' resources and also to advise on the implementation of regional policy; in addition they are to advise the central Government on the regional implications of national economic policies.[16]

The Councils are advisory bodies consisting of members appointed by the Secretary of State having a wide range of knowledge about their regions. The Boards consist of senior Civil Servants drawn from the various government departments concerned with regional planning and their functions are 'in co-operation with the Planning Councils to help formulate regional plans and to co-ordinate the work in the regions of the government departments concerned with regional planning'. Although the Councils are purely advisory and have no executive powers nor are they charged by central government with any responsibility for the preparation of plans they have in fact produced some regional plans, for instance, The Strategy for the South East (1967)[17] and West Midlands—Patterns of Growth (1966).[18]

However, control over the expansion of existing industries and new industrial development, and in some parts of the country, office development, rests with the Department of Trade and Industry (DTI). These powers are related to encouraging the growth of new employment in areas where traditional industries are declining and areas which have high levels of unemployment. This control is exercised by the granting or withholding of industrial/office development certificates which must be obtained, with some minor exceptions, before a planning authority can grant permission for such development. Additionally the DTI operates a system of inducements, mostly financial, to industrialists to encourage them to locate in particular areas. This dual approach of 'sticks and carrots' and its successes and failures is described by McCrone.[19]

The DTI has also recently set up a series of Regional Industrial Development Boards[20] in Scotland, Wales, the North, the North West, the South West, Yorkshire and Humberside regions. These are intended to advise generally on 'regional industrial opportunities and on application for selective financial assistance for the development of industry in their regions'. These Development Boards will be linked with the Regional Economic Councils and Boards so that 'the process of industrial regeneration in a region and the overall planning of its land-use and other physical resources are properly co-ordinated'.

Development Control

The control over development is an integral part of the operation of physical planning. The 1947 Act gave local authorities wide powers of control and, although amended to cover new circumstances, they still form the basis of current legislation relating to the control over development. These powers give a local planning authority control, with some specific exceptions, over all development taking place within its area. Development is defined in the 1962 Town and Country Planning Act[21] as being 'the carrying out of building, engineering, mining or other operations in, on, over or under the land, or the making of any material change in the use of any buildings or other land'. This definition indicates that not only do local planning authorities normally have control over building operations but also they have powers of control over the way that land or buildings are used. There are some major exceptions to this. For example, planning authorities do not have powers to control the ways in which agricultural land is used nor over buildings used for agricultural purposes.

With some exceptions, anyone wishing to carry out development as defined above must obtain planning permission to do so. The local authority in determining whether or not to grant permission is generally guided by the provisions of the development plan. For example if someone wishes to build a house on land zoned for a cemetery he would probably not be granted permission to do so. In addition to this the authority will be guided by such factors

97

as the appearance of the proposed building in relation to other buildings, the provision for car parking and access to the building, the likely intensity of use of the building, the capacity of the sewage and drainage systems to cope with any effluent from the building and so on. Thus, although a proposed building and its use may be in accordance with the general zoning of the development plan it does not necessarily follow that permission would be granted to build it. In considering a planning application a planning authority can make use of three decisions. They can approve the application; but attach conditions to it, i.e. a condition to retain some existing trees and plant some new ones might be attached to a permission for a new housing development; or they can refuse permission for the development to take place. If they refuse permission then the applicant has a right to appeal to the Secretary of State against the decision of the local planning authority.

If leave to appeal is granted then an inquiry may be held at which both the appellant and the local authority have the opportunity to present their case in front of an independent Inspector appointed by the Secretary of State. Under the provisions of the 1971 Act[22] the decision as to whether or not the appeal should be allowed is normally made by the Inspector unless the Secretary of State wishes to determine the appeal himself.

Development Plans

The preparation and implementation of development plans has been the backbone of the operation of physical planning since 1947. The 1968 Act introduced major changes in the legislation which affect the nature, form and content of development plans. The underlying reasons behind these changes are complex and to develop an understanding of why they were introduced and what they are intended to achieve, it is necessary to go back in time.

Pepler, in reviewing the progress of plan making in the first twenty-one years after the 1909 Act, remarked that 'in our good old English way we prefer to reverse the order of logic and to work up to the general from the particular'.[23] This referred partly to the way that the scope of plans which could be produced had evolved from the narrow to the comprehensive. The 1909 Act generally restricted the preparation of plans to schemes for new development. Thus a town planning scheme may be made as respects any land which is in course of development or appears likely to be used for building purposes, with the general object of securing proper sanitary conditions, amenity and convenience in connection with the laying out and use of land and any neighbouring lands.

The 1947 Act, in contrast, introduced a comprehensive system of planning covering the whole of towns, cities and countryside through the medium of development plans. These plans were intended to indicate

the manner in which a local planning authority propose that land in their area should be used, whether by the carrying out thereon of development or otherwise and the stages by which any such development should be carried out.

Thus the plan should

define the sites of proposed roads, public and other buildings and works, airfields, parks, pleasure grounds, nature reserves and other open spaces or allocate areas of land for use for agricultural, residential, industrial or other purposes.

These development plans had to be prepared on the basis of a comprehensive survey of a wide range of factors which mainly related to the use, condition and quality of land and buildings which, together with an analysis of trends and needs relating to population, employment, shopping etc., would influence the aims of the local planning authority in preparing their plan. The documents which comprised the legally defined development plan, when approved, were a written statement and a series of maps. A written statement usually contained a brief summary of the main proposals of the plan without any substantiation of the basis on which the proposals are made. For County Boroughs the main maps were a Town Map and a Programme Map drawn to a scale of six inches to one mile, and for County Areas the main maps were a County Map and a Programme Map drawn to a scale of one inch to one mile. County Councils could also, as part of the development plan, prepare more detailed maps for part of their area. Usually these were prepared for urban areas within the county and took the form of Town and Programme Maps similar to those for County Boroughs.

Town and County Maps were prepared with great precision and indicated in detail the proposed use of land and buildings in the areas which they covered. The Programme Maps were intended to cover a twenty-year time period and therefore indicated the priorities of the local planning authority. Under the 1947 Act, the minister required that all development plans should be submitted to him for approval by 1951. In fact very few plans were submitted by that date and it took until the early 1960s before all the development plans were submitted and approved. The culmination of this was that the plan-making machinery for the country as a whole was out of phase which often made co-ordination between the plans of neighbouring authorities very difficult and that the plans therefore were becoming increasingly unrealistic in a rapidly changing society. Many development plans were outpaced by events and were often out of date before they were approved. Thus in the early sixties it was realised that the development plan machinery as it existed was inadequate in a number of ways.

The Planning Advisory Group

A study group, the Planning Advisory Group, was set up in 1964 to assist the then Ministry of Housing and Local Government and the Ministry of Transport in a general review of the planning system. The Group's terms of reference covered both the system of development plans and the methods of control over development. They initially concluded in their report (the PAG report)[24] that 'the main defect of the present planning system lies not in the methods of control but in the development plans on which they are based and which they are intended to implement'. The Group therefore focused their attention on the defects of the 1947 Act development plan system and on measures which might be introduced to overcome them. The main criticisms of the development plans are summarised by James[25] as follows:

(a) they are deficient in policies, particularly those not directly related to land use, and they are inadequate as guides to developers and as bases for control;

(b) they concentrate on detail and on what are often misleadingly precise boundaries;

(c) they try to illustrate in standard forms different kinds of information, much of which is not relevant to positive promotion or control of development;

(d) they are ill-equipped to influence the quality of development as distinct from its location;

(e) finally, their inflexible form and content are not adaptable to new techniques and concepts, and the centralised procedures required for amendment impose long delays on attempts to deal with rapidly changing circumstances.

As examples to illustrate these kinds of defects the Group particularly emphasised that the development plans did not enable the proper integration and development of land use and transportation policies and that this factor alone 'goes . . . to make a radical revision of development plans necessary'. Again, they pointed out that 'the relationship between regional policies and local development plans has been ill-defined and uncertain' and that there has been 'no effective means of co-ordinating the plans and proposals of contiguous planning authorities in a conurbation or throughout a region'. At the more local level the Group said that although development plans gave a good indication of land-uses they did not give any real indication of how the land might be developed or redeveloped or what else might be done to improve the environment. Similarly the detailed land-use proposals gave very little indication to the public or guidance to developers of the quality of environment or design which the plan sought to promote. The report also criticised the process by which plans were approved particularly the long delays caused by hearing of a large number of objections to detailed proposals contained in the plans. The Inquiry into the Greater London Development Plan, for example, lasted for nearly two years and considered some 28 000 objections. Although this is perhaps an extreme and unrepresentative example it does illustrate the time, cost and delays which can be incurred in dealing with formal objections arising from the detailed proposals of a new development plan. Thus one of the major conclusions of the PAG report was that the main defects of the development plan systems arose from the abandonment of the concept that development plans should be concerned with 'indicating the general principles upon which development in an area will be promoted and controlled'.

Finally the Group in summarising their criticisms concluded that the present development plan system is too detailed for some purposes and not detailed enough for other purposes. It brings before the Minister issues of major importance but in a form which may be incomplete and out of context, and also many issues of local interest which have no policy significance requiring the Minister's approval. Yet it does not provide a satisfactory medium for positive environmental planning at the local level.

On this basis the Group recommended that a number of changes should be made to the form and function of development plans and that the responsibilities and powers of central and local government should be recognised.

The changes in the form and function of development plans envisaged by the group were numerous and radical. They recommended the introduction of new forms of development plans for counties, county boroughs and other urban areas over 50 000 population size. These plans, termed county structure and urban structure plans, would be limited 'to the major issues of policy affecting the area concerned and those matters in which the Minister has an interest'. Thus these plans would not contain detailed land use proposals but would be primarily statements of policy issues accompanied by diagrams and illustrations together with a diagrammatic 'structure' map. The structure map would indicate the main characteristics of the physical proposals and the main elements of the transportation network. These plans would be submitted to the Minister for approval.

In parallel to the structure plans, a series of local plans would be required to indicate detailed aspects of the broad policies contained in the structure plans. The local plans would provide a guide to development control and also be concerned with providing a framework for more positive environmental planning. The PAG group visualised local plans being prepared for small towns, villages, town centres and parts or districts of urban areas. They stressed the importance of a particular form of local plans, action area plans, which they envisaged as being prepared for local areas where major changes were likely to take place in the relatively near future. The Group emphasised that the policies and proposals of local plans would have to conform with the policies laid down in the structure plans. Through this mechanism the preparation and adoption of local plans would be the responsibility of the local planning authority concerned and would not need to be submitted for ministerial approval.

The PAG group also recommended that both structure and local plans should be prepared within a regional context set out in plans prepared by the Regional Economic Planning Councils and Boards. It would be 'necessary to associate local planning authorities with the regional planning process and to ensure that their plans give effect to the intentions of the structure plan'. In certain circumstances the Group envisaged that it would be necessary to prepare 'sub-regional' plans which would give a more detailed basis for the formulation of structure plan policies within a particular area.

The Group recognised that the system they proposed would change the nature of an individual's rights of objection. They considered that 'the preparation and adoption by the local planning authority of local plans will mean that the individual is better informed and more consulted on planning matters'. The local authority would have to publish a draft local plan and at this stage an opportunity would have to be made for comments, representations or objections to the proposals of the plan. In the case of structure plans, because they would only deal with major policy issues any objections to the proposals of the plan could only be made on issues of general principle and policy. In this way, the Minister, in considering any objections to the structure plan would be concerned with major issues rather than detailed local matters.

The Minister published the PAG report for public comment and dicussion before deciding upon any action which he might take in accepting or rejecting the proposed changes. Generally, the proposals of the report were welcomed by practising planners. However, a number of criticisms were expressed many of which focused on the largely political questions related to the relative responsibilities of central and local government together with the rights of individuals in relation to these responsibilities. The question was asked 'For whose benefit is this reform intended, is it intended for the planner or the planned?'[26] Related to this 'the main aim (of the PAG group) seems to have been nothing more than to produce a system of planning that gives the least possible trouble to planners' and to 'regard an interested public as a collection of possible enemies to be placated (even sedated) with sweet generalities but to be deprived as far as possible of opportunities of being a nuisance'.[27] The proposed power by which local planning authorities would not only prepare but also adopt local plans was criticised from the point of view that this, in effect, made the authority both judge and jury in its own court.

The Town Planning Institute,[28] in its formal observations on the PAG report, made three major criticisms of principle as follows:

(a) The analysis of the defects of the current machinery was not sufficiently penetrating.

(b) The proposals were limited in that they concentrated on the Development Plans and did not sufficiently cover the whole of the planning process. The Council recognised that this was a criticism of the Group's Terms of Reference rather than of its work.

(c) Some of the proposed changes from current practice seemed to be unnecessary because they were unlikely to produce improved results.

The New Planning System—the 1968 Town and Country Planning Act

Despite these and other criticisms the main proposals of the PAG group were accepted by the Minister and formed the basis of the 1968 Town and Country Planning Act. The Act made provision for local planning authorities to prepare Urban or County structure plans and local plans along the lines of the PAG recommendations. Subsequently, the publication of *Development Plans—A Manual on Form and Content*[29] together with a number of circulars and advice notes have amplified aspects of the legislation and it is perhaps useful to compare the major provisions of this Act, as far as development plans are concerned, with those of the 1947 Act.

Under the 1968 Act the 'development plan' of an area has a substantially different legal meaning than previously. The term 'development plan' now includes

the structure plan and any alterations to it with the Minister's notice of approval, together with any local plans and alterations to them with the [planning] authorities' resolution of adoption or the Minister's notice of approval.

Thus 'development plan' is now a general term covering the structure plan for an area together with any local plans for parts or the whole of that area.

The form of the development plan is also substantially different. The structure plan consists primarily of a written statement together with supporting diagrams and illustrations but no map. Local plans will consist of a written statement and a map giving detailed proposals. The written statement must include a summarised substantiation of the decisions which will be required including 'a description of the examination of alternative decisions that may have been considered'.

Local planning authorities are no longer required to carry out a five-yearly review of their development plan proposals. The frequency of any review is at the discretion of the local planning authority informed by continuous monitoring of change affecting the area' and a local planning authority may 'undertake a partial amendment, alterations being confined either to a particular area or areas or to a particular subject or group of subjects'. This procedure is designed to allow much greater flexibility than the procedures of the 1947 Act in adapting planning proposals to meet changing or unforeseen circumstances. The five-yearly review system, which in practice often meant the preparation of a new plan, did not allow for any real flexibility in times of rapid change. Additionally the procedures for amending development plan proposals were often long-winded and cumbersome.

The programme map, which was an essential part of the Development Plan, is not replaced by formal requirement for a similar map. Instead it is suggested that account should be taken of the placing of proposals and the time factor in four ways. Firstly, by highlighting short-term projects, i.e. those which are to be completed within ten years—these of course will include a number of projects to which the local authority is already committed. Secondly, the stages of implementation should be summarised and the key dates and stages clearly identified. Thirdly, the anticipated population levels at 1981 and 1991 should be set out, as population levels obviously determine the scale of social and land-use provisions which may be necessary. Fourthly,

to recognise that some policies in the plan will be open ended, long term and in broad outline only and that it would be inappropriate to attach dates or a precise programme to the implementation of such policies in the more distant future.

The scope of the coverage of the structure plan is much wider than that of the Development Plan though there has been and still is debate on how wide this scope should be. The scope of the Development Plan was largely concerned with land utilisation and the provision of sites for particular uses. In contrast the potential scope of the structure plan is extremely wide and allows for the integration of social, economic, transport and environmental policies. However, the Layfield Report makes the point that

one of the most important differences between the situation in 1947 and now, is that in 1947 the planning authority was considered to be the initiator or controller through its formal development plan procedures, of most important development and physical change in its area, whereas now it is not. The schemes of Government Departments and statutory undertakers not subject to the normal planning processes, the informal processes of regional plans, general improvement areas or conservation areas, do not stem from the development plan machinery.

Local planning authorities are required to take account of regional policies and proposals as a context for the development of structure plan policies. In some cases this was also the situation for Development Plans. For example, Development Plans for London and the South-East region were intended to be prepared within the context of the Greater London Plan prepared in 1944. Some of the problems of attempting to do this are described by Cullingworth.[30] However, for most of the country there was no system of regional planning into which the preparation of development plans could fit. A form of regional machinery now exists through the Regional Economic Councils and Boards but for some areas additional regional and sub-regional plans have been prepared largely to provide a context for structure plans. Examples of these include the sub-regional plans for Leicester and Leicestershire,[31] the Coventry Study mentioned earlier, and the Notts-Derby Study.[32] Examples of regional plans include the Strategic Plan for the South-East[33] and the West Midlands Regional Study.[34] All of these sub-regional and regional plans are advisory and although they may exert profound influence on the major policy decisions affecting urban and rural areas they have no legal status.

People and Plans

A major difference between the development plan and the structure plan concerns the way in which people are involved in the plan-making process. Under the 1947 Act there is no legal requirement that an opportunity should be given for people to become involved in the process of formulating the policies and proposals of the development plan for their area. There is simply provision that people, under given circumstances, can make formal objections to proposals and have these objections heard in an inquiry, the outcome of which is decided by the Minister. The 1968 Act, however, introduced the idea that people should have a legal right to participate in the formulation of the planning proposals themselves apart from the legal right to make formal objections. The provisions of the Act state that the local planning authority must

take such steps as in their opinion will secure that adequate publicity is given in their area to the report of survey and to the matters they propose to include in the plan—that persons who may be expected to desire an opportunity of making representations to the authority with respect to those matters are made aware that they are entitled to an opportunity of doing so;—that such persons are given an adequate opportunity of making such representations. Additionally, the local authority is required to make copies of the structure plan available for inspection and submit the plan to the Secretary of State together with a statement of the measures which have been taken to comply with the requirements and of consultations which have been carried out with other persons.

Additionally, the Act specifies that the Minister has the power to return the structure plan to the local authority if he is not satisfied that they have taken adequate steps to comply with the above requirements.

The introduction of the concept of citizen participation into the plan-making process led to the setting up of a committee[35] to clarify the processes and procedures which local authorities might adopt in carrying out these requirements. The committee made a number of rather obvious recommendations 'of a mundane nature' in their report which nonetheless stimulated a great deal of public discussion. Many of these recommendations together with further clarifications are contained in circular 52/72[36] which expresses ministry policy guidelines on public participation to local planning authorities

Lessons from the Greater London Development Plan

At this point in time few structure plans have been through the whole process and therefore it is difficult to assess how successful the new Act will be in practice. However, some lessons can perhaps be drawn. The Greater London Development Plan, although technically not a structure plan, gives some indications of the kind of problems likely to arise in the preparation of structure plans. The Layfield Report indicates a number of general defects which 'are likely to be present in other structure plans unless action is taken to ensure that they are not'. These defects include over-ambition in terms of what the plans may be able to achieve. Examples are given of assumptions that the policies of a plan can alter settled population trends when no policies of a local authority (in a democratic country at least) can effectively change settled population trends in the short term. Also that the plan tried to forecast the supply and demand of employment for substantial periods ahead and 'to translate those into terms of floor-space allocations for various sectors of London'. When as the report goes on to say 'the G.L.C. had neither the information to make employment forecasts nor the ability to relate them to floor space'. This led the panel to conclude that these might be a danger of treating the structure plan as

being the unique document in which all major decisions must be taken even those decisions which, while there is no information at present upon which to base them and no indications that they could lead to any useful or ascertainable result, the authority would like to take.

A second general defect was the inconsistent treatment of the matters contained within the plan. Examples of this were that 'the information upon which the plan was founded differed widely in degrees of specificity and depth' and that this wide variation was reflected in the formulation of the plan. Also, the GLC tended to concentrate in their plan upon those proposals which it had the power to carry through itself. The panel pointed out that even if some of the problems were perhaps made more acute by the governmental structure of London the new local government structure after re-organisation looks as though it may raise similar difficulties.

A third defect concerned the way in which information about problems and planning issues was related to policies to deal with them. Thus the panel states that 'one of the most notable features of the GLDP is the independence of the policies in the Plan from the facts gathered in the Report of Studies and other documents'. The panel in many instances, found great difficulty in seeing how the facts led to some of the solutions put forward. They considered that the

GLC when examining a range of alternative solutions to a problem 'chose one on political grounds and then presented it as inevitable'. The panel recommended that if a solution is arrived at on political grounds then 'it should be presented as a choice preferred for political reasons amongst alternatives and not represented as the only logical consequence of technical information'.

A fourth problem relates to the way that the policies in the plan relate to the aims of the plan and the way in which the aims themselves are expressed. The panel state that they 'found it extremely difficult to discover what the precise aims were that many of the policies in the GLDP were supposed to fulfil', and that 'it is only by reference to aims that policies can be judged necessary or likely to be successful'. These points are also connected with the way in which the aims are expressed and the panel found it necessary to make the comment that 'the GLDP written statement is full of statements of aims which do not mean anything because they can mean anything to anyone'. They give examples of these kind of aims—'to give new inspiration to the onward development of London's genius'—'development schemes throughout London should provide as many new dwellings as a good standard of environment will allow'—'the Council's policy is the objective of improving public transport in all possible ways'. The panel point out that there is a great temptation for local authorities, who have to try and please a great number of authorities and interest groups, to word the aims of their plans in a very general way 'in order not to offend anyone too deeply'. The panel indicate the dangers of this temptation and state that if it is not resisted then 'the whole system of structure plans will fall into disrepute'.

A final problem identified by the panel was concerned with the distinction between broad policy issues appropriate to a structure plan and more detailed material appropriate to a local plan. This distinction is, as the panel accept, not always an easy one to make and yet it is crucial to the relationship between structure and local plans as envisaged by the act. For example, a structure plan might indicate in broad terms the line of a proposed road of national importance and the building of this road and its general costing might be closely related to improving public transport and removing through traffic from other areas. The detailed line of this road could probably be included in local plans and if the local authority was forced to abandon road proposals through some areas because of opposition from residents then the whole broad transport strategy of the structure plan might have to be substantially changed. If the parts of the transport strategy were derived from regional or national policies then these in turn might have to be modified—'from little acorns do mighty oak trees grow'.

To a certain extent this example illustrates the nature of the relationship between national, regional, structure and local planning policies. The example indicates that the relationship between these spatial levels of planning is not a simple hierarchy. This point is made by Burns.[37] Rather, the relationship is iterative. In other words

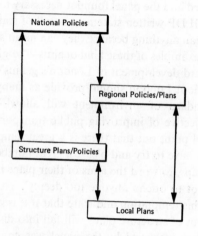

Fig. 1   Iterative relationship between spatial levels of planning

the policies and proposals of one level of plan-making interact with those at another level in such a way that a continuous process of modification takes place until some kind of finality is reached. The broad outline of this process is indicated in Figure 1. The structure plan, under the arrangements of the 1968 Act, can be seen as a pivotal point in this iterative process. This makes the role of public involvement in the processes of formulating structure plans even more important and extensive than the protection of the individual's rights to protect his interests.

Public Participation and Structure Plans

As yet there have been very few analyses of the different methods and procedures adopted by local authorities to involve the public in the plan-making process. Certainly there has been a wide variation in the approaches of different local authorities. These have included the production of brochures, films, leaflets and newspapers; static and mobile exhibitions (Birmingham City has had a Structure Plan Bus for example) talks in schools, local meetings and large public meetings. Also, some local authorities have employed public relations consultants to advise them in the preparation of material to be presented to the public. Although there has not as yet been a complete analysis of the success or failure of these measures some indications of major problems arising can be seen. A local magazine concerned with planning issues in the West Midlands[38] has monitored some aspects of participatory procedures in that area. Some of the problems they identify relate to the nature of structure plans themselves and reflect some of the points made in the Layfield report. Many structure plans do, in fact, express their aims in general terms— 'better housing', 'more jobs', 'more public transport', 'better roads' and very few people would quarrel with these kinds of statements. However, the implications of these aims as expressed in different policies are often not very clear and the conflicts between them are not necessarily specified. Thus a policy of 'better roads' may mean that the local authority may have less to spend on 'better houses' or a 'better environment' and similarly a policy of providing more open space in the suburbs of a city, may mean that the authority will have less to spend on improving educational facilities in the less privileged parts of the city. It is clear that the authorities in formulating these kinds of policies are not just concerned with land utilisation, traffic movement or environmental quality but are also concerned with making major decisions on the levels of investment which will be available to implement these policies and it may well be that many people would take issue with the priorities given to different policies by an authority. Put another way 'a structure plan is a political document —it says some shall have, and others shall not.'[39]

If a general conclusion can be drawn from the views expressed above it is that the apparent apathy of the public towards involvement in the structure planning process reflects a failure on the part of planning authorities to make clear to the public just what their policies and proposals mean and the extent to which the public have real influence on the priorities implied by these plans.

Local Plans

Local plans as described earlier now form a separate part of the plan-making machinery. This is, however, somewhat complex in that the legislation upon which many local plans may be based does not stem from Town and Country Planning legislation. The Development Plans manual defines a local plan as a 'general term for any plan adopted by a local planning authority, or under certain circumstances approved by the Minister, for part, or all, of an area already subject to an approved structure plan'. The provisions of the 1968 Act allow for the preparation of three general types of local plan. These are action area plans, district plans and subject plans.

Although the 1947 Act did not provide for the preparation of local plans as such, it did make provision for the preparation of Comprehensive Development Area plans (CDAs). CDA plans although they technically constitute amendments to a development plan are similar in purpose to action area plans. Also many authorities have prepared Town Centre Maps[40] which, although non-statutory plans, are effectively local plans prepared to guide the development of town centres. Many county authorities have prepared non-statutory village plans again intended to guide the detailed development of small settlements in their area. The 1967 Civic Amenities Act[41] requires local authorities to prepare plans for the conservation of historic and architecturally important areas with cities, towns and villages. The 1969 Housing Act[42] gave local authorities powers to declare General Improvement Areas to help in the rehabilitation and revitalisation of older areas of housing. A recent White Paper[43] proposes that local authorities should declare Housing Action Areas in areas of great housing stress within cities. All of these in some measure constitute local planning proposals or policies.

The Development Plans manual specifies four functions that

local plans are meant to perform. Firstly, they are concerned with applying the general policies and proposals of the structure plan to particular areas in a precise and detailed way and thus indicating the developmental and land-use proposals necessary to achieve the aims of the structure plan policies and proposals. Secondly, from this they are intended to provide the detailed basis for the control of development by giving 'more precise information to developers by allocating sites for particular purposes by defining the areas to which development control policies will apply and by explaining those policies in terms of standards and other criteria'. Thirdly, local plans are intended to provide a specific framework within which public and private development and expenditure in particular areas can be co-ordinated. Fourthly, by interpreting structure-plan policies in a more detailed way 'a local plan will be concerned to draw the attention (of the public) to more detailed planning issues', affecting the area in which they live or have an interest. Thus, local plans, like structure plans, are intended to be decision documents by making clear to the public what is proposed for an area, showing why such proposals are needed and 'how, when and where they will be implemented'.

The general form that local plans are intended to take, for instance a written statement and accompanying map, has been mentioned earlier. For local plans, the written statement is meant to include an explanation of the structure plan policy as it affects the area; a description of survey information about the area; an explanation of how decisions were arrived at together with a substantiation of the proposals made; and a summary, where alternatives have been examined, of the arguments which have led to the choice of particular alternative. The map should show as precisely as possible the boundaries of land allocations and include any proposals for new development, redevelopment and improvement. The map should indicate the exact extent of the areas covered by other policies (for example, conservation areas). Also the map should show which properties or lands are to be acquired by public authorities and

it is important that where there is a firm decision on the part of the planning authority to acquire land for planning purposes or on the part of another public authority for their own purposes, this should be made clear as part of the policy for implementing the proposals.

The provisions for the public participation in the process of formulating local plans are similar to those of structure plans and again the Secretary of State has the power to refer back plans if he is not satisfied that the authority has met with the requirements. However, the local authority who prepares the plan is also, except in certain circumstances, the authority who approves the plan. Given the extremely wide and comprehensive coverage of local plans these are potentially very wide powers.

District Plans

The range of local plans as previously mentioned includes three general types of local plan: these are district plans, action area plans and subject plans. District plans are defined as being 'for the comprehensive planning of relatively large areas, usually where change will take place in a piecemeal fashion over a long period'. The relatively large areas can range from the whole of a town or city to parts of a town, city or country. Thus a district plan could cover, for example, the whole of Birmingham, Manchester or Leeds; alternatively it might cover a large part of a county which needed fairly detailed planning action and control.

The time-scale over which proposals in the district plan can be made is not fixed and can be extended over the full time period of the structure plan to which the district plan relates. District plans are also meant to be comprehensive in the sense that they must take all planning factors into account together with other public policies which affect the area covered by the plan.

The functions of the district plans have the common element of functions of all local plans described earlier. However, the particular emphasis of district plans is that they are intended to be concerned with setting out of the planning policies for an area, restating and amplifying the long-term intentions of the structure plan as they affect that area in terms of specific proposals and the laying down of development control criteria. Also for urban areas they should apply the structure plan policies for environmental planning and management—these could include, for instance, policies of traffic management and the district plan would indicate the areas affected by traffic management policies; or alternatively the structure plan might contain policies for housing improvement and the district plan would indicate those areas scheduled for improvement. For rural areas the district plan should apply the structure plan policies for managing the rural environment.

Action Area Plans

Action areas plans are defined as being 'for the comprehensive planning of the areas indicated in the structure plan for improvement, redevelopment or new development or combinations of these actions, starting within a period of ten years'. Thus they are distinctively different from district plans in that they are limited to a specific range of planning issues and that the time-scale is tied to a period of ten years ahead. Also they must be indicated in the structure plan.

The areas covered by action area plans may well be sub-areas of a district plan. For instance, a district plan may be prepared for a large area of old housing within a city parts of which are considered to be in need of intensive change. In this case an action area plan could be produced for the redevelopment of some areas and the improvement of others. Alternatively, a district plan might be prepared for a substantial area of new development which is programmed to take place over a long period of time. In this case action area plans might be produced as a brief to developers in the development of the earlier stages in the total development.

In addition to detailed proposals of developmental change, action area plans are also intended to indicate the means by which the plan will be implemented and give as precise dates as possible to the stages of implementation. Also, where appropriate the financial implications at various stages in the implementation of proposals should be set out with particular emphasis on those costs likely to be incurred by the public sector.

Subject Plans

Subject plans are defined as being 'for dealing with particular planning aspects in advance of the preparation of a comprehensive plan or where a comprehensive plan is not needed.' These local plans are intended to deal with two particular circumstances. Firstly, where there is a need to develop a particular policy contained in the structure plan which because of its urgency cannot be fitted into the time period required for the preparation of a comprehensive district plan. Secondly, where the nature of the issues are insufficient to justify comprehensive treatment. Examples of the latter might include a plan to convert an abandoned railway line into a linear park and walkway or a plan for the development and control of mineral workings in a county. Thus a subject plan will be usually confined to a single aspect of planning.

It is anticipated that district plans when they are prepared may incorporate subject plans in a similar way to action area proposals. Also it is possible that one subject plan, for example for the abandoned railway line, could cut across the area of several district plans.

'All Change is for the Worse' (Dr Johnson)

So far this chapter has outlined a number of changes in the operation of physical planning and has indicated some of the problems and implications arising from these changes. As a form of conclusion it is perhaps useful to examine some of these further.

Central Government and Change

Changes in the organisation of central government indicate a number of trends. The setting up of the DOE represents an attempt to achieve better co-ordination between those activities of government which directly and perhaps indirectly affect people and their living environment. It also reflects a realisation that many of these activities inter-relate with each other. Thus, for example, for the first time responsibility for regional planning lies with the same department which is responsible for physical planning at other spatial levels. The dilemmas posed by the the separation of these responsibilities in the past are described by Self[44] and are aptly stated by the Strategic Plan for the South East study team as follows:

On the one hand [regional planning] is an extension of local planning, dealing particularly with those matters—the movement and distribution of population and employment; the complex interaction of social and economic needs, the provision of major recreational facilities and the main communications network, for example—which can only be decided for areas much larger than the areas of existing local planning authorities,

On the other hand it is concerned with inter-regional flows of population and employment, with the availability and use of resources, and with the long term economic prospects which cannot be properly considered except in the context of the balance to be achieved between growth in one region and growth required in other parts of the country, on which only the Government can decide.

But major problems still remain. There is no formal regional planning machinery with executive powers directly answerable to an electorate. This fact is important in considering the relationship between regional, structure and local plans. Regional plans are meant to set the policy context for the preparation of structure plans and as such could considerably influence the range of alternative policies which could be considered in a structure plan. This raises questions related to the idea that people, by participating in the formulation of plans for their area, have a real choice in the alternatives with which they may be presented. How far is this idea negated when many of the aims and proposals of a structure plan may be derived from policy decisions outside the control or influence of the people in an area? Additionally, the setting up by the DTI of another system of advisory, *ad hoc*, regional boards with functions somewhat similar to those of the Regional Economic Planning Councils and Boards could, apart from raising confusion in the minds of the public, create additional problems in formulating and developing co-ordinated regional policies.

A second feature of change in central government is the increased devolution of power and responsibility to local authorities in their plan making functions. This reflects the traditional relationship between central and local government in that the main concern of central government is with the major issues of national importance whilst local government is concerned with the resolution of local issues. How successful the devolved powers will be in producing more effective plans at the local scale remains to be seen.

Local Government and Change

The re-organisation of local government into the new authorities is intended to overcome a series of deficiencies which exist in the current system. These deficiencies, outlined in the White Paper[45] on local government reform, mainly relate to irrelevance of existing local authority boundaries to present conditions and the fragmentation of powers between local authorities. Thus the current re-organisation involves a greater centralisation of powers into the hands of a smaller number of enlarged authorities. This centralisation of powers has been frequently criticised on the grounds that it will increase the remoteness of the individual from authority and that it could increase the gap between the planners and the planned. Also, the relationship between the planning powers of the new Counties and those of the Districts is likely to be highly complex[46] and subject to continuous political debate. This could well lead to inconsistencies between the planning powers of local authorities, particularly Districts, in different parts of the country, thus breaking the concept of a consistent system of planning powers between local authorities which was a major feature of the 1947 Act.

Changes in the internal structure of many local authorities mirror the kinds of changes which have taken place within the structure of central government. However, the rearrangement of management structures does not in itself ensure more efficient management. Taking a lot of fish from a number of small tanks and putting them into one large tank makes it possible for the fish to meet but it does not ensure that they will do so. Equally it does not ensure that the cross-fertilisation between different fish will be more efficient, rapid or result in bigger, fatter fish. Similarly the introduction of corporate management arrangements into local authorities does not in itself immediately ensure changes in the traditional attitudes, beliefs and demarcation lines between various local authority departments. The impending re-organisation of local government may help to overcome some of these problems through the attention which has been paid to the staffing structure[47] of the new authorities and the volume of work and levels of interdepartmental co-operation which will be necessary to make the new authorities operate effectively.

The Plan-making Process and Change

New institutional arrangements and new legislative procedures imply new processes and techniques of plan-making. Legislation, however, only indicates the nature, form and content of plans and does not specify the technical processes by which they might be prepared.

The introduction of new forms of plans implies that the technical means are available to achieve them. Certainly over the past decade many major changes and developments have been introduced into the plan making process. The underlying rationale of many of these developments and the ways in which they have been adopted is complex and a full discussion is beyond the scope of this chapter. Many of these changes have arisen through a greater understanding of the nature of physical plans based upon operational experience. For example, the idea of a physical plan as a once and for all blueprint of the future has been replaced by ideas of continuous planning and of plans which are flexible and adaptable to meet changing circumstances. Other changes have, for example, stemmed from developments in computer technology. These developments have enabled the innovation of techniques and methods which would be almost impossible to operate without the aid of computers. Additionally the increasing realisation of the inter-relationships of physical planning with other forms of planning and societal activities has led to changes. For example, increased understanding of the relationships between land uses and transportation has led to the development of a wide range of new techniques.

A major feature of change in approaches to plan-making over the past decade has been the introduction of systemic approaches which attempt to provide a rational methodology for decisions relating to the solution of planning problems. These approaches can take a number of forms, but the general stages they involve can be outlined as follows:[48]

(a) Definition and clarification of future problems and the inter-relationships between them.

(b) Identification of future conditions which might arise from the problems identified.

(c) Identification of constraints which determine the range of possible solutions to the problems.

(d) Determination of goals and objectives which plans are meant to achieve.

(e) Formulation of alternative ways of achieving the goals and objectives which plans are meant to achieve.

(f) Evaluation of the alternatives.

(g) Recommendation of preferred alternatives.

This process also involves the development of methodologies to monitor the progress of a plan towards the achievement of its goals and objectives. The results of the monitoring arrangements are meant to feed back into the above processes so that modifications to the proposals or policies of the plan can be made, if necessary, in response to changing circumstances. In general terms this is meant to form the basis of a continuous plan-making process. However, the development of techniques and methodologies for the monitoring of plans has lagged behind the development of techniques for plan formulation. This factor may prove a serious problem in achieving the reality of a continuous planning process which is quickly responsive to change.

The need to more clearly identify and express problems in quantitive terms has led to the development of techniques from the social sciences. Many of these are still in early stages of development which partially reflects the relatively recent entry of social scientists into the field of planning.

The collection, analysis and interpretation of the vast amounts of data which are often required for the identification and quantification of problems has been helped by the use of computers. However, the availability of suitable up to date information often remains a major problem which hinders the full indentification of problems and particularly the relationships between them.

Considerable developments and refinements have taken place within predictive techniques although this, almost by definition, remains a difficult area. Many of these developments relate to attempts to simulate possible future changes and to assess their implications through the use of mathematical modelling techniques. The computer has had a considerable influence upon the development of modelling techniques but the extent of their operational usefulness has still not been fully explored. The need to evaluate and assess the implications of possible alternative plans has led to the application and development of a wide range of evaluative techniques. These have been mainly aimed at quantifying the differences between possible alternative plans. The use of cost-benefit analysis, for example, as a technique to measure the costs of proposals and the benefits arising from them has been fairly widespread. These techniques have often been criticised when their use has been extended to cover matters which are difficult to quantify and therefore measure.

Will All Change be for the Worse?

The theme of this chapter has been concerned with change. It has tried to indicate the processes of change in the physical environment and the ways in which physical planning intervenes in these processes; it has tried to indicate what the operation of physical planning is attempting to achieve by this intervention; additionally it has tried to indicate the role of physical planning in relation to other forms of planning.

Physical planning stands yet again on the threshold of major changes in its operation. This chapter has attempted to show how and why some of these changes have evolved and indicate some issues arising from them. How effective the changes in legislation and organisation will be is difficult to predict and the directions in which physical planning will evolve in response to these changes is also difficult to foresee. Unfortunately, the least developed of all predictive techniques is that of predicting the future of physical planning itself. The indications are that the next ten years will be times of great challenge and opportunity to those working within the field of physical planning and one hopes that the gloomy forebodings of Dr Johnson will prove to be unfounded.

References

1 J. B. McLoughlin, *Urban and Regional Planning. A Systems Approach* (Faber and Faber, 1969).
2 J. B. McLoughlin, 'Notes on the Nature of Physical Change', JRTPI, vol. 51, no. 10 (1965).
3 D. L. Foley, 'British Town Planning: One Ideology or Three', *British Journal of Sociology*, vol. 11 (1960). See also Faludi, *A Reader in Planning Theory* (Pergamon, 1973).
4 Coventry—Soluhull—Warwickshire Sub-regional Planning Study. A Strategy for the Sub-region 1971.
5 J. B. Cullingworth, *Town and Country Planning in England and Wales* (Allen and Unwin, 1972).
6 W. Ashworth, *The Genesis of Modern Town Planning* (Routledge, 1954).
7 Housing, Town Planning etc. Act 1909.
8 Town and Country Planning Act 1947.
9 New Towns Act 1946.
10 Local Government Act 1972.

11 P. Self, *Metropolitan Planning, Greater London Papers No. 14* (Weidenfield and Nicholson, 1971).

12 Department of the Environment, Greater London Development Plan Report of the Panel of Inquiry, vol. 1 (HMSO, 1973).

13 White Paper—The Reorganisation of Central Government Cmnd 4506 (HMSO, 1970).

14 Town and Country Planning Act 1943.

15 Department of Economic Affairs, The National Plan (HMSO, 1965).

16 B. C. Smith, *Regionalism in England*, vol. 3 (Action Society Trust, 1965).

17 Department of Economic Affairs, A Strategy for the South East (HMSO, 1967).

18 Department of Economic Affairs, Patterns of Growth (HMSO, 1967).

19 G. McCrone, Regional Policy in Britain (Allen and Unwin, 1969).

20 Treasury Information Division, Economic Progress Report No. 32 (October 1970).

21 Town and Country Planning Act 1962.

22 Town and Country Planning Act 1971.

23 G. Pepler, *Twenty-one Years of Town Planning in England and Wales* (Town Planning Institute, 1946).

24 Ministry of Housing and Local Government, The Future of Development Plans: A Report by the Planning Advisory Group (HMSO, 1965).

25 J. James, *The Future of Development Plans*, Summer School papers (Town Planning Institute, 1965).

26 'Pragma', *JRTPI*, vol. 51, no. 8, Sept./Oct. (1965).

27 T. Sharp, 'Planning Planning,' *JRTPI*, vol. 52, no. 6 (June 1966).

28 Town Planning Institute, 'The Future of Development Plans', *JRTPI*, vol. 52, no. 3 (March 1966).

29 Ministry of Housing and Local Government, Development Plans—A Manual on Form and Content (HMSO, 1970).

30 J. B. Cullingworth, *Housing Needs and Planning Policy* (Routledge, 1960).

31 Leicester City and Leicester County Council, *Leicester/Leicestershire Sub-Regional Study* (1969).

32 Nottinghamshire/Derbyshire Sub-Regional Planning Unit, *Nottinghamshire/Derbyshire Sub-Regional Study* (1969).

33 South East Joint Planning Team, A Strategic Plan for the South East (HMSO, 1970).

34 West Midlands Planning Authorities Conference. *A Developing Strategy for the West Midlands* (1971).

35 Committee on public participation in planning, People and Planning (Skeffington report) (HMSO, 1969).
36 Department of the Environment, Circular 52/72, (HMSO 1972).
37 W. Burns, 'National and Regional Planning Policies—England', *JRTPI*, vol. 58, no. 7 (July/Aug. 1971).
38 Community Planning Associates, see series of articles in *West Midlands Grassroots*, nos. 5 to 9 (1973).
39 Community Planning Associates, *West Midlands Grassroots*, no. 8 (1973).
40 Ministry of Housing and Local Government, *Town Centres; An approach to renewal*, Planning Bulletin no. 1 (HMSO, 1962).
41 Civic Amenities Act 1967.
42 Housing Act 1969.
43 White paper, '*Better Homes—The Next Priorities*', Cmnd 5339 (HMSO, 1973).
44 P. Self, 'Regional Planning in Britain'. *Regional Studies*, vol. 1, no. 1 (1967).
45 White Paper Reform of Local Government in England, Cmnd 4276 (HMSO, 1970).
46 F. J. C. Amos, 'The Local Government Bill: Planning Provisions', *JRTPI*, vol. 58, no. 2 (1972).
47 Department of Environment, The New Local Authorities—Management and Structure (Bains Report) (HMSO, 1972).
48 A. J. Catanese and A. W. Steiss, 'Systemic Planning', *JRTPI*, vol. 54, no. 4 (April 1968).

5. Economic Planning

James T. Hughes

Economic Planning Defined

The term 'economic planning' has a very comprehensive air. It has been defined as 'the systematic management of the nation's assets in pursuit of more or less well-defined objectives'.[1] It has, however, never been possible to plan such a complex mechanism as the functioning of the entire economic system. Even in socialist economies of Eastern Europe, where economic planning has been developed to a high degree of sophistication, it has not been thought desirable to plan in detail the output of foods at all levels. The goal tends to be to maintain a balance between the output of key goods and commodities by setting broad targets and controlling the flow of investment resources and key raw materials. Outside the manufacturing sector, in agriculture and service industries, an even greater freedom of action exists. There is a wide literature on the problems of comprehensive economic planning.[2] Briefly, the main difficulties are the retention of incentives at all levels of production, the specification of targets, the need to respond to consumer preferences and the correct allowance for unforeseen difficulties and delays. There is a difficult balance in all forms of economic planning between detailed control and the flexibility required to prevent a rigid schedule breaking-down when disrupted by a relatively minor hitch.

Although the technical problems of planning the economy place constraints upon any comprehensive planning system, governments do have more or less well-defined economic goals and in a number of important areas intervene directly in the economy to obtain their fulfilment. Economic planning is one type of economic policy which a government will employ depending upon its chosen goals and the responsiveness of the economy to alternative measures. In particular the stage of economic development is an important determinant of the need for economic planning; in the early stages of growth the competing claims of growth and higher consumption and the slower rate of economic adjustment have tended to lead to a greater degree of economic planning. The goals of economic policy have been specified in a form which has gained fairly general agreement as follows:[3]

(a) equity—a 'fair' distribution of income;
(b) stabilisation of fluctuations in national income and employment;
(c) the efficient allocation of resources between current, private and public wants;
(d) the optimal allocation over time between consumption and investment leading to a desired rate of economic growth.

Although it is increasingly difficult to distinguish between economic planning and other types of economic policy, it tends to describe measures which have a direct and immediate influence over the use of economic resources. The growth of economic planning has been associated with the increasing proportion of the Gross National Product (GNP) which is spent by the government. During the twentieth century there has been an increasing awareness of the social responsibilities of the State towards its citizens. Whereas previously it was thought that the prime function of the State was to provide security from foreign and internal threats to the life and property of its citizens, the list of threats has been widened to include items such as bad health, unemployment, the uneven distribution of economic power and environmental pollution. In some cases, the economic policies employed have been restricted to regulation and quasi-judicial review such as with monopolies and restrictive practices. In other cases, even though expenditure was transferred to the public sector, as when the National Health Service was instituted, the organisation and provisions of medical services remained relatively undisturbed. The later sections of this chapter will discuss the principal areas of economic planning policies, namely postwar planning for reconstruction and indicative planning to increase the rate of economic growth, budgetary planning, stabilisation of national income and employment, and regional planning.

The growth of physical planning has been one aspect of the increased role of government in recent decades. Development control and zoning policies are basically regulatory policies, but they are closely allied to the powers of local authorities to build housing, and to initiate broader development and redevelopment schemes. The policy of developing New Towns has been closely allied to regional economic development policy in certain respects. In large measure economic and physical planning run parallel to each other, motivated by similar social forces. Economic planning has considerable implications for physical planning and related policies, insofar as the rate of growth of GNP and budgetary policy will be major determinants of the resources available for social policies. However, there are only a few examples of an examination of the economic consequences of planning standards and decisions[4] or of the extent to which the spatial factor influences the efficiency of economic processes. There will, therefore, be a brief discussion in the concluding section to the chapter of how economic planning and physical planning may be more closely related.

Economic Planning in Postwar Britain

The extent and form of economic planning in any country is partly dependent upon the prevailing political and social philosophies. This chapter is limited to a discussion of planning within the modified capitalist framework of postwar Britain. In this context economic planning has typically referred to two sets of government action. Firstly there was a period of direct (or 'interventionist') control of economic resources during the extended period of reconstruction which followed the Second World War. Secondly, around 1960 a new form of 'indicative' planning was set up by a Conservative government with the more particular goal of increasing the rate of economic growth which seemed to be so much lower in the UK than in other European countries.[5]

During the first period of planning the great shortage of economic resources available to repair the devastation of war and to renew neglected economic and social capital created two principal goals. The first, by means of rationing and high taxation, limited the goods available for personal consumption. Consumer goods were directed to export markets and imports strictly controlled. The other main task was to allocate the available materials to priority industries by means of quotas, licences and to a lesser extent by nationalisation. Although the mobilisation of the national economy for the war effort had worked reasonably well in Britain and had created a unique fund of experience for economic planning, postwar planning created a climate of opposition and disillusionment. The reasons were numerous: popular solidarity of purpose broke down in peacetime; the problems of allocation were more numerous and subtle when applied to the complex task of reconstruction; the reservoir of able temporary civil servants was drained; the longer planning continued in operation the more mistakes were available as evidence against it; as planning became more comprehensive more people were brought up against its restrictions and prohibitions. Thus for a variety of reasons, real and imaginary, economic planning fell into disuse and in the mid-1950s it seemed appropriate only to a condition of national emergency, being economically wasteful and, above all, politically unpopular. It may be interesting to observe, however, that while the national structure of economic planning was being dismantled (even before the 1951 election) the primarily local administration of land-use planning under the Town and Country Planning Act 1947 and New Town Development Corporations was being set up.

The resurgence of economic planning in the 1960s was clearly differentiated from the earlier neo-socialist attempts. Its goal was not the optimal allocation of national resources but the more limited one of increasing the rate of economic growth. The mode of planning was not by rationing and quotas (negative measures) but by persuasion, the spread of information and the creation of a favourable climate of business confidence. To some extent the change in aims and method may be attributed to doctrinaire differences between the Labour government of 1945-51 and the Conservative administrations by which the new indicative planning was initiated. There were, however, more immediate reasons which are apparent when the origins of the new planning are more fully considered.

During the second half of the 1950s[6] there was an increasing awareness in the UK of the low rate of domestic economic growth when compared not only to the traditionally high-growth economies of the United States and Germany but also to France, Italy and other countries in Europe. Perhaps the most surprising feature of this international comparison was the high rate of growth in France which had been generally regarded as handicapped by conservative social and disruptive political forces. On further examination it appeared that the new force in French economic life was the influence of the Monnet plans. These plans, normally for four years ahead, laid down broad guidelines for public investment and mapped out an agreed programme of output growth and investment for the private sector which was consistent with the overall capacity of the economy. There was some diversity of opinion as to how far the growth of the French economy could be attributed to planning and especially upon which aspects of planning, the spread of information, change of expectations or regulatory devices. Nevertheless an overwhelming weight of opinion favoured the establishment of a British version of the Commissariat du Plan.

Accordingly in 1961 the Chancellor of the Exchequer initiated negotiations with both sides of industry on setting up the National Economic Development Council (NEDC or 'Neddy'). From early 1962 it carried out 'a joint examination of the economic prospects of the country stretching five or more years into the future . . . above all . . . to establish what are the essential conditions for realising potential growth'.[7] It was assisted in this task by the National Economic Development Office (NEDO) and in 1964 by the Economic Development Committees ('little Neddies') in all the main industries. In 1963 the NEDO produced a document which examined the consequences and feasibility of a 4 per cent rate of growth of GNP.[8] However, there was never an explicit statement as to how the work of the NEDC would change decision making in the economy. Each of the principal units in the economy, large firms, nationalised industries, central and local authorities, had their individual plans which related to varying time periods and were formulated in different ways. Indicative planning was not filling a vacuum; it was hopefully changing a myriad of separate sets of expectations and reactions to the future. Unless one subscribes to the naive view that people changed their minds about the future course of events because they read it in an official document, there was considerable scope for disagreement as to how and over what period it was possible to change the rate of economic growth. A major obstacle to the discussion of these issues was the belief that critical debate would negate any element of self-fulfilling prophecy which might exist. Thus in Alan Day's terminology[9] there grew up the 'myth' of 4 per cent growth.

In 1964 the agency of planning changed when the Department of

Economic Affairs took over many of the responsibilities of the National Economic Development Office. The NEDC remained as a forum for the exchange of views among government, industry and trades unions but the revised and expanded version of the 1963 document was entitled the National Plan[10] and described as a statement of government policy. The policies pursued by DEA are open to the same criticisms as NEDC of specifying growth rates—in this case 3·8 per cent per annum—by assumption rather than in the light of current economic circumstances. The prospective target of a 25 per cent increase in national output by 1970 was made impossible initially by the measures which the Government implemented in 1966–7 to restrain domestic demand to protect the value of the pound. But even without the handicap of an overvalued currency it is very doubtful if the rate of increase in productivity could have sustained the hoped-for increase in output.

Following the devaluation in November 1967 a second planning statement was prepared by DEA.[11] It was introduced, in the words of the first sentence of the first chapter by the disclaimer 'This is not a plan . . .' The form of publication was a Green Paper, a document for discussion rather than a precursor of government action as in the case of a White Paper. The discussion of future growth was placed in the context not of a single growth rate well above that which had been sustained for any substantial period in the past but of three possible rates. A 'basic' rate of $3\frac{1}{4}$ per cent per annum was regarded as not the lowest which may be achieved (there was a 'lower' rate of 3 per cent) but one which could be improved upon by pursuit of the right policies. A more desirable rate was the 'higher' rate of 4 per cent per annum. There was no detailed survey of industry but the rates were discussed mainly in the context of the balance of payments and in particular the probable rate of growth of exports, a major gap in the National Plan. The fortunes of indicative planning seemed to have gone full circle when later in 1959 the DEA was abolished and the Treasury resumed its former unchallenged leadership in economic affairs and association with the NEDC.

The history of indicative planning is, to say the least, not one of outstanding success. The most immediate flaw was the inability to increase domestic demand without creating a balance of payment crisis. A widespread criticism was that growth had been sacrificed on the altar of a fixed (and, by 1965, overvalued) sterling exchange rate.

However, it was by no means clear that it was within the power of indicative planning to raise the level of investment in the long run nor that domestic economic problems such as inflation would not place constraints upon growth. It is also possible to argue that the experiment created problems in other respects. For example, many public expenditure and investment programmes assumed a much higher rate of growth of output than was achieved resulting in an unmanageable public sector deficit in the late 1960s and substantial overcapacity in some nationalised industries.

The main danger, however, may be that indicative planning is regarded as ineffective for reasons which are more apparent than real. There is evidence that the proponents of indicative planning based their enthusiasm on a highly simplified, not to say misleading view of how French planning operated. It would be unfortunate if this type of planning which seems *prima facie* suitable for a mixed private-public sector economy were to be discarded for equally insubstantial reasons. One of the questions which should be considered in a book covering a number of planning areas is whether the principles and lessons of indicative planning could be applied in other fields and to goals other than raising the national rate of ecomonic growth.

There is a detailed examination of the theory and principles of indicative planning by J. E. Meade.[12] Beyond the simplistic belief that the postulate of a target *per se* will bring about the desired result, the effectiveness of indicative planning may be justified on three grounds. Firstly, the postulate of an improved economic performance coupled with research into the major associated decisions may have the effect of reducing uncertainty about future events. It was hoped that this reduction would reduce the extent to which an individual producer discounted estimates of future sales or alternatively reduced the margin for risk which he added to the expected rate of return. A reduction in avoidable uncertainty would improve the rationality of any type of business or household decision. Thus a reduction in uncertainty associated with geographical distance might improve locational decisions and add to the effectiveness of a regional policy.

Secondly, indicative planning could serve a useful purpose by identifying the major obstacles to the attainment of any policy goal. Perhaps the difficulties associated with changing the overall rate of economic growth, in particular developments in the field of inter-national trade, are among the most unpredictable and uncontrollable economic variables. In other areas of planning the constraints may be more readily identifiable and influenced to a greater extent by public action. Thirdly, indicative planning may allow more efficient co-ordination of decisions by business, households and government. Probably the most obvious element of co-ordination is in timing but there are many other aspects of each decision and its background which would be of significance to other agencies. It might be a matter of considerable surprise and concern if it were more fully known how many business and governmental decisions were made in ignorance of the activities of apparently closely related bodies. The main prob-lem of planning for economic growth in this respect is to make allowance for the difference between the best firms and the worst. The better firms, it is clear from evidence to inquiries such as the Radcliffe Committee on the working of the monetary system, have from the 1950s operated within their own long-term plans divorced from short-term fluctuations. An extension of indicative planning might, for example, have to allow for the wide differences in the efficiency of local authorities.

In the field of spatial and physical planning there may be a more convincing case to be made for indicative planning. In some senses the move towards structure plans following the PAG Report in 1965 has created a more 'indicative' type of physical planning in that there should be a greater recognition of the limited extent to which development plans may control land-use where there are contrary social and economic forces. However, there remains a need to establish a national statement of goals and strategy. The potential contribution of local and regional plans has been reduced by the fact that collectively they do not add up to a rational national strategy. For example, most plans tend to over-estimate either the area's attractiveness to people and industry or the government's intention to create sufficient incentives to location in the area. Consequently the composite population projections which would be obtained from adding together separate regional or local plans is considerably in excess of those done on national demographic data. Also local planning strategies could lead to a considerably more efficient land-use pattern if they were more consistently related to

131

each other. In part local political autonomy and taxation considerations are responsible for lack of co-ordination but there is also a marked lack of mutual knowledge and guidance. The Select Committee on Scottish Affairs has recommended a regional indicative plan.[13] Whereas there remains a need to examine in greater detail the contribution of such plans for land-use, they may well prove more successful in creating a favourable background for implementation of local policies than their macro-economic counterparts.

From the lessons of the recent past, a summary of the merits of indicative planning should end on a clear statement of what it *cannot* achieve. An indicative planning document, either from a quasi-public agency or from a Department of State, whether it be called a Plan or not, does not commit the government to a predetermined set of policy priorities regardless of the consequences. The initiation of indicative planning does not of itself improve the knowledge and measurement of the preconditions for change nor of its consequences. Finally, the existence of planning machinery which involves all the major interest groups does not obviate the conflicts which most major changes imply. Although the current degree of confrontation between public and private sectors, between employers and employees, between social classes or income groups may be unnecessarily exaggerated, any plan in which there appeared to be no conflict of interest is, it may be suspected, either very perfect or at a very generalised level.

Economic Growth and Physical Planning

Many environmental and physical planners (and certain economists) may well take another view of the 'failure' of economic planning in stimulating a higher rate of economic growth. There has been an increasing awareness that economic growth, at least in terms of the conventional measurement of output as an indicator of welfare, creates social costs for the community at large. These costs are well recognised in the growth of the Victorian city and as such have been a major stimulus to the emergence of town planning in the twentieth century as a means of checking such social and physical abuses. Only recently, however, has there been a school of thought within the economics profession which has presented a case for slowing the rate of economic growth on the grounds that the costs not only partly offset but may actually outweigh the benefits of increased output. For example, an addition to the number of motor vehicles will add to the congestion on the existing road system imposing costs on other users, and additional pollution and noise for those living beside the roads. Alternatively, the extension to the road network 'justified' by the increased traffic will use public expenditure and construction resources which could be better used for the public good in other uses. The new roads, in particular urban motorways, also create social costs and dislocation in clearing other uses and exploring neighbouring uses to the side-effects of traffic. There are numerous other examples of how 'progress' or 'growth' contribute to a deterioration in the quality of life.[14]

What should be the response of economic planning to these arguments? On the one hand, it is possible to deny that growth has such costs exclusively attached to it. Although we live in an age of national affluence in developed economies, there remains a large sector of the community which lacks many of the material comforts of life. The benefit which the spread of motor cars, televisions and dishwashers brings to these groups outweighs the costs which accrue to the rest of the community from this 'catching up' process. Such arguments *pro* or *con* are ultimately indecisive and rest heavily upon differing social values. Is it possible to resolve the issues more rationally and conclude with recommendations for public policy? Firstly it is necessary to recognise the difference between projections of the future at differing levels of probability. The predictions of the 'ecodoomsters', that we shall exhaust the physical resources of our planet, seem to rely for their fulfilment on relatively unlikely combinations of circumstances. Nevertheless it may be advisable to take precautions to avoid such irreversible disasters even if there is only a 0·1 per cent or even a 0·0001 per cent probability of their occurrence. Most public policy, however, will have to weigh the probable benefits against the costs of controlling growth. One set of policies would identify the goods which are the principal offenders and ensure that their ownership or use bears the full economic costs associated with them. As examples, motor vehicles could be charged for the use of congested roads in city centres or charged a cost for petrol which reflects not its current supply costs but the higher prospective costs of the forthcoming 'energy crisis'. These policies make use of market pricing to reduce the noxious use. A second set of policies would require the pollutors to bear the costs of offsetting the results of their activities, for example water purification and air-cleaning schemes by industrial users. Thirdly, the government may take direct action to forbid certain activities, e.g. fertilisers, or spend public funds on environmental improvement or conservation. All three sets of policies require the close co-operation of physical sciences, engineering and a wide variety of technologies, to identify the effects of physical and environmental damage. In particular physical planning on a rural and urban scale is necessary to establish the priority programmes in such an extension of planning policies. Current apparent lack of progress in this area may derive both from seeking physical solutions to problems which have powerful economic forces causing them and from ignoring important facets of economic growth policies. Economists must clearly extend their measurement of economic welfare from the narrow assumptions of the calculation of GNP.

Budgetary Planning

In one sense budgetary planning is the point at which other forms of planning are 'planned'. Most forms of planning require the expenditure of public funds to implement their proposals. Indeed most forms of planning depend upon public money to finance the planning function itself. Planning public expenditure has traditionally been in the hands of the Treasury which has always re-emerged as the fount of economic public policy following experiments with the Ministry for Economic Affairs after the Second World War, and more recently the DEA. In strict accounting terms 'Treasury Control' has been relaxed since 1945 but, on the other hand, the increasing size and diversity of claims for resources in public expenditure programmes has placed an even greater premium on the work of the department responsible for financial co-ordination.

There are two timescales for planning public expenditure, the establishment of the estimates of expenditure for the forthcoming financial year and 'forward looks' for five years ahead. The preparation of estimates begins for the major spending departments soon after the beginning of the current financial year in the early summer. They prepare estimates of expenditure internally for submission to the Treasury in September. These estimates are then the subject of discussion by officials and, ultimately, at ministerial level until January; then they are published in advance of the Budget. This hectic and often highly contentious process clearly does not allow a great deal of scope for discussion of fundamental issues and frequently the inevitable process of political compromise leads to an inefficient allocation of resources in a series of half-measures. These problems together with dissatisfaction in other departments at the rigour of the Treasury control led to the reforms of the budgetary process suggested by the Plowden Committee.

One of the most significant proposals of the Plowden Committee in 1961 was to institute 'forward looks' of proposed expenditure over a five year period. Many decisions on public projects will have their main expenditure impact three or four years afterwards. A decision to build a major motorway, for example, will entail limited expenditure on design and planning for some time before the main construction contracts begin. There will remain a substantial part of expenditure which cannot be planned in this way since there are 'open-ended' commitments dependent upon factors outside the immediate control of the public sector, for example unemployment benefit upon the level of unemployment and investment grants upon the level and location of business investment. It was hoped that the necessity of examining the total implications of current and proposed programmes would act as a stimulus to view them against the background of available national resources. In this context it would, it was hoped, be clear that the essence of budgetary decisions was not in the traditional role of the Treasury in trimming expenditure of waste and extravagance—often called the 'candle-ends' approach—but involved the fundamental and far-reaching priorities of our society. Unfortunately the planning of public expenditure still falls far short of these ambitions. The procedure of 'forward looks' has developed into a routine which occupies the late spring and early summer and tends to be built from the bottom up with insufficient feedback. The Treasury would probably complain that the projects which enter into the forward programmes are justified by words like 'highly desirable' and 'essential' rather than specified criteria of assessment. A further complaint lies in the reliability of cost estimates. Costs are often based on very optimistic assumptions since no department will raise the obstacles and problems which *might* arise. There is normally an allowance for contingencies but little is known about the adequacy of these allowances. For its part, despite substantial changes in the past fifteen years, the Treasury is not necessarily well organised to promote departmental efficiency in the manner which Plowden suggested.

In order to play its full part in economic planning budgetary planning should ensure that the scale and distribution of public expenditure is considered in relation to the available national resources. There are criticisms of the procedure by which the requirements of the public sector are arrived at but beyond a period of two or three years the greatest weakness probably lies in the forecast of overall economic growth. Secondly, the process of planning public resources should be evaluative and should ensure the choice of projects which make best use of the available resources. There has been increased application of economic evaluation in techniques such as cost-benefit analysis and cost-effectiveness, although also an increasing awareness of their limitations in solving complex questions or ones where the choice has not been specified correctly. Thirdly the process of economic evaluation should be closely allied to other forms of planning. In some instances, for example, economic evaluation and transport planning, this marriage has occurred despite the tensions which naturally occur between disciplines. The combination of economic, physical and social planning in, say, urban renewal, faces much more serious problems. Finally, as a procedure which has to be carried out by administrative units such as civil service departments, local authorities and *ad hoc* bodies, budgetary planning must be administratively convenient and efficient. As an administrative activity, planning, although *a priori* the means of improving the effectiveness of public programmes in the interests of all, has to become a routine activity to compete with the short-term operational requirements of these departments. Once this dilemma is faced it is necessary to abandon a strict betrothal to the principles of economic planning, efficiency and general welfare, in order to arrive at the best practical solution.

Stabilisation Policy

The form of economic planning of which the ordinary man is most aware is government policy to avoid short-term fluctuations in National Income and employment. The roots of stabilisation policies lie in the mass unemployment and consequent social problems in the 1930s and in 1944 all major British political parties accepted responsibility for pursuing policies to maintain a high level of employment. However, during the postwar period two other main goals of short-term economic management have emerged, namely avoiding an unacceptable rate of inflation and ensuring equilibrium in the balance of payments. At certain times one goal was predominant in determining short-term policy, for example the balance of payments in the period 1964–7 when we were trying to stave off a devaluation, but usually stabilisation policy has had to strike a balance which would minimise a combination of evils.

There are three principal groups of policies by which the government can achieve equilibrium in the economy at the aggregate level:

1. *Fiscal policy*, which involves adjustments in the level of taxation and public expenditure designed to increase or decrease the level of aggregate demand in the private or public sectors respectively. The Budget tends to be the main focus of fiscal changes but the use of the Regulator by which indirect taxes (purchase tax and excise duties) may be changed by up to 10 per cent has increased the flexibility of such changes.

2. *Monetary policy*, which is designed to influence expenditure by changing the supply and terms of credit. Since a great part of investment and consumer durable expenditure is financed by credit, a restriction in the availability of credit and a rise in the rate of interest will induce businessmen and consumers to abandon or postpone certain items of expenditure. There is a great deal of dispute on the precise operation of monetary policy and the transmission of the expenditure effects but it has been widely used since its re-introduction in 1952.

3. *Incomes and prices policy*, which was first used on a largely voluntary basis by Sir Stafford Cripps to protect the advantage given to British exports by the 1949 devaluation. It has been used to an increasing extent since the first pay 'freeze' under Selwyn Lloyd in 1961. The main justification for its use has been evidence that cost inflation may be currently more important than demand inflation. The various packages of such measures have set an upper limit for increases in incomes or for prices and incomes, but in practice the need to allow mutual bargaining and for productivity differentials has considerably reduced their effectiveness as a means of restraint.

The result of the short term adjustments in policy has been periodic changes in the rate of growth of aggregate demand and output. Although fluctuation of the so-called 'stop-go' cycles have been much smaller than trade cycles in previous periods in British modern economic history, there has been criticism that stabilisation measures have been so mistimed as to aggravate rather than reduce any inherent cyclical behaviour in the economy. There have also been occasions when the different types of policy have been pulling in opposite directions. In 1955 while monetary policy was restrictive, fiscal policy remained expansionary; in 1968–9 while increases in taxation made fiscal policy appear highly restrictive, public expenditure was still rising at a rapid rate. However, the principal objection to 'stop-go' was on the ground that the frequent changes of direction were inimical to long-run growth. The success of stabilisation planning, therefore, is at best doubtful and the need to give priority to the short-term goal of retaining equilibrium in the balance of payments was the immediate cause of the failure of indicative planning in 1966–7. There is no means of knowing how far the economy would have behaved without detailed intervention. It might have been preferable to avoid making policy so sensitive to deviations from the short run goals and to pursue longer term planning goals within broader limits or tolerances; but many of the reasons for the attempted 'fine-tuning' were dictated by domestic political and international pressures.

Regional Planning

It would appear from the brief descriptions and analysis in the preceding sections that the three forms of national planning have no spatial dimension. This is nearly but not entirely true. Stabilisation policy measures seldom have the capability to be discriminatory although monetary policy has been moderated for the Scottish and Northern Irish Banks. Budgetary planning has important implications for the distribution of expenditure in all parts of the country but it is not clear how many times the spatial element is an explicit and important part of the criteria by which the expenditure is justified. However, a major element in the measures promoted by Department of Economic Affairs to increase the rate of economic growth was a policy to stimulate economic growth in the regions with high unemployment. Although the DEA laid more emphasis upon the role of regional development in contributing to national growth, regional policy has a much longer history.

With the designation of Special Areas in 1934 the Government first recognised the need to take positive steps to reduce the high rates of unemployment in the depressed areas of Wales, the North of England and Scotland. The measures pursued in the 1930s were *ad hoc* but the Barlow report[15] in 1940 presented a much broader case (although heavily dependent upon the need to avoid vulnerability to strategic bombing) for examining and taking action to influence the spatial distribution of population and employment on a national scale. Accordingly, the Distribution of Industry Act 1945 contained the aim of a 'proper industrial balance'. The Act laid the foundations of regional policy in the postwar period by increasing and making more comprehensive the financial incentives for industrial expansion in the Development Areas (note the change to a more positive terminology). In addition to the 'carrot' of financial incentives there was a 'stick' to control development. The control was made possible by the 1947 Town and Country Planning Act which stipulated that planning permission for manufacturing premises of more than 5 000 square feet was conditional upon an Industrial Development Certificate from the Board of Trade. In the immediate postwar years the Development Areas received a very high proportion of new industrial development but much of this apparent success could be attributed to the availability of wartime factories in these areas. The control which the economic planners had over key materials and building licences was a further reinforcement of the policy. However in the ten years following 1948 the effectiveness of regional policy greatly diminished.

Regional planning following the Distribution of Industry (Industrial Finance) Act 1958 entered a period of rapid change and adaptation which is continuing to the present day. The first moves appeared to be a retreat from the concept of regional development. The primary concern of the 1960 Act was to relieve unemployment in local areas where it was over twice the national average. However, the new detailed concern with the spatial differences within the Development Areas took a more constructive form when the White Papers on Central Scotland and the North East were published in 1963.[16] These documents initiated policies, which had their roots in

139

local thinking and initiative to stimulate development in 'growth areas' or 'growth zones'. There was the world of difference between the 1960 Act and 'growth areas' policy but they each had a common stimulus from the increasing concern that the diversion of industry to possibly unfavourable locations in the regions would injure national growth prospects. One reaction is to minimise the regional effort to areas in greatest need; another is to concentrate upon areas with the greatest growth potential. From empirical studies it seemed that the costs of production did not vary substantially between alternative locations.[17] The choice of the most favourable areas in the regions, therefore, would mean that regional growth could be stimulated without the cost of reducing national welfare. For example, in Central Scotland the New Towns were identified as the major growth points together with centres of expanding modern industry such as petro-chemicals at Grangemouth. These growth points were planned to grow by the immigration of Glasgow overspill. Similarly in the North East of England the area east of the A1 was chosen as having growth potential to receive migration from the mining communities farther inland. A major consequence of the growth point policy was that the national policy to influence the location of industry was allied to physical planning policies to create areas attractive to incoming industrialists and the resident population.

This was the approximate stage of development when the Department of Economic Affairs took over responsibility for regional planning, although the basic framework of industrial financial incentives continued to be operated by the Board of Trade.[18] A major element in DEA's regional role was to provide co-ordination at the regional level of the many strands of policy and planning by central and local government and *ad hoc* bodies such as hospital boards. Part of the case for greater regional co-ordination arose from the frictions which existed between the responsible bodies. It was also felt that from 1961 onwards the co-ordination of many regional development functions in Scotland in the Scottish Development Department had contributed a great deal to the evolution of the new ideas about growth points referred to above. In particular these ideas seemed to represent a marriage of physical and economic planning for regional development.

Physical planning is important for regional development in order to create an attractive environment which will attract industrialists and satisfy the existing population. Equally a great deal of physical planning in the form of local development plans prepared under the 1947 Act was being frustrated by the constraints imposed by local authority boundaries. Regional co-ordination of development plans was in theory done when the plans were submitted to Whitehall for approval. However, the formal nature of these submissions was not conducive to constructive criticism; the co-ordination should have moulded the plan at an early stage, not forced modifications on a completed document; the extent of regional study and planning within central government was minimal. Although some regional initiatives existed in the North West, the North East and a study of the South East was completed in 1964, the main attempt to provide a general co-ordination of physical planning and to relate economic and physical planning began under the D E A's aegis.

In eight English regions, Scotland and Wales, Regional Economic Planning Councils were established. They were advisory bodies comprised of local public figures and were served by the staff of the parallel regional Boards. The function of this new machinery was

(a) to evolve a strategy for each region in the light of its available resources and opportunities,

(b) to advise on the national policies required to realise regional objectives,

(c) to co-ordinate the work of central government departments and national bodies in the region,

(d) to encourage local authorities and *ad hoc* bodies to frame their policies with the aim of furthering regional goals.

The most obvious result of this regional planning effort is the series of regional reports or plans which appeared in a steady stream between 1965 and 1971. There was also a valuable contribution persuading central administration to be more sensitive to regional issues and opinions, a change which may improve the effectiveness of the regional structure to be created by the Redcliffe–Maud proposals to reform local government. There was widespread recognition throughout this period that effective regional planning required active physical planning to create new centres for industry especially as compensation for the declining industrial cities and new environmental background to replace grimy cities and landscapes scarred by

141

industrial and mining activity. Transportation planning played an important role partly in decreasing transport costs but, perhaps more important, in reducing the psychological barrier of distance. These factors were not new but in face of the administrative difficulties of functional co-ordination and the large sums of public expenditure involved their implementation was no insignificant achievement.

Following the publication of the Hunt Report[19] regional policy moved from the sharp division into the areas eligible to receive financial assistance and those without the system of regional incentives. Although the concept of 'two nations' the prosperous South and the depressed North and West, was an important part of the popular case for a regional policy to equalise the disparity,[20] in fact the assumption that all the areas without aided regions had no economic problems was quite unwarranted. Between the prosperous areas of the South East and (although it is now a more dubious inclusion) West Midlands and the depressed Development Areas, there are 'grey' or Intermediate Areas in which economic problems exist to a varying degree. They are areas such as South Yorkshire, South-East Lancashire, Humberside, Derbyshire which have experienced a relatively slow rate of economic growth and in which there is a concentration of stagnant industry, low participation rates,[21] a low rate of industrial and commercial investment and in local pockets high rates of unemployment. The changes during 1958–60 in regional policy were intended to take account of the fact that some areas in Development Areas were relatively prosperous. It is perhaps a mark of the new positive attitude to regional policy in 1969 that additional measures were taken to aid the Intermediate Areas on a scale somewhat below that of Development Areas. At the same time the areas of greatest need were designated Special Development Areas where higher levels of investment grants were available and increased public investment was planned.

When the Department of Economic Affairs was dissolved by the new Conservative administration in 1970, the system of regional planning was transferred to the new 'super-ministry', the Department of the Environment. During the early months of the new, or reshuffled, regime the system of regional financial incentives and investment grants was substantially reduced. However, in face of rising unemployment and the collapse of a number of 'lame ducks', the reduction in regional aid was reversed in 1971. The new industrial policy was operated through the Department of Trade and Industry within which were located the new regional industrial executives, with wide powers of initiative to attract industry. In principle, therefore, there might be expected to be less co-ordination between public investment policy and industrial development. On the other hand, the newly strengthened policies for industrial expansion could not have been channelled through the Department of the Environment (or Scottish Development Department).

Problems of Regional Planning

The administration of regional planning reflects the differing views on whether regional policy is mainly a question of industrial location or comprises a much more comprehensive approach to co-ordinating public investment and services throughout the country. In large measure the answer to this dilemma lies in the causes and nature of spatial inequalities and the reasons for rectifying them. The early ideas of diversifying the industrial structure of the depressed areas from the inheritance of Victorian heavy industries has given way to the realisation that the pace of industrial change requires a continued attention to regional balance and that the Victorian heritage extends to social capital as well as industrial capital. The experience of regional planning is the difficulty of separating a national policy for the distribution of industry from the entire allocation of public investment resources between regions. Similarly the optimal distribution of investment between regions is closely bound up with the intra-regional distribution.

To be fully effective, therefore, regional economic planning should co-ordinate the activities of central and local levels of administration and relate decisions in the public and private sectors to each other. If regional policy is restricted to incentives for the relocation of industry coupled with IDC controls, the effects could well be offset by other budgetary decisions which resulted in the concentration of new social investment in the prosperous areas. Indeed if population increase, including migration from the depressed regions, is the justification for that investment, there is clearly the possibility of accelerating rather than improving regional decline. Conversely, the application of large slices of the national budget together with

the diversion of private investment could, despite the strong economic arguments for greater regional balance, lead to a considerable
waste of resources unless it is accompanied by a regional strategy.

Improvements in Economic Planning

Inevitably the history of economic planning in its several aspects
has laid more stress upon the problems rather than the achievements. Such is the nature of a critical review. It is also difficult to be
very specific about what the achievements of planning have been. We
have experienced much greater stability of income and employment
in the postwar period but at times, it would appear from the evidence,
stabilisation policy has aggravated endogenous fluctuations.

The principal problem however, is that we do not know, except in
the very short term, what course economic events would have taken
without stabilisation policies. Similarly although indicative planning
failed to reach 'target' rates of growth, the underlying growth of
productivity and productive potential in the British economy did
appear to rise in the mid-1960s to levels above that of the 1950s.
Was it a consequence of planning or the accompanying propaganda
for growth? There is no definitive answer and any attempt to establish the causes of changing circumstances is particularly hampered in
Britain, which is more open than most other major economies to the
external effects of international trade and finance.

Regardless of the difficulties of establishing the results of economic
planning there is wide agreement on the need to improve its effectiveness. However, there is a substantial minority opinion which
opposes economic planning on two main grounds.[22] The first is that
economic planning runs counter to the operation of a democratic
society by giving a preponderant influence to the central government.
This objection is much stronger against economic planning than in
the case of other forms of planning since it tends to be more centralised. The second ground of objection to economic planning is
that economic forces are capable of adapting to the changing needs
of society more efficiently (that is, with less waste of economic
resources) through the operation of the market mechanism than by
means of any human agency. Non-economists may be astounded
that such a view could be tenable but it may be worthwhile to reflect
on the extent of economic change which has been 'unplanned' at

least by any national or governmental agency. Few anti-planners would wish to dismantle the whole structure of planning which has been described above but would tend, where the results of any policy were not reasonably clear, to give the free operation of individual decisions the benefit of the doubt. There is a temptation to identify the anti-planners with conservative political views but their arguments carry equal weight against the right-wing aims of national socialism and the fascist 'corporate state'. There is no space within the limits of this chapter to take up these fundamental arguments.[23] It is possible to circumvent these objections by arguing, as Oulès does, that economic planning is necessary for full individual freedom, and, that whereas the market mechanism or *laissez-faire* may give better results than bad planning, successful planning is best of all. If, however, we recognise their partial validity, it may be a useful discipline to recognise that economic planning involves economic and social costs and that the history of such experiments is littered with plans which have turned out to be based on wildly unrealistic assumptions both about the existence of conditions favourable to their fulfilment and on the administrative capacity for implementation.

The Current Lessons of Economic Planning

In conclusion, with some trepidation and only limited supporting argument some of the more important requirements for improved economic planning may be suggested.

1. As one weapon of economic policy the implementation of economic planning should follow upon a close examination of the existing decision-making framework and of how the proposed planning structure might compare under a range of circumstances; favourable and unfavourable. Economic planning is being used in both socialist and democratic countries not to replace other decision-making units but to superimpose a more co-ordinated or centralised dimension upon them. Consequently it is important to specify as exactly as possible how the system of decision is likely to be changed.

2. Much of the difficulty in being specific about the consequences of economic policy changes lies at the door of economic science. There is a dearth of economic theories which are sufficiently tested in the real world to make them suitable frameworks for economic policy.

3. Tinbergen, the most celebrated of the influential Netherlands school of quantitative planning economists, lays great importance upon the existence of forecasts of the future economic situation assuming no change in economic policy as a means of establishing the requirements of an exercise in economic planning.[24] In all spheres of British economic planning, there is a need to improve the availability of current economic statistics in a form which is useful to planners.

4. In common with most other forms of planning, the impact of economic planning will be related to the flexibility of the plan specification (whether that document be termed a 'plan' or not). Flexibility, however, requires not only that the plan can be changed to meet new circumstances but that there should be some means of quickly translating the changed assumptions into altered planning goals and policies. There are of course limits to the type of shocks which the plan may be expected to withstand; for example, a major international trading crisis would clearly be too major and unlikely an event to include in normal economic planning.

5. A close relationship between economic planning and other forms of planning is necessary on two general grounds. On the one hand, the economist relies upon other disciplines involved in complementary activities for judgements on the technical efficiency of alternative solutions. On the other, if economic evaluation and planning is distant from other planning functions there is a danger of decisions being reached which are optimal within the bounds of the individual functions but ignore wider costs and benefits. Above all it is necessary to ensure that other planning policies do not set goals and adopt means which run counter to macro-economic goals for the economy as a whole or to the broader operation of the price mechanism.

Finally, it would be surprising if there were not more general lessons to be learned by a broad comparison of economic and other forms of planning. To some extent this cross-fertilisation must rely on individual stimuli when individual planners are faced with particular problems. If there is one general advantage to be gained from the lessons of economic planning, it is the need to take account of decisions in the uncontrolled sector. Economic planning, as was pointed out at the beginning of the chapter, has always had to come to terms with the fact that a substantial proportion of economic decisions cannot be directly controlled, at least not without a large bureaucracy and infringement of individual freedom. It has, therefore, been necessary to take account of the social preferences as expressed in the market place and of the trends which will emerge regardless of the approval or disapproval of planners. Physical planners have tended to overestimate their power to control the factors affecting land use and to regard 'trend-planning' with disfavour. Only a frank recognition of the powerful forces of consumer preferences, business decisions and technological change will lay the foundations of sound planning policies. There is, of course, no need to accept these factors as unchangeable but there is a need to explore methods of influencing them. In this respect indicative planning may prove a fruitful line of research.

References

1 Neil W. Chamberlain, *Private and Public Planning* (McGraw-Hill, NY, 1965).

2 For an introductory text and bibliography see H. Kohler, *Welfare and Planning* (John Wiley, NY, 1966).

3 R. A. Musgrave, *Public Finance* (McGraw-Hill, NY, 1959).

4 P. A. Stone, *Urban Development in Britain: Standards, Costs and Resources 1964-2004. vol. 1, Population Trends and Housing* (Cambridge University Press for NIESR, London, 1971).

5 *Economic Planning and Policies in Britain, France and Germany*, chapter 4 (Allen and Unwin for PEP, London, 1968).

6 See, for example, Michael Shanks, *The Stagnant Society* (Penguin, 1961)—although as early as 1954, R. A. Butler as Chancellor of the Exchequer referred to the possibility of 'doubling the standard of living in twenty-five years'.

7 Hansard, House of Commons (July 26, 1961).

8 Growth of the United Kingdom to 1966 (HMSO, February, 1963).

9 *Westminster Bank Review* (November 1965).

10 The National Plan, Cmnd 2764 (HMSO, September, 1965).

11 The Task Ahead: Economic Assessment to 1972 (HMSO, February, 1969).

12 J. E. Meade, *The Theory of Indicative Planning* (Manchester University Press, 1970).

13 ' . . . we believe that there is a need to prepare an indicative plan for Scotland on a national scale which will show how it is intended to utilise the land for urban, industrial and recreational purposes. To prepare such a policy plan it will be necessary to take into account the views of planning authorities, industrialists, trade unions and many other interested parties.' Report from the Select Committee on Scottish Affairs, Land Resources Use in Scotland, vol. 1, Session 1971-2 (HMSO, London).

14 See E. J. Mishan, *The Costs of Economic Growth* (Staples Press, 1967), for an early example of the arguments.

15 Report of the Royal Commission on the distribution of the population, Cmnd 6153 (HMSO, 1940).

16 Central Scotland: a Programme for Development and Growth, Cmnd 2188 (HMSO, 1963), The North-East: a Programme for Regional Development and Growth, Cmnd 2206 (HMSO, 1963).

17 See R. J. Nicholson, The Regional Location of Industry, *Economic Journal*, vol. 66 (1956), pp. 467–81; Report on the Scottish Economy, 1961 (Toothill Report), (Scottish Council, Development and Industry, Edinburgh; 1961); W. F. Luttrell, Factory Location and Industrial Movement (National Institute for Economic and Social Research, London, 1962).

18 Later incorporated into Mintech (Ministry of Technology), and subsequently DTI (Department of Trade and Industry).

19 The Intermediate Areas, Cmnd 3998 (HMSO, 1969).

20 *The Economist* went so far as to propose a new national capital in the vicinity of Marston Moor as a countervailing attraction to London.

21 The participation rate may be defined as the proportion of a population of working age which is available for work or habitually, though not constantly, in work.

22 For example, see John Jewkes, *Ordeal by Planning* (Macmillan, 1948).

23 Economists may refer to A. P. Lerner, *The Economics of Control* (Macmillan, London, 1946), for non-economists try Firmin Oulès, *Economic Planning and Democracy* (Penguin, 1966).

24 See J. Tinbergen, Central Planning—Studies in Comparative Economics, No. 4 (Yale University Press, New Haven, 1964).

6. Social Planning

Graham M. Lomas

There has been a relatively long history of the use of the term 'social planning' in what is increasingly referred to as the Third World—those countries facing the triple crisis of a low standard of living, a high rate of population increase, and rapid urbanisation. The importance of social planning in this context is not difficult to discern. It arises from a number of needs; firstly, the need to make the most effective use of very limited resources by deciding on certain priorities for action, knowing that these will have immense social consequences; secondly, the need to pursue economic development in ways that will lead to the increasing use of the nation's manpower rather than the immediate exploitation of it; thirdly, the need to control the process of urbanisation and physical development in order to marshal the process of migration from rural to urban situations, and thus stave off the ill-effects of massive migration flows; and fourthly, the need to develop a population policy that will equip people with the competence to undertake family planning.

Planning on this scale has sometimes led social planning to be called 'societal' planning for it involves the deliberate, and often massive, intervention by government in the 'market forces' operating in a country and a conscious and pervasive influence on people's living conditions. Planning on this scale too inevitably means, in developing countries at any rate, that basic decisions are in the hands of a relatively small elite among the population.

The use of the term social planning is much less frequent in the developed countries of Western Europe. In relatively sophisticated urban societies there is an inbred suspicion of something that smacks of societal planning. It is not easily forgotten that the first efforts at national planning were begun in the USSR, in Nazi Germany, and in Fascist Italy. Until very recently, therefore, the term social planning was never used in the United Kingdom.

Nevertheless State intervention influencing economic affairs, and physical and social conditions in this country is recognised and broadly accepted. Indeed it can be argued that government influence in the widest sense on living standards in Britain far exceeds that in any developing country, or even in totalitarian countries. The distinction that has to be made, of course, in judging the merits of social planning, is whether the policies pursued are really in the interests of the whole population and whether people willingly go along with them. The definition of social planning is important.

Some Problems of Definition

The word 'planning' itself poses problems. It is sometimes used interchangeably with 'policy'. Sometimes the word policy is given wider meaning to denote the principles underlying a broadly defined course of action and the word planning used more narrowly to denote the methods by which the policies are implemented. More often in the literature, however, it is the word planning which is used in the wider context, and policy given the narrower interpretation: thus 'social planning is the scientific preparation for policies, and social policy the instrument whereby social planning is put into practice'.[1]

The word 'social' poses more problems; in particular because there is the fundamental difficulty of delimiting the boundaries between *social* planning, *economic* planning and *physical* planning. Kenneth Boulding makes one useful distinction in the following way: 'if there is one common thread that unites all aspects of social policy and distinguishes them from merely economic policy it is by unilateral transfers that are justified by some kind of appeal to a status or legitimacy, identity or community'.[2] In other words grants, gifts and non-market transfers of resources, including cash, are essential hallmarks of social policy. An attractive and brief definition is François Lafitte's 'through collective action in particular by imposing the state's directing power on the forces of the market, we seek to steer society along paths it would not naturally follow . . .'[3]

A working definition of social planning might read as follows. It seeks to achieve expanding opportunities for the raising of the standard of life of the whole population, through deliberate steps initiated in the main by government, influencing both economic activity and the physical environment when necessary, to achieve this end. Such definitions carry important implications. First of all they suggest that whilst economic growth may be a necessary condition for increasing welfare, it may not be a sufficient condition in itself, and that there may well be circumstances when economic growth disadvantages sections of the community. Government interference might be needed to offset this. A second implication is that social planning has the edge over economic planning in certain circumstances: the steering of industrial development to those regions of the country displaying structural unemployment—referred to sometimes as 'taking work to the workers'—is an illustration of this. It may be popular with neither economists nor industrialists, but it is deemed important socially. A further implication flowing from our definitions is that social planning is a positive activity in quite another sense in that it requires government to be on the look out not only for ways of responding to and guiding events, but to be prepared to strike out in quite new directions. Good examples of this view of social planning are the British New Towns. The New Towns movement as it might be more accurately described is a unique blend of three major areas of governmental policy: economic, physical and social. But the guiding spirit is social; for without the social goals (summed up in Ebenezer Howard's three magnets diagram and the phrase 'social cities')[4] the economic activity and the physical infrastructure that now exist in the new towns would have taken other forms elsewhere.

It is in the relationship between physical planning and social planning, however, that the most difficult problems of definition lie. This arises not for semantic reasons, but for professional reasons. Few would question that much physical planning is in the broadest sense undertaken for 'social' reasons but few physical planners would accept a state of affairs in which physical planning was to be regarded as a tool of social policy, or as a set of techniques to be employed at the behest of social policy makers. On the contrary many physical planners would regard themselves as makers of social policy. The problem is compounded by the fact that other groups of administrators in the past have large excluded

151

physical environmental matters from their sphere of active concern. Richard Titmuss' definition of social policy as late as 1968 makes this clear.[5]

The relationship between social service, housing and education experts and physical planners is becoming an issue partly because management reforms in local government are giving greater emphasis to policy formulation, as well as defining whose responsibility it is, and also because of the increasing use of the term 'social planning', itself the outcome of growing concern about the limited relevance of so many ongoing policies to conditions in different parts of the country.

Recognition of the fact that there are some underlying and persistent social problems that do not seem to yield in the face of sustained economic growth, or with continuous improvement in the physical environment which has been largely responsible for the emergence of an interest in social planning in the United Kingdom over the last decade. The term is still used sparingly, but the hallmarks are there in the call for a 'total approach' to social issues at central and local government levels; in the call for policies which have a greater element of positive discrimination in favour of the more disadvantaged sections of the community; in the recognition that poverty is still present in our society (and that social planning measures are most needed at this level); and finally in the recognition that many people are fundamentally ill-equipped to cope with life in a sophisticated but rapidly changing urban situation.

Having looked now in some detail at the origins of social planning, its purposes and its meaning, we can now turn to examine more closely the range of subjects and issues that might be considered to be of major concern in social planning.

Subjects of Major Concern in Social Planning

The diagram shown in Figure 2 attempts to set out the subjects that might be considered of major concern in social planning. It recognises four major areas—the economic base, the individual person (social planning literature uses the more euphuistic title of 'human resources'), the social context, position and relationships of people, and fourthly, the agencies which have come into being to help maintain people's welfare and security. The diagram is highly

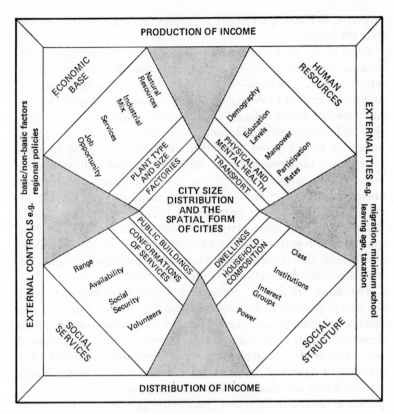

PRODUCTION OF INCOME

ECONOMIC BASE

Natural Resources

Industrial Mix

Services

Job Opportunity

PLANT TYPE AND SIZE

FACTORIES

HUMAN RESOURCES

Demography

Education Levels

Manpower

Participation Rates

PHYSICAL AND MENTAL HEALTH

TRANSPORT

EXTERNAL CONTROLS e.g. basic/non-basic factors regional policies

EXTERNALITIES e.g. migration, minimum school leaving age, taxation

CITY SIZE DISTRIBUTION AND THE SPATIAL FORM OF CITIES

PUBLIC BUILDINGS

CONFORMATIONS OF SERVICES

DWELLINGS

HOUSEHOLD COMPOSITION

Class

Institutions

Interest Groups

Power

Range

Availability

Social Security

Volunteers

SOCIAL SERVICES

SOCIAL STRUCTURE

DISTRIBUTION OF INCOME

Fig. 2   Subjects of major concern in social planning

generalised, and certainly does not draw out adequately—perhaps no mere diagram could—the highly complex inter-relationships which exist between the four 'sectors'.

The sectors, and their subdivisions, are familiar enough as categories but the really important point is that only now are all the sectors being seen as of direct concern in social planning. Indeed some—as for example the economic base—have only recently become subject to any form of state planning. Regional economic development, for example, even now is only tentatively studied by economic planners. It follows that not nearly enough attention has been paid to the side-effects of intervention in any one sector, nor to the

153

powerful, if highly fragmented, influences that each sector exercises over the others.

Some of the inter-relationships are suggested by the way the diagram is constructed: sectors diametrically opposite each other have strong causal connections—social structure to the regional economy, and social services to the region's human resources. Again, the sectors correlate rather differently if one thinks in terms of the production and consumption of income. Adjacent sectors of the diagram appear to have a strong functional relationship one with another: for example the demand for labour influences, and is in turn influenced by, the supply. The supply of labour is related to household composition; and in various ways the social services too are involved: for instance the provision of pre-school play groups and day nurseries will affect married women's activity rates; and there may be certain parts of the city where more social services are needed because of the concentration there of non-family households— itself a consequence of the city's economic base.

The chains are endless; and emerging from these four sectors are the spatial patterns of human settlements: the urban hierarchy, the location of industry, and the appearance of distinctive zones within these settlements. The diagram also recognises that the subjects of major concern for social planning do not form a closed system—at a regional or metropolitan scale for example there will be factors operating that are 'external'. Instances are given in the diagram—in particular the impact of central government policies on industry and commerce and the social services. On the social structure and human resources side, the influence of state policies are no less strongly felt.

One other aspect might be clarified, at this point. The diagram does not suggest where planned intervention starts nor why it is necessary at all. It is about the major *concerns* in social planning; not the *problems*. But of course a similar diagram could be drawn to illustrate social problems or the types of intervention needed to combat social problems. The categories would be legion:

Economic Base	*Human Resources*	*Social Structure*
Structural decline	Unemployment	Racial discrimination
Low regional product	Low incomes	Broken homes
Manpower shortage	Low education standards	Drug addiction
Etc.	Etc.	Etc.

The Social Planner

We have discussed social planning. But who is the social planner? Social planning in fact has an army of practitioners, yet no one in Britain has the title Social Planner. There are social workers. There are social development officers in the new towns. Increasingly there are community workers in a variety of departments of local government. All have a social planning role, though none is customarily regarded as a social planner, still less *the* social planner. Architects, engineers and town planners too have a social planning perspective in their work, and whilst such planners are increasingly involved with subjects that were placed more peripherally in the diagram discussed above, nevertheless the spatial arrangement of activities is, as we noted earlier, still their central concern.

Economic planners have been largely concerned with the inter-related subjects contained in the outer sections of the diagram; not with the sector labelled Economic Base alone; but their involvement is spreading inwards—instance the economist Professor Ford writing on social theory and social practice.[6]

Social planning therefore is not a profession but a process of change and development taking place within a community, enveloping physical, economic, political and cultural components. Because of its diverse content and method it requires within its total framework the skills of many academic, professional and technical disciplines. In a sense this defusion is useful since there is less danger of vital concepts and approaches being subjugated to a narrowly professional outlook, or to the regimentation imposed by departmental boundaries in local and central government. At the same time there is a real risk of losing sight of the animal entirely in the present jungle of professional and departmental vested interests.

This brief description perhaps allows one to answer more clearly questions as to who is the social planner. Some possible misconceptions have been nailed. One is not saying that social planning lies in the domain of one profession, or even that a profession so titled could emerge. One is not implying that any person involved in social planning should be expert in, or even conversant with, all the subjects just discussed. One is not arguing that social planning is superior to, or even *primus inter pares* with, economic or physical planning on every front, nor is one suggesting that social planners should automatically exercise control over either the factors of production or a neighbourhood plan.

It is reasonable to suppose however that social planners will want to influence those who do exercise control over industry and development plans. One should recognise that there are no neat boundaries to the field and that it is more important to acknowledge this than to start hedge laying. One should also be aware that there is in practice no neat progression from one type of planning to another. Most important of all is that social planning, no less than economic and physical planning, is a political activity suffused with ideological issues; and that in practice role differentiation between the politician and the administrator is rather one of milieu than of comparative power and responsibility in a decision-making process.

The Institutional Framework of Social Planning

If there are no clearly defined professional groupings but rather a situation in which social planning policies have to be conceived and made operational by a wide range of officials working together (and of course with the public), then the institutional framework for social planning becomes the more important.

The present framework is far from ideal. There are no Departments of Social Planning in either central or local government. The links between local and central government both in formulating and implementing social policy are tenuous. The collection, analysis and interpretation of data in the field of social policy is haphazard. With the major exceptions of the field agencies serving the Department of Employment (the employment exchanges) and local health and social security agencies relating directly to the Department of Health and Social Security, it is local government which is the operational home of social policy. Yet the local town hall has its main channel of communication into Whitehall via the Department of the Environment, whereas the social policies of central governments lie *increasingly* with the Home Office, and continuingly with the Department of Health and Social Security, and the

Department of Education and Science. There is poor co-ordination between these departments of state particularly in so far as policies work themselves through at local scales.

Many changes are occurring in the management system of local authorities, but it is not yet apparent that these changes, coupled with innovations in planning terminology, are leading to a more effective approach to social planning. In searching for the unifying planning concepts that might give a greater sense of direction and purpose to local government three new planning processes have emerged: corporate planning, community planning and strategic planning. Each has a place and a contribution to make; but none is a proxy for social planning. It may be sufficient in the present context to say that with corporate planning there is more than a temptation for the medium to become the message, for community planning to drift along with such disarming notions as 'the greatest good of the greatest number' and for strategic planning to go for the main chance, ignoring on the way all the little local difficulties. Undoubtedly an interdepartmental approach to policy analysis can provide two benefits in the long term. It can lead to more relevant problem definition, and it can lead to more comprehensive and internally consistent sets of objectives; but whilst the new terms, and their institutional setting, are part of an attempt to differentiate the issues involved in local government into various scales of magnitude, it is becoming evident that where economic, physical and social planning problems are most appropriately integrated, namely at a metropolitan area scale, the institutional framework is least helpful. Within London for example the powers and responsibilities of the Greater London Council in respect of the three main fields of planning are quite limited and splintered.

The importance of the metropolitan scale in social planning might be underlined here: first of all, because an increasingly large section of our society lives in metropolitan areas rather than simply urban areas; secondly, because governmental systems are evolving which increasingly recognise the metropolitan area as a meaningful physical and socio-economic system within the state; thirdly, because the metropolitan area, whilst it is of a scale where a combination of processes and methods could most readily effect change, is also, paradoxically, the area where the changing nature of the social order is probably least understood.

Having raised the subject of problem definition once again we might now turn to the kind of social planning issues that seem of most concern in the British planning context in order to examine the methods and techniques that social planning would seek to bring to bear to resolve them.

Poor Jobs, Low Pay and Bad Housing: Key Issues in Social Planning

Social planning may be concerned with the whole social condition but it is inevitably preoccupied with aspects that are recognised by many observers as social problems: in particular the problems that beset what Patrick Geddes sixty years ago called 'the submerged fifth' in society.

There is some debate—currently rather heated[1]—about how far certain problems have become ingrained within this group through a 'culture of poverty'. There is little doubt that dead end jobs and low pay coupled with inadequate housing in the run down part of a city set in train other social problems; and whilst there may be argument over what might be called the multiplier effects, there is wide agreement that something should be done about poor jobs, low pay and bad housing. But what? It is necessary to remind ourselves first of some uncomfortable facts about these problems in embarking on social planning.

In a metropolis like London, for example, 40 per cent of all resident male workers fall into what might be described as the 'less skilled' categories of occupation.[8] Ten per cent of the labour force is unskilled, and there has been very little change over the last half-century[9] in the proportion of the workforce that is low skilled—though some significant shifts from blue collar to white collar unskilled work. It is still the case that a quarter of all school children in London leave at the minimum leaving age[10] and whilst some of these will eventually take up apprenticeships,[11] current data shows that two-fifths of the 150 000 school-leavers in Great Britain in 1970 who had no paper qualifications, went to non-trainee employment.[12]

It is estimated that something like 20 per cent of households with an adult male earner, in London, has an income of less than

£20 week. And the change to a service economy—particularly marked in metropolitan areas—is eradicating neither low skill nor low pay, since these factors are even more prevalent in service than in factory work. Poor jobs and low pay are continuing problems.

Indeed the demand for less skilled labour was such in the metropolitan areas of Britain in the 1950s and 1960s that sizeable quantities of migrants from the New Commonwealth arrived to fill these jobs: 55 000 men into London alone.

The low pay question is taking an ironic twist at the moment, through the working wife. In most parts of London now, one in two wives goes out to work, recruited in the main to do less skilled work. So much for Women's Liberation? There is surprisingly little social class variation in married female activity rates,[13] so that in terms of household incomes the working wife is in practice sustaining income inequalities and very probably widening those between the top and the bottom of household income scales. Thus the low-skilled head of household is in all probability not increasing his relative purchasing power through higher income even though his wife is going to work ostensibly to try to enhance the household's purchasing power.

The connection between low pay, low skill and poor accommodation needs to be considered also. Each year brings new records in our achievements in the housing field: new techniques of building, at higher standards; higher output and more rehabilitation. Yet the end of slums always seems a decade away. Until recently, ministerial speeches on this question had barely altered since Sir Hilton Young's day. Now a new note has been sounded. It is to the effect that only a 'hard core' problem exists, one confined to the conurbations.[14] The impression created is that adequate housing for all is just round the corner. It is, of course, an illusion. In the first place the argument relates only to a balance between households and dwellings, ignoring the galloping obsolescence which is overtaking much of the older housing stock. More importantly it ignores the fact that as long ago as the end of the First World War the problem of a deficit of dwellings compared with households was confined to the conurbations. In 1921 the area outside the six emergent English conurbations had a near balance between households and dwellings. Shortage of dwellings was even then a metropolitan problem. It remains one because the conurbations are still major reception areas for less skilled migrants.

In new towns fully controlled development has meant that industrial growth and the provision of housing are geared to each other. This is not the case in the conurbations, and we have seen the effect of this disjointedness in the 1950s and 1960s especially. Whilst the influx of labour (especially Commonwealth immigrants) seemed automatically[15] to adjust itself to labour demand without planning, housing supply did not. And our incipient twilight areas became full-blown problems—with the overcrowding, the stress, and the conflict over rehousing priorities that the conurbations have today.[16]

The housing problem is no easier, and like the labour market questions just discussed, it is compounded by the (essentially) irrelevant issue of race.

The Social Planning Response

Money is clearly fundamental; and government is now committing itself more forcefully to intervention on this level by way of an incomes policy applied through flat rate wage increases, negative income tax, family income supplements—in effect a minimum wage policy geared to varying types of household composition—and all these related to other social policies with an incomes basis, such as rent and rate rebates. These measures amount in effect to continuous State influence over the earnings of wide sections of the work force, and increasingly therefore to a planned economy carried through on the assumption that improvement in the living standards of a large part of the population requires them.

Whilst these measures are important advances in the attempt to redress some of the more extreme social inequalities in our society; nevertheless some deepseated obstacles which remain, for the really fundamental problem is that our society does not want equality. Even equality of opportunity—that less headstrong and more practical minded brother—whilst becoming acceptable Party manifesto material of the right as well as the left in post-war years, has been adopted into social policy only hesitantly.

Thus the most necessary of goals are far easier to spell out than to achieve. In 1938, under the strangely vogue title of 'The Strategy of Equality', R. H. Tawney was declaring:

If the first use which a sensible society will make of its surplus is to raise the general standards of health, and the second to equalise educational opportunities, the third is not less obvious. It is to provide for the contingencies of life, and thus to mitigate the insecurity which is the most characteristic of the wage earner's disabilities.[17]

and again—

If every individual were reared in conditions as favourable to health as science can make them, received an equally thorough and stimulating education up to sixteen, and knew on reaching manhood, that, given a reasonable measure of hard work and good fortune, he and his family could face the risks of life without being crushed by them, the most shocking of existing inequalities would be on the way to disappear.[18]

For Tawney these were, in a sense, starting points rather than goals!

Of course some progress has been made since 1938. The school leaving age has just been raised to 16; and we have a minimum household income level through social security (though not yet a national minimum wage). But the trouble with the minimum income is that it is minimal; and as many writers have pointed out, jacking up the lowest incomes can spark off a host of regressive side-effects; even of widening the definition of poverty. The vital point however is that raising the lowest income to a critical minimum floor level does not, alas, enable the low paid to gain better housing: 'standard' housing, as the Americans would say, is not there to be had.

We could make good the housing question in the medium term by the State pouring much more resources into rehabilitation and new building, whilst at the same time knocking down the unfit dwelling, and giving adequate allowances to enable everyone to pay for better housing. But society is unwilling to do this.

One major difficulty in forming a judgment of these unhappy metropolitan characteristics—and a major problem in any attempt to resolve them—is that the social planner still has no model enabling him to equate the demand and supply of housing for different socioeconomic groups at the metropolitan scale: defining the labour catchment areas within the metropolis is difficult enough; assessing the *availability* of dwellings as against the stock even more difficult. This explains no doubt why the Francis Committee was just as reluctant to control the furnished rented sector of the housing market as the medical officers were to use the Torrens and Cross Acts a century ago.

There are grave dangers in a partial approach to social planning. Attempts by planners to eliminate bad housing may also extinguish any chance of social mobility for those wishing to migrate from rural to urban economics—like New Commonwealth migrants. Erasing the poorer districts of the city, preventing low paying industries from establishing themselves, setting objectives like the maintenance of average incomes, could conceivably mean driving the poor out of town. It is not impossible that the new big city governments backed by an irrecusable PPB system could in future pursue their interests as restrictively as a medieval city guild. A balance has to be struck.

Conflicts and Compromises

Social problems become even more tangled when we try to formulate social policies for specific parts of the city. In the past social workers have responded to social pathology symptom by symptom. Physical planners on the other hand have responded with comprehensive redevelopment hoping perhaps that bull-dozing the buildings would banish the problems. The two sides have rarely exchanged notes. Now, sixty years after Beatrice Webb challenged fellow social workers not just to bale out the water but drain the swamp, social workers are at last talking about social problems related 'to the whole environment'. Planners meanwhile are learning the hard lesson that redevelopment, whatever it may do to the appearance of the city, shifts some problems along the road to the next twilight area, whilst others pop up again in the new council estates.

We must not fall into the trap of despising even small advances in welfare rights and social security. Equally we must not excuse our failure to research and monitor by making a scapegoat of the physical planner. It is not enough to say 'it was the place's fault'. There is need to establish which social problems (if any) are the price for city life, and which could be reduced if the planners used their wits. We must distinguish more clearly whether it is certain parts of the city which continually display sets of problems or people: our all too infrequent survey snapshots usually fail to note the rate at which population in an area is turning over (unacknowledged, even the classic area for family and kinship[19] stability lost half its population in twenty years).

162

A critical yardstick in judging whether an area is in good shape may be social mobility. There are hunches about the way low skill socio-economic patterns have been maintained over several generations but we are still not able to test the David Glass Index of Dissociation in the various problem areas of the metropolis; and are thus a long way from devising viable measures to combat low indices in households with low skills. Social mobility via migration may be a personal success story, but it could be a pyrrhic victory for community and kinship ties. There are signs that upward social mobility is indeed becoming the central concern of social planning, hastened on by the bleak theories about the metropolis which suggest that we have an inner city problem of growing magnitude. Concern over the future of people living in the inner areas of the major British cities therefore features prominantly in current issues in social planning. The concern expressed above pointed to a continuing, if not widening, gap between the standard of life of the population living in parts of the inner city and those elsewhere. People in such areas are increasingly referred to as 'deprived' or 'disadvantaged' and the repetition of such problems in these areas through succeeding generations of inhabitants is referred to as 'the cycle of deprivation'.

In looking at methods of approaching the particular issue of the inner city it is well to recognise that deprivation defined in this way will have a number of counterparts, and that all of these will require differing methods of treatment and remedy, and in a situation of scarce resources they may even compete with one another for priority. Deprivation may be defined as arising in the following ways.

1. Among the elderly in the population who have lost power, status and income.

2. From disablement and progressive handicaps.

3. From a declining economic base in an area whose economic development has lead to sophisticated urban patterns.

4. In areas with a heavily biased social class structure arising from a narrow range of job opportunities and with poor services, and limited leadership qualities.

5. In older urban areas which are now losing middle-income groups through migration as the urban regional economy expands.

6. Among specific groups within a generally prosperous population who suffer either poor education and health or 'cultural' obstacles to promotion or personal advancement.

7. In its most complex form, among parts of the total population that are handicapped through a poor home life and low motivation; a condition which, where it exists at all, is not readily pin-pointed within the population.

Social planning measures to tackle these seven categories usually fall under three broad headings; social work, social security (income maintenance), and efforts to effect the general functioning of society. Unfortunately it is rare for all three to be tackled simultaneously.

Social Planning and Community Development

The question of raising people's expectations and their ability to help themselves, especially in a situation where rapid improvement would normally appear unlikely, returns us to the opening theme of this chapter, and the Third World; for the need to find methods of bringing ordinary people together in efforts to improve their own welfare, in their own local communities, has always been seen as an indispensable feature of economic and social planning in the Third World. The process is called community development.

Since 1969 the concept has been increasingly commonly used in Britain. Staff, often with the title 'community workers' have been appointed to various departments of local government to assist the process in local neighbourhoods. Central government too is involved through commencing a number of experimental programmes in a dozen locations throughout England, mainly in the older urban areas of large cities. Whilst it was charitable (voluntary) organisations in the main who pioneered community development[20] in this country, the need for it has gained such acceptance that it is now becoming an aspect of local authority work.

Whilst community development, no less than social planning, requires specific kinds of technical expertise to assist its progress, community development work (and community work) is not itself a profession. Indeed the rigidities imposed on many community workers by having to work to departmental codes of practice in local government has given rise to the suggestion that such workers should be grouped in the office of the chief executive or town clerk. In a number of authorities this is happening.

The link between social planning and community development has perhaps been most clearly expressed by those workers who have been involved in giving technical advice in developing countries —work which has often required a return to first principles of planning and innovation, under primitive conditions—and who see applications for their methods in the most disadvantaged areas of cities in advanced urban societies. Understanding of the problems in these areas has been aided too by social anthropologists and sociologists studying the peasant leaving the Indian, West Indian or African village to find low-skill work, and shelter, in the rooming-house quarter of North-West European cities. Many social planners are thus beginning to speak a common language based on the concepts and practice of community development.[21]

An added spur towards a significant change in the orientation and style of local government has come about through the growth of community action groups. Some of these argue that because of the 'failure' of planned change, all physical change should be stopped, and that the whole of the resources devoted to infrastructural improvements should be focused on people: that software programmes should replace hardware programmes. They see little difference between the so-called 'gentrification' of inner London and the 'big bang' methods of the housing authority. Those with an historical turn of mind will argue that there are instructive parallels between the renewal of Smithfield or the Law Courts in the nineteenth century and Covent Garden in the twentieth. They say it is time we began talking to the people themselves, at the same time giving them power to plan for themselves.

Perhaps the most significant evidence of any changes of approach has been the move to decentralise some departmental activity in local government to district and even neighbourhood centres. It may be too early to say whether the new community action groups and neighbourhood councils are challenging or simply underlining traditional social planning objectives; but they are certainly challenging its methods.

Some Conclusions

Social planning has developed through recognition that collective action is needed to advance social welfare. It is still weak both as a body of knowledge and as a theoretical structure, and it proceeds through the setting of priorities that cannot be done by economic calculations alone. Social planning operates through political decisions and therefore is at heart much affected by social norms, and the range of social values, in a society. By dint of this, social planning is made the more hazardous; its outcome is essentially a compromise between the market, the public and the government.

Yet it would be altogether negative to conclude simply that social planning is a helpful notion that lies behind many of the concepts, and the organisation and methods of government in a developed country like our own. The malfunctioning both of society and of government requires a more purposeful approach. It is sometimes argued that social planning should not be vested in any group within government because the same interests are already represented by existing groups: 'it is clear that there cannot be a breed of planning separate from structure planning or corporate planning or separate from the many types of departmental plans within the local authority'.[22] But as we discussed earlier, these brands of planning emerging within local government do not add up to social planning: their frame of reference is still too narrow. There may well be value in having within the Civil Service Department of central government and within the chief executive's office in metropolitan government, a group of staff, whose experience is wide, whose technical knowledge is deep and varied, who could review the development and implementation of social policies and advise on future strategies, without the normally heavy commitment to departmental responsibilities. This grouping could be called a social policy unit. There could emerge a close relationship between community workers and these social planners. Something along these lines is now emerging within the Home Office at central government level oriented to inner city problems. It is yet to emerge in metropolitan government. There is an added reason for it so doing: with a greater degree of understanding of the processes of economic and physical change, and with increasing control over the levers of change at the city regional level, we can begin to ask basic questions about the direction in which we want to go—what form development should take, what priorities should be set, and who should benefit,[23] in the knowledge that, for better or worse, action could have some impact.

References

1 *Social Policy in Europe*, 6th European Symposium of the International Conference in Social Welfare, Edinburgh, 1971. Commission 2, p. 16.

2 K. E. Boulding, The Boundaries of Social Policy, *Social Work*, vol. 12, no. 1, pp. 3–11 (1967).

3 F. Lafitte, *Social Policy in a Free Society*, Inaugural Lecture, Birmingham University, p. 9 (1962).

4 Sir Ebenezer Howard, *Garden Cities of Tomorrow* (first published 1900, see Faber and Faber, reprint, 1965).

5 R. Titmuss, *Commitment to Welfare*, Chapter 1, p. 22 (Allen and Unwin, 1968).

6 P. Ford, *Social Theory and Social Practice* (Irish University Press, 1968).

7 U.S. Department of Labour, *The Negro Family: The Case for National Action*, (Washington, 1965).
W. Ryan *Blaming the Victim* (Orbach and Chambers, 1971).
N. Keddie (editor), *Tinker, Tailor . . . The Myth of Cultural Deprivation* (Penguin).

8 G. M. Lomas, *Labour and Life in London. London: Urban Patterns Problems and Policies* (Heinemann, 1973).

9 National Board for Prices and Incomes, *The General Problems of Low Pay*, Report No. 169 (HMSO, 1971).

10 Greater London Council, *Annual Abstract of Greater London Statistics*, see table 6.11 (1969).

11 Schools Council, *Young School Leavers*, p. 142 (HMSO, 1968).

12 Department of Employment and Productivity, Young Persons Entering Employment in 1970. *DEP Gazette* (May 1971).

13 Registrar General, *Census of Population 1966—Household Composition Tables*. See table 46, p. 347.

14 Gillian R. Vale, *Is the Housing Problem Solved—A Review of Recent Estimates*. Centre for Urban and Regional Studies, University of Birmingham (Published by Housing Centre Trust, 1971).

15 E. J. B. Rose, *Colour and Citizenship*, A Report on British Race Relations, part 2, section 7, 'The Dynamics of Migration'. (Oxford University Press, 1969).

16 J. A. Rex, *Race, Class and the City*, Presidential Address to the British Association (Sociology Section) Annual Conference, Swansea (1971).

17 R. H. Tawney, *Equality*, Chapter 4 (Allen and Unwin, 1938).

18 *ibid.*

19 P. Wilmott and M. Young, *Family and Kinship in East London* (Pelican, 1962).

20 G. M. Lomas, 'Community Development: the Lessons of London', *Municipal Journal*, 12 January (1973).

21 Gulbenkian Foundation, *Community Work and Social Change* (Longmans, 1968). See also *Current Issues in Community Work* (Routledge and Kegan Paul, 1973).

22 T. Eddison, *Local Government: Management and Corporate Planning*, p. 96 (Leonard Hill, 1973).

23 M. Webber, 'Planning in an environment of Change', *Town Planning Review*, vol. 39, pp. 179–185 and pp. 272–295 (1969).

7. Transport Planning

Michael J. Bruton

Introduction

At first sight the purpose and content of transport planning appear obvious. The problems and difficulties associated with moving about within the towns and cities of the industrialised world are readily apparent and publicised and feature daily in the lives of the majority of urban dwellers. Although these problems are not new, they have taken on more dominating dimensions in the last twenty-five years with the growth of urban populations and the rapid increase in motor vehicle ownership and usage. In an attempt to alleviate these problems, whilst at the same time still utilising the full range of transport modes available for movement, the transport planning process has been developed. The aim of this process, until comparatively recently, has been purely traffic functional. That is, it has aimed to produce proposals for capital investment and construction in existing and new transport facilities, which will improve the operating conditions of the estimated future movement flows where they are expected to overload most seriously the existing transport networks, and to ameliorate those obvious inefficiencies of the current transport systems such as congestion, accidents, and pollution. This approach is attractive both to the political decision-makers, and to those members of the public not directly affected by the proposals put forward, because it is quite clearly seen to be an attempt to correct visible and foreseeable ills. What it fails to do however, is to utilise the potential of transport to shape the urban environment by influencing the accessibility of locations within the urban area, to produce the optimum urban structure for whatever goals might be adopted and whatever constraints might be imposed. Indeed, Stone argues that 'transportation acts as the most effective single form-determining element in the man-made environment'[1] and although much has been written of the potential of this interaction between land use and transport, little attempt has yet been made to put into practice those 'form-determining' aspects of transport planning. Perhaps the way in which the proposals for Cumbernauld New Town were prepared and implemented, provides the most obvious example of one of the rare attempts to utilise the transport planning process as an integral and constructive element in the production of urban structure proposals. Although the approach adopted was simplistic, it was nevertheless a genuine attempt to utilise accessibility to produce the most appropriate structure for the town. Since then, with the exception of some of the more recent New Town proposals such as Runcorn and Milton Keynes, and the Teesside Study which was completed in 1968, few attempts have been made to integrate land-use planning and transport planning. Indeed Proudlove's comment, although made in 1968 in relation to the West Midlands study, aptly summarises the attitude adopted by land-use—transport planners when put into the position of practising their profession: 'the present round of studies . . . whilst acknowledging the place of land-use in travel generation, do little more than incorporate it as a control in the preparation of estimates of future travel needs.'[2] Yet if the efforts of planners are to be successful in creating an urban environment which is an efficient, attractive and pleasant place to live and work in, then it is essential that the dual role of transport planning be recognised and implemented. It is important that the traffic functional problems, which are primarily short or mid-term problems, be dealt with as an integral part of the transport planning process. Equally it is essential that the long-term influence of accessibility, and changes in accessibility brought about by the implementation of transport proposals, be considered as an integral element of transport planning.

Causes of the Transport Problem

A variety of causes have been identified to account for the 'transport problem', most of which tend to relate to the fact that developments in technology, new forms of transport, and the way of life in the industrialised nations of the world, have occurred at a rate far more rapid than the traditional cycles of urban renewal. The result is that today the majority of the towns and cities in the world are neither designed nor equipped to cope with, or realise the potential of, comparatively new modes of transport such as the motor-vehicle. The Traffic in Towns Report puts this point quite emphatically:

The manner in which the buildings and streets are put together is basically unsuitable for motor traffic. This soon became apparent after the invention of the motor vehicle because it soon exerted a strong influence towards changing the form of towns by encouraging the outward spread and sprawl of development.[3]

Changes in the way in which people live compound the issue. Higher incomes and increased car ownership enable more families to occupy homes in sub-urban areas; changes in transport technology e.g. the construction of motorways, the development of large load-carrying trucks, have reduced the dependence of manufacturing industries on central locations, whilst the development of new production techniques requiring comparatively spacious but ground level layouts has caused many industries to move to sites on the edge of urban areas—a trend which has been encouraged by planning policies applied in this country certainly since 1947. These changes in location patterns have given rise to changes in the pattern of travel. Previously most people travelled along well-defined corridors of movement to either a central location (town centre) or an area of concentrated employment activity. Today, travel patterns are increasingly diverse, incorporating sub-urban to town and city movements, and large cross-town flows which are not capable of being handled by the established public transport systems.

Traffic Functional Elements of the Transport Problem

The 'transport problem', which has been defined by Creighton 'as the summation of the things which people don't like about transportation',[4] is perhaps the most readily identified problem of the world's urban areas, and is certainly one of the longest recognised of the 'serious urban problems'. It is obvious as a problem because every town dweller, at some time or another, uses the different systems of movement available in urban areas, and suffers directly from their inefficiencies e.g. delay, accidents, noise, pollution. Not only is the problem obvious, but also the very nature of transport allows it to be easily and directly quantified, as for example traffic in the streets, person movements, cost of delays in time and money.

Despite the ease with which the transport problem can be identified and measured, and despite the fact that it is generally regarded as 'a serious urban problem' the importance which it merits in both the eyes of the public and the politicians tends to vary with time. For example, during the late 1950s and early 1960s in Britain, transport was regarded as the dominant urban problem. Concern for other urban problems such as poverty, racial tension and environment was relatively low, with the result that considerable effort and finance were expended in an attempt to alleviate the transport problem, possibly at the expense of the other urban problems. However, since the late 1960s there has been a greater commitment to other significant social concerns, so that there is now a tendency to regard transport 'as a luxury problem which can be given priority only by an affluent society that has solved its more fundamental ones'.[5] Such a position, although easing the collective social conscience, can only be accepted with great qualification. Transport is inextricably related to population and economic activity, and the spatial distribution of population and production. Consequently transport problems are related to the other problems of urban areas, although the nature of this relationship is not always recognised or understood. Any attempt to solve the more obvious social problems of the urban areas could be self-defeating unless careful consideration is given to the nature of the transport problem in the area under examination and the way in which transport and these other urban problems are inter-related.

Perhaps the most visible, and therefore most irritating, dimension of the transport problem is the loss of time and money resulting from inefficiencies imposed on the normal movement of people and goods through congestion and poor accessibility, e.g. it is estimated that in 1970 the cost of road traffic congestion in Great Britain was the equivalent of £35 per family per annum.[6] Allied with the problem of congestion is the unreliability of transport systems affected by it, and it is unreliability and lack of comfort which tend to give rise to the greatest dissatisfaction with the suburban railway services of the larger towns and cities in this country. For example, according to *Motorways in London*[7] in December 1968, 40 per cent of all Southern Region trains were late, whilst a high proportion of peak hour travellers are forced to stand throughout their journey. Much of the dissatisfaction with rail travel stems from capacity limitations at junction bottlenecks at termini, arising from antiquated signalling and short platforms.

Accessibility in urban areas gives people considerable freedom of choice in deciding where they will live, work, shop and play. It also enables commercial activities to choose the optimum location for their production and distribution activities. Conversely poor accessibility can result in a loss of freedom for the people affected and the frustrations caused can have a variety of unforeseeable repercussions, e.g. poor accessibility in the Watts area of Los Angeles is held by the McCone Commission to be one of the causes of the riots in Los Angeles in 1966.[8]

Accidents constitute perhaps the most dramatic element of the transport problem and it was estimated that in Great Britain in 1971 the cost of fatal accidents was £375 million.[9] Approximately 75 per cent of all casualties occur in built-up areas and the consistency with which accident statistics recur, tends to suggest that the only radical improvement of the situation will stem from sweeping physical changes designed to reduce the opportunity for conflict between vehicles and pedestrians.

Since the publication of the Traffic in Towns Report the environmental aspects of the transport problem have been given considerable emphasis, and register with many as perhaps the most intractable of all the problems associated with transport. Delays in traffic jams, and difficulties associated with parking receive publicity, yet the deterioration of the urban environment is often allowed to pass unnoticed.

Safety should be a prime consideration in producing satisfactory living and working conditions in urban areas, and the point of view put forward in the Traffic in Towns Report is held by most urban dwellers—'To be safe, to feel safe at all times, to have no serious anxiety that husbands, wives, or children will be involved in a traffic accident are surely prerequisites for civilised life.'[10] Yet the number of urban streets where this condition is met are few— parked cars, delivery vans, and through traffic tend to result in the continuous movement of vehicles up and down most urban streets, including residential streets, to the detriment of safety standards.

Noise from motor vehicles, aircraft, and other transport rolling-stock constitute another aspect of the urban transport problem. Indeed the Wilson Report on the problem of noise concluded that in London and other large towns and cities 'road traffic is, at the present time, the predominant source of annoyance, and no other noise is of comparable importance.[11] Fumes, smell and air pollution form yet another environmental aspect of the transport problem. In contrast to the situation in the United States of America, in Britain engine fumes do not yet rank as a major cause of atmospheric pollution, although there is little doubt that they contribute a great deal towards making many urban streets extremely unpleasant.

Transport systems in urban areas tend to produce visually intrusive side-effects which contribute significantly to the deterioration of the urban environment. The parking of motor vehicles in every square yard of space in the centre of towns and the associated clutter of street signs and other paraphernalia associated with the use of the motor vehicle tend to destroy architectural and townscape qualities. The ugliness of vast monolithic transport structures, which are completely out of scale with the areas through which they pass tend to arouse great public antagonism, and contribute significantly to the transport problem.

For some years now the above aspects have been recognised as important elements of the transport problem. In more recent years the public outcry over the construction of some major transport proposals such as the westway route in West London, and the proposed 'motorway box' in London indicate that there is yet another significant factor to be considered—namely the public at large need to be convinced that at any particular moment in time investments proposed through the implementation of transport plans are sound, necessary and constitute the best possible solution for the problem in hand.

In an attempt to eliminate or ameliorate these traffic functional elements of the transport problem, the transport planning process has been evolved. The evolution has occurred over a period of some 30 years, from comparatively simple movement studies of road traffic to the relatively complex transport studies involving the analysis of the relationship between land-use and the movement flows generated by that land-use.

Development of the Transport Planning Process
The Basis of the Urban Transport Planning Process

The urban transport planning process is based on a range of assumptions and principles the most basic of which are that:

1. Travel patterns are tangible, stable and predictable.
2. Movement demands are directly related to the distribution and intensity of land-uses, which are capable of being accurately determined for some future date.

Although such assumptions can be subjected to critical academic debate, nevertheless they do at present provide a basis from which the planner can attempt to deal with the problems of movement and land-use. The fact that urban transport planning has not, in the eyes of the public, achieved many worthwhile results is due as much to the limited way in which the process has been applied to traffic functional elements of the transport problem, as to the short-comings of the fundamental assumptions.

N. America

Prior to the early 1950s problems of urban movement were seen in terms of road traffic only, and transport planning consisted primarily of the application of crude growth factors to existing traffic flows to estimate future movement. In 1954, however a major break-through in the development of the transport planning process occurred with the publication of the classic work, *Urban Traffic—A Function of Land Use*, by Mitchell and Rapkin.[12] Following an analysis of movement and land-use data for Philadelphia, they established that different types of land-use generate different and variable traffic flows, and went on to indicate how this inter-relationship could be applied in operational terms. This approach brought about fundamental changes in the study and understanding of movement, and shifted the emphasis from the study of road traffic flows to the study of the land-uses that give rise to the flows. It was successfully applied in large *ad hoc* studies such as the Detroit Area Traffic Study (1953), the Chicago Area Transportation Study (1955), the Pittsburgh Study (1958) and the Penn–Jersey Study (1959), and eventually became declared national policy in 1962 when the Highway Act 1962 required all metropolitan areas with cities having a population of

50 000 persons or more, to produce a comprehensive transport plan embracing all modes of travel, and taking land-use plans into consideration. To assist in the development of these comprehensive transport plans the United States Department of Transportation Bureau of Public Roads produced a 'package' of techniques for transport analysis, which is readily available for purchase. The objectives adopted by these studies were purely traffic functional; they aimed to ameliorate the various elements of the transport problem such as congestion, delay, poor accessibility and accidents, by producing proposals for 'capital investments in new transportation facilities, or in funding the operation of certain transportation services such as mass transportation facilities'.[13] Indeed the prime objective of the Chicago Area Transportation Study is typical of many of the early studies undertaken in the United States, and emphasises how much attention was focused on the traffic functional aspects of the problem, and how little attention was given to the structure-influencing aspects of transport on urban form. This bias can be seen from the Chicago study:

what then is the dominant objective of a transport facilities plan? It is to reduce travel frictions by the construction of new facilities so that people and vehicles . . . can move about within the area as rapidly as possible, in a manner consistent with limitations of cost and safely.[14]

Great Britain

In Great Britain the development and application of the transport planning process received its first major impetus in the late 1950s, when the Ministry of Transport encouraged the local authorities in the major conurbations to co-operate in producing long-term highway plans for their areas. The objectives adopted for studies such as the *London Traffic Survey* (1960)[15] and the *SELNEC Highway Plan* (1962)[16] were limited and purely traffic functional. For example the objectives of the London Traffic Survey were basically:

1. To survey the origins and destinations of traffic movement within an area extending beyond the boundaries of the then London County Council.
2. To survey journey times.
3. To develop a method to estimate the amount of traffic on a road network.

4. To indicate areas where travel capacity was limited and travel conditions poor.

5. To present the results in a form suitable for the preparation of a comprehensive road plan for the County of London.[17]

Although these objectives were limited, the significance of developments in transport planning in the United States were realised in the early stages of the studies. Gradually amended objectives were incorporated which required land-use and public transport analyses to be carried out as part of the process. Following the publication in 1963 of the Traffic in Towns Report, which established the need for comprehensive movement studies involving land-use analysis, the then Ministries of Transport and Housing and Local Government issued a joint circular in 1964 advocating the use of land-use – transportation studies to achieve a co-ordinated approach to land-use and transport planning.[18]

In April 1964 the first of these land-use – transport studies, the West Midlands transportation study, was commissioned, and was followed in later years by the studies for Greater Glasgow (1964), Teesside (1965), Belfast (1965) SELNEC (1965), Merseyside (1966), West Yorkshire (1967), Tyneside (1967), and many other studies for smaller urban areas such as Worcester, Colchester, and Brighton and Hove. With notable exceptions, e.g. the Teesside study the objectives generally adopted for these studies were again traffic functional, although the interaction between land-use and movement was seen to be an integral element in the process. The objectives for the West Midlands transportation study and the Belfast study are perhaps typical of this type of study and illustrate quite emphatically that their aims were to produce solutions to the traffic functional elements of the transport problem:

1. West Midlands—'to undertake a comprehensive survey of all forms of transport in the West Midlands conurbation, and to analyse its relationship to types of land-use and all other factors affecting the demand for and movement of transport; and to make forward projections with the aim of providing guidance on the desirable pattern of road development and public transport facilities.'[19]

2. Belfast—'to carry out a transportation study which would lead to the preparation of a long term transportation plan for the improvement of communications in Belfast, i.e. a plan to provide for

the efficient movement of persons and goods by all forms of transport.'[20]

The Structure of the Traffic Functional Transport Planning Process

The structure of the traffic functional transport planning process, as it has been applied to date, can be illustrated in many different ways. However, when generalised it can be reduced to the simple line diagram shown in Fig. 3, and the principal steps identified as:

1. The explicit formulation of goals and objectives for the study.

2. The collection of land-use, population, economic, and travel pattern data and the development and calibration of land-use and movement models for the base year of the study. (This stage of the exercise quantifies the relationship between land-use and movement.)

3. The development of a land-use plan, and the estimation of the pattern of movements associated with that plan, for the target year of the study. (This stage of the exercise applies the land-use and movement models established for the base year to estimate the future pattern of movements.)

4. The development of alternative highway and public transport networks 'to fit' the land-use plan and accommodate the estimated pattern of movements.

5. The assignment of the estimated future movements to the alternative networks to test their traffic carrying capabilities.

6. The evaluation of the alternative networks in terms of both economic and social costs and benefits.

7. The selection and implementation of the most appropriate network.

Although the principal steps in the process can be readily identified and isolated, the relationship and interaction between them is vitally important. Indeed it has been said that '. . . they are interdependent and individually almost meaningless'.[21]

The Formulation of Goals and Objectives

In any systematic planning process the formulation of explicit goals and objectives is essential, as the objectives become the criteria

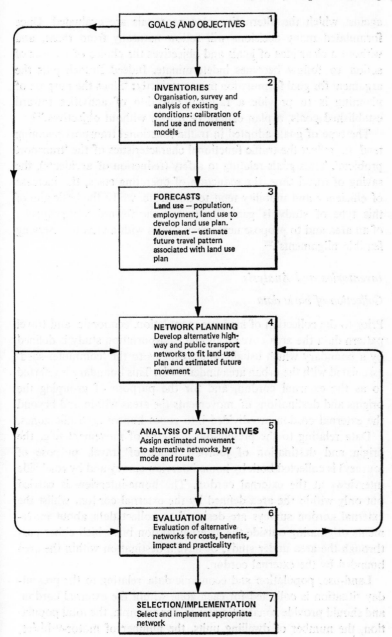

Fig. 3   Traffic functional approach to transport planning

against which the alternative plan proposals are evaluated. Once formulated many decisions will follow naturally from them, and without a clear idea of goals and objectives the choice of courses of action to follow becomes indeterminate. Indeed Branch puts the argument for goal formulation most succinctly: 'Since the purpose of planning is to provide a rational direction of activities toward established goals, a plan cannot be drawn without objectives.'[22]

The type of goals adopted in traffic functional transport planning tend to reflect the traffic functional characteristics of the 'transport problem'. Thus goals relating to safety (reduction of accidents), the saving of travel time, the reduction of operating costs, the increase of efficiency and mobility tend to dominate, whilst the basic aim of this type of study is generally 'to test the foward route capacity of an area and to propose new urban routes with a view to reserving feasible alignments'.[23]

Inventories and Analysis

Collection of basic data

Prior to the collection of land-use, population, economic, and travel pattern data the area covered by the transportation study is defined by a boundary which usually approximates to the 'commuter-shed' associated with the urban area under study. This boundary is referred to as the external cordon, and for the purpose of grouping the origins and destinations of movements the areas within and beyond the external cordon are divided into zones known as traffic zones.

Data relating to the present-day patterns of movement (e.g. the origin and destination of journey, mode of travel, purpose of journey) is collected both by home-interview survey and by road-side interviews at the external cordon. The home-interview is carried out only within the area defined by the external cordon, whilst the external cordon surveys are designed to collect data about movements originating outside the external cordon but which either pass through the area under study, or have a destination within the area bounded by the external cordon.

Land-use, population and economic data relating to the present-day situation is collected for each zone within the external cordon, and should provide zonal estimates of, for example, the total population, the number of dwelling units, the number of motor-vehicles, household income, the number of jobs available, the volume of retail sales, school attendance, and the area of land given over to different uses. In addition to the planning and movement data, an inventory of the existing transport facilities is completed, including parking surveys, travel time surveys, highway and public transport capacity and volume studies.

Establishment of quantifiable relationships between movement and land use[24]

By using statistical and mathematical techniques relationships between land-use and movement data for the present-day situation are established and quantified. For example multiple linear regression analysis can be used to establish the relationship between the number of person or vehicular movements produced by a defined traffic zone and the zonal characteristics of that zone such as total population, population density, and income. For the same zone the number of trips attracted to that zone can be estimated by the same technique, but this time relating the movements to such factors as the number of jobs available, the volume of retail sales, and school attendance within the zone. This stage of the process is generally referred to as trip generation. Similarly the present-day pattern of movements, that is, the distribution of movements within and beyond the area under study, can be reproduced by applying mathematical models such as the 'gravity model', whilst the actual routes taken by present-day movements can be reproduced by using traffic assignment models such as the 'all-or-nothing' or 'capacity-restraint' assignment procedures. The trip generation and trip distribution relationships thus established are used in stage 3 of the process to forecast the future origins, destinations and distribution of movements associated with the developed land-use forecasts, whilst the assignment relationships are used in stage 5 of the process to evaluate alternative network proposals.

Forecasts

Prediction of future land-use, population and economic characteristics, and preparation of land-use plan.

Demands for movement are related to activities pursued by people,

181

and these activities are reflected in the distribution and characteristics of a range of different land-uses. By using the relationships established between land-use and movement for the present-day situation, and applying them to future estimates of land-use distribution and characteristics, it is possible to derive estimates of the future pattern of movements associated with a particular set of land-use proposals. Thus the development of estimates of the future land-use characteristics and distribution, and the preparation of a land-use plan are fundamental aspects of the transport planning process. Indeed, it is essential to have estimates, on a zonal basis and for some future date, of population, economic activity, vehicle ownership and land-use characteristics. In the United States, where there is little history of strong regulatory planning powers, the forecasting of future land-use distribution and characteristics has for some time been based on the use of land-use distribution models, such as the Garin-Lowry residential allocation model. In the absence of land-use controls, these models attempt to estimate the effect on urban areas of incremental growth resulting from the actions of individuals and corporate bodies intent on maximising their own benefits.

In Britain, however, with its long history of comparatively strong land-use controls the approach to the forecasting of future land-use distribution and characteristics has been somewhat different. Indeed, it could be argued that in Britain no real attempt has been made to forecast, on a systematic and comprehensive basis, estimates of the future land-use characteristics and distribution. Rather, *ad hoc* estimates of land-use distribution tend to be produced, based on generalised and rather crude predictions of population and employment. The assumption implicit in this approach is that the land-use regulations are sufficiently strong to control the pressures influencing the distribution and characteristics of land-use, with the result that there is no apparent need to be able to forecast accurately what is likely to take place. However, such an approach ignores the susceptibility of land-use to market forces, and in more recent studies land-use allocation models are being used to produce forecasts of estimated land-uses.

The end product of the land-use forecasting stage of the process, in both Britain and the United States, tends to be similar—one land-use plan or set of land-use estimates, relating to a date some 20 years in the future.

Prediction of future travel pattern associated with estimated future land-use distribution

This stage of the procedure is concerned with predicting the future origins, destinations, and distribution of movements associated with the estimated future land-use distribution and characteristics. Future trips produced by and attracted to each zone are estimated through the 'trip generation' process, whilst the pattern of movements within the area are estimated through the 'trip distribution' procedure. Both stages utilise the relationships established between the present day land-use and movement characteristics and rest on the assumption that this relationship will not alter materially in the future.

Network Planning

The network planning stage of the process involves the development of alternative transport networks for the selected land-use plan. These alternative networks generally take the form of complete systems serving the whole of the area under examination, and include networks for both public transport and the motor-vehicle. Each alternative network should ideally reflect different policies regarding the extent, location, characteristics and cost of the network.

The procedure generally adopted in the traffic functional transport planning process involves the consideration of such factors as the density of trips produced by or attracted to an area, trip length, land-use characteristics, network design criteria and investment costs, although the way in which these factors are considered, and the influence they have on the design of the alternative networks varies from study to study.

Highway Networks

In the United States, a generalised but fairly typical example of the procedure which tends to be adopted in the development of alternative highway networks as part of the traffic functional transport planning process could take the following form. For the selected land-use plan and the estimated demand for movement associated with it:

1. Determine the optimum number and spacing of major links

in the highway network. Here 'optimum' tends to be equated with cost, and thus optimum spacing generally attempts to minimise the sum of both travel costs and network construction costs.

2. Consider the fundamental design principles to be applied at the network design stage, and determine design standards and criteria, e.g. design speed, capacity.

3. Assess the constraints likely to influence the design of alternative network proposals, e.g. committed proposals to improve existing network.

4. Produce layout plans of alternative networks.

In Britain a variety of approaches have been adopted towards network planning, all incorporating to a greater or lesser extent the steps, if not the procedure, outlined above, although work on Oxford[25] by the city council and their consultants, and on Guildford[26] by C. D. Buchanan and partners, indicates how network planning can be made less intuitive.

Public Transport Networks

The design of alternative public transport networks involves the same general procedure as that adopted for the development of highway networks, although the factors which need to be considered are completely different. In addition, the way in which these factors are considered will also differ according to whether public transport is seen solely as only one component in the overall transport system, or whether it should be looked at in relation to other aspects of urban and social planning, e.g. by supporting the existing central area.

Two basic alternative modes of public transport are generally examined in the development of alternative public transport networks. Firstly, rapid mass transit (e.g. underground or suburban railways) and secondly the motor-bus. The establishment of firm criteria for the development of complete public transport systems is complex in the extreme, especially as experience of recent developments in this field is limited to such ventures as the Bay Area Rapid Transit District in San Francisco. Indeed, most existing public transport systems were developed prior to the widespread ownership and usage of the motor vehicle, and frequently in areas of high population density, and central area congestion.

In general terms the procedure followed in developing alternative network plans is one of gradually identifying the constraints within which alternative solutions must be found. Indeed the report of the Chicago area transportation study summarises the approach generally adopted.

The actual planning of new transportation facilities is not done on a clean slate; the process, rather, is one of successively imposing limits within which the solution must be found. Existing expressways, boulevards and transit lines are one set of limits. Land-uses (such as housing developments, industrial districts and commercial centres) impose other limits. The forecasts of future traffic demands fix the magnitude of the improvements which must be made. Finally, objectives and standards control the solutions greatly.[27]

Analysis of Alternatives

The purpose of this stage of the process is to determine whether any of the alternative proposed transport plans would in fact be capable of carrying the estimated movement volumes for the target year. This is achieved by simulating the choice of travel mode (modal split), and the route chosen from point of origin to destination (traffic assignment), for person movements derived from stage 3 of the process.

Modal split—or the allocation of the total number of person movements to different modes of travel—can be derived in a variety of ways.[28] All, however, are based on the assumption that of a given total travel demand the proportion carried by bus, underground, surface railway, or private motor-vehicle will depend on the standing of each mode in relation to its competitors. The measure of this competitiveness is usually derived from an analysis of:

1. The characteristics of the journey to be made, e.g. purpose, length.
2. The characteristics of the person making the journey, e.g. social standing, income.
3. The characteristics of the transport system, e.g. travel time and cost involved, comfort, accessibility.

The allocation of all movements, by mode of travel, to appropriate routes between each pair of origins and destinations is achieved through the traffic assignment process. A variety of techniques have been developed to simulate this route selection. The most significant of these are the 'diversion curve', the 'all-or-nothing' and the 'capacity restraint' assignment procedures. The 'diversion curve' procedure is based on empirical studies, and in general terms estimates the number of persons likely to transfer (or divert) from an existing facility to a new or improved facility. The proportion of diverted traffic is usually related to such parameters as cost, distance, or speed.

The 'all-or-nothing' assignment is based on the assumption that all movements between each pair of origins and destinations will take the shortest route between the zones, whilst the 'capacity restraint' assignment procedure attempts to take account of congestion which builds up with increased traffic volumes.

The output from this stage of the process takes the form of movement volumes on each part of the network, including turning movements at major intersections. This output is analysed and evaluated for each alternative, and modifications and amendments can be incorporated to take account of traffic overloading, and other factors such as environmental considerations. In this 'testing' phase the original objectives come under close scrutiny, as the test results may well indicate that some of the objectives and standards are mutually inconsistent.

Evaluation of Alternative Transport Plans

Within the limitations imposed by the numerous assumptions made, it is a comparatively straightforward task to assess whether the alternative network plans will meet the estimated travel demand with adequate capacity, safety and standard of service. However, the problems associated with developing a reliable assessment of the economic and social costs and benefits, resulting from the implementation of any of the alternative networks, are considerable. If, as so often is the case, the objectives originally adopted for the study are primarily economic, then the benefits derived from, for example, a reduction in accidents, and time saved, can be compared with the cost of constructing, maintaining and operating the alternative networks. Through an interactive procedure it is possible to determine which type of plan will provide greater reductions in the cost of transport in return for increased investment. Eventually a preferred plan will emerge. However, if the social implications of alternative networks are included in this evaluation it becomes much more difficult to decide on the preferred solution—invariably economic interests are in conflict with social or environmental interests.

The Traffic in Towns Report[29] indicated one evaluation approach which could be adopted in addition to the more straightforward economic evaluation, in an attempt to compare the intangible and unquantifiable effects of alternative transport networks. Basically this approach involves the subjective ranking of the performance of the alternative networks against certain criteria such as accessibility and environment. A numeric benefit–cost ratio, and an incremental benefit-cost ratio are derived for each alternative, to enable a comparison to be made. This approach was put into practice in the Canterbury study carried out by Buchanan and partners[30] and although it can be criticised on the grounds that it is subjective, and the allocation of ranking values is arbitrary, it nevertheless does attempt to take account of the many factors which are difficult to quantify. Indeed Barrell in his analysis of the use of cost-benefit analysis in transport planning states 'the Canterbury traffic study demonstrates a considerable conceptual advance . . . in its attempt to integrate intangibles within the evaluation . . .'[31]

Selection and Implementation of Preferred Plan

The decision as to which transport and land-use plan best serves the need of the community is not the logical and final output of the traffic functional transport planning process. Rather the judgement of professionals and politicians is applied to the various stages of the process to determine what, in their opinion, constitutes the optimum transport and land-use solution. In this respect the transport planning process is an aid to decision-making, and not the precise instrument that some people like to think it is.

In deciding on a 'preferred plan' it is vital to ensure that any proposals put forward are not so rigid as to impede the course of progress. With changes in the demographic, technological, economic and social spheres occurring at increasingly rapid rates, it is impossible to forecast accurately for periods of more than five to ten years in advance. Consequently it is important that the 'preferred plan' should be flexible enough to accommodate any changes brought about by future trends.

After implementation, the way in which the network performs

should be kept under constant review. In addition to long-term policies, up to and beyond the target date, short-term predictions are generally made, and these are used as a check against what actually happens on the network at different stages of the construction programme. If the comparisons are good then no changes are necessary to the long-term policies. If the comparisons are poor then the assumptions made at the outset must be reviewed and up-dated. If necessary the long-term policies should be modified.

Relationship of the Traffic Functional Transport Planning Process to the Land-use Plan-making Process

The relationship between the traffic functional transport planning process and the traditional land-use plan-making process varies from country to country, as different political, legal and administrative frameworks inevitably give rise to different traditions and processes. In the United States, the legislative and other controls which exist for the preparation and implementation of land-use plan proposals are limited. Consequently the opportunity of producing and implementing plans which call for change and improvement are also limited. As a result of these limited opportunities for planning, a reliance on the forecasting of future land-use requirements has tended to be substituted for planning the future pattern and characteristics of land-use. Given the reliance of most forecasting techniques on the extrapolation of existing trends, the derived land-use forecasts have inevitably indicated that 'more of the same' is required. From this basis of 'more of the same', the transport planning process is then utilised to 'test the forward route capacity of an area and to propose new urban routes with a view to reserving feasible alignments'.[32] The attitude adopted towards the integration of land-use and transport planning tends to be negative. Land-use forecasts are used as inputs to the transport planning process, merely as a control factor which will influence the output of the process in terms of network proposals. Little or no attempt is made to examine alternative land-use plans or to assess the inter-relationships which might result from the imposition of an optimum transport system on a set of land-use forecasts.

In Britain, where there is a long tradition of strong legislative powers to control the development and implementation of land-use proposals, the situation is only slightly better. One plan for change and improvement in the distribution and characteristics of land-use is usually produced for each major settlement as opposed to the North American tradition of forecasting likely change and using that as a plan. However, with notable exceptions, the transport planning process then utilises this plan as the best available set of input variables from which to develop traffic forecasts and transport networks. Although the procedure involves the consideration of alternative transport systems, it is inevitably based on only one land-use plan. Solesbury and Townsend put this relationship between land-use and transport planning most succinctly. 'Methodologically, the transportation forecast has been grafted to the normal plan making process as an evaluative measure.'[33]

In an attempt to overcome this serious short-coming, the traffic functional planning process was gradually modified during the 1960s to incorporate a consideration of alternative future land-uses. At the same time the overall process and procedure became more sophisticated as a consequence of a better understanding of the nature of the problems involved. Figure 4, which is taken from the Bureau of Public Roads publication *Urban Transportation Planning*, illustrates the modified nature of the process. Although it was argued that this process should be a continuing, co-operative and continuous planning process, in actual fact leading practitioners generally took the view that 'urban transportation planning is designed to develop and continuously evaluate short and long-range highway and transportation plans . . .'[34]

Deficiencies of the Traffic Functional Transport Planning Process.

Even with the evolution of the transport planning process incorporating the consideration of alternative land-use proposals, severe deficiencies can readily be discerned at both the operational and conceptual levels.

Operational deficiences

Much criticism has been levelled at the different stages of operation involved in the traffic functional transport planning process. Despite the modified process incorporating the consideration of alternative

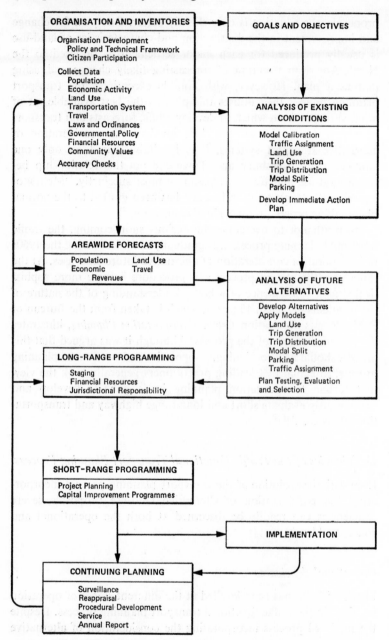

Fig. 4   The traffic functional transport planning process II

SOURCE Bureau of Public Roads, *Urban Transport Planning*, General Information and Introduction to System 360.

land-use proposals it is criticised on the grounds that too few alternatives are considered, and that in many instances the so-called
alternatives are nothing more than variations on the same theme.
For example, the London traffic survey originally defined twenty-
three 'alternative' road networks, and several combinations of
improvements to public transport, without making public the
methods by which any of the 'alternative' network plans were
prepared. Of the twenty-three 'alternative' networks, three road
networks and two public transport networks were tested, but the
minimum road network formed part of the middle-range road network, which in turn formed part of the maximum road network.

In the United States an analysis of thirteen metropolitan area
land-use transportation studies carried out by Boyce, Day and
McDonald emphasises this inability to produce true alternative
policies or plans. They establish quite clearly that for the period
under review 'the attempts of [land-use-transport] programmes to
prepare different land-use and transportation alternatives fell far
short of the aspirations of these programmes'.[35] They found that:

1. In those programmes using urban development models to
elaborate alternative land-use patterns in which only transport
policies were varied, no significant differences in the land-use patterns
were identified among the alternatives.

2. In those programmes in which land-use patterns exhibiting
significant differences were used as the basis for testing a single
transportation system, including both highways and transit, no large
differences in network performance and costs were demonstrated for
the land-use alternatives.

3. In those programmes using urban development models to
elaborate land-use alternatives in which both transportation policies
and land-use policies were varied, the resulting land-use patterns and
transportation requirements were not sufficiently different to provide
a technical basis for policy decisions.[36]

In general terms the main reasons put forward to account for the
lack of real difference between alternatives can be summarised as
follows. The land use and transportation policies tested were too
similar and conservative for significant differences to obtain; the
models and methods available to evaluate alternatives were 'too
blunt' to respond sufficiently to alternative policies; the scale of

aggregation for forecasting development and travel was too large to detect differences in land-use-transport interactions.

Another major operational criticism of the modified traffic functional transportation planning process is that the setting of goals and objectives tends to be inadequately carried out. They are derived either through discussion and concensus, which inevitably means that the generation of any true alternative land-use and/or transport policies is made extremely difficult from the outset, or they are specified in such a general way that any alternative could fulfil them.

The evaluation stage of the process is also heavily criticised. Traditionally evaluation is based on economic methodologies, yet evaluation based only on economics has the serious disadvantages that minority viewpoints are obscured through the high degree of aggregation involved. Those factors which are readily expressed in monetary terms tend to be over-emphasised, whilst little attention is paid to 'fairness'. Considerations of the relative efficiency of alternatives tend to predominate. Similarly, the use of forecasting techniques which tend to perpetuate the existing situation, simply because these techniques are based on the reproduction of existing individual and aggregated patterns of behaviour, is also heavily criticised.

At a more general level the process is criticised by politicians, the public and land-use planners on the grounds that it is far too concerned with the technical problems associated with the traffic estimation, and network planning stages of the process, and too little concerned with the transport needs of the community at large. It is criticised for favouring the motor vehicle in any solution produced, and ignoring the possibilities of public transport. It is criticised for not involving the public more in the process.

Conceptual Deficiences

Although the operational deficiencies of the traffic functional transport planning process are serious enough, fundamental conceptual deficiencies arise as a result of the extremely narrow viewpoint adopted by most practitioners.

Despite the requirements both in Britain[37] and the United States[38] that the transport planning process should be comprehensive and incorporate on an integrated area-wide basis the consideration of economic and population factors, land-use, social and community values and the role of different transport modes, what generally tends to emerge is a highway plan designed to fit one particular land-use plan. A comprehensive approach tends to be interpreted as full coverage of the technical aspects of the planning process in relation to highway networks, with lip-service being paid to the needs and values of the community, whilst public transport demand becomes a residual after motor-vehicle trips have been estimated. This attitude has resulted in the development of a comparatively sophisticated methodology to estimate future traffic-flows and derive alternative networks. At the same time it has led to the production of proposals which threaten jobs and houses and are totally unacceptable to the public.

A panel of experts brought together in Paris by the OECD in 1971 to consider the strengths and weaknesses of transport planning emphasised that the narrow conceptual approach adopted on the part of practising transport planners was perhaps the greatest weakness in the process. They found that investment in transport proposals derived from land-use transport plans tends to be evaluated against six main traffic functional criteria.

1. The satisfaction of observed demand.
2. The reduction or elimination of bottle-necks in the existing network(s).
3. Enhanced efficiency in the existing or proposed network(s).
4. Net user benefits.
5. Capital costs involved in the construction of the network(s).
6. The economic return on investment.

They argued that although this

allows for the satisfaction of internal, system specific demands, it ignores the wider external effects of transport. Yet transportation is only a part of a larger urban or regional complex and every change within the transport system reverberates throughout the larger complex, producing multiple impacts that reach out beyond the confines of the transportation system.[39]

This comment highlights what is perhaps the most significant criticism which can be levelled at transport planners—the failure to recognise and utilise transport planning as one of the most important tools for guiding and shaping the development of the urban environment. Rather than take the opportunity of designing a framework of interaction for urban communities, urban transport planning has been seen and applied as an engineering exercise to design a physical transport system. Indeed Wingo and Perloff state quite categorically that 'the choice of a transportation system is the core developmental decision that the metropolitan region can make . . .'[40] and it is surprising that, with notable exceptions, planners have made little attempt to use this tool to shape the physical urban environment.

Perhaps the root of the problem lies in the definition generally implied or adopted for a transportation system. For example, the definition of a transport system adopted by the Washington transportation plan is typical: 'a set of facilities for the movement of goods and people, including highways, parking facilities and public transit'.[41] This may be an acceptable definition for a physical system, but the transport system of any urban area is something more than a physical system. Its performance can have far reaching consequences for all individuals, businesses and other bodies relying on it. These consequences can be both long and short-term. In the short term they influence the origin and destination, the time, the mode and route, of all trips made. In the long term they can result in a change of location of activities in order to adjust to the transport system. In the transport studies completed to date, changes in the location of activities (and ultimately land-uses) in respect to the implementation of transport system proposals are not considered as part of the process. The reasons for this are:

1. That the physical transport system is designed to 'fit' a pre-determined land-use plan, and
2. it is argued that little can be done in twenty years (the normal target period for transport studies) to change current trends and commitments in the distribution of activities.

This state of affairs leads to the anomalous situation of recommending long-term proposals based on an analysis of the short-run transport behaviours of the users of the system, and inevitably policy is implemented on a project by project basis.

Such an approach, although often self-correcting, is wasteful. Specific problems may be rectified as they arise, but the long-term consequences for the locational behaviours of businesses, individuals, and hence the structure of urban areas, are haphazard and unpredictable.

Arising from this narrow outlook other 'lower-level' conceptual deficiencies can be identified. For many years the complex nature of the transport planning process, and the difficulties involved in applying the methodology were underestimated. This tended to lead to the operational deficiencies already identified, and the production of plans and proposals which were over-simple. For example, plans were produced for an 'end-state' situation some twenty years in the future, with no real attempt to assess how the area was likely to evolve during the plan period or after the target date was reached. At the same time, the narrow conceptual basis led practitioners to think of plans and proposals in terms of a physical plan form—social and economic activities were seen in terms of physical land-use systems, whilst the transport systems were seen solely in physical terms as, for example, highway networks/systems. Although this makes it relatively easy for alternative proposals to maintain a consistent approach, it can be argued that a reliance on the physical plan form inhibits a full exploration of the wide range of policies that one might expect in a set of alternative plans.

New Approaches to the Transport Planning Process

In an attempt to off-set the many deficiencies associated with the traditional traffic functional approach to transport planning, a variety of alternative approaches have been put forward. The most significant of these new approaches are the systems approach and the cyclic approach.

The systems approach towards urban planning evolved from the work of engineers and planners involved in the early transportation studies, such as the Chicago and Detroit studies, and from the work of Mitchell and Rapkin[42]. In the view of these men, the city was seen as a set of interconnected parts—a system of component parts (land-uses) connected by different forms of communication, especially road traffic. As we have seen, a series of transportation plans was produced, based on the view that if the land-use pattern of a town or city could be defined for some future date then the associated traffic pattern could also be determined and a suitable transport system designed to fit it.

In the early sixties objections were raised to this view. People like

Wingo and Perloff argued that the city should be seen as a system which evolves, where land-uses and traffic flows are interdependent. Thus, they contend, it is not realistic to define land-use distribution for some period of time twenty years into the future and derive a traffic pattern for it, for this approach fails to recognise that traffic flows alter in response to changing land-use patterns and vice versa.

In an attempt to overcome the preoccupation with physical form, Wingo and Perloff claimed that a transport system should be seen as 'a set of facilities and institutions organised to distribute a quality of access selectively in an urban area';[43] that the 'location behaviour of businesses and individuals are affected by the implementation of transport proposals', and that 'these induced locational changes affect the performance of the transport system in the long run'. Indeed they are of the opinion that 'the accumulation of these consequences is in fact the shape and structure of the metropolitan region a generation or more hence'.[44]

In an attempt to utilise the systems approach and to encourage the use of transport as a 'structure-forming' tool, Wingo and Perloff argue that:

1. Transport facilities fulfil a 'market role' in determining the amount of land that is available for development at different levels of accessibility.

2. A transport system should not be chosen exclusively on its ability to meet travel demand, as the side-effects from this sort of choice may be so overwhelmingly negative in the field of public services, that the short-run benefits on which the choice was based are cancelled out. At the same time the locational consequences of businesses and individuals may accumulate in such a way as to impair the performance of the transport system as a whole.

3. The design of a transport system should be achieved by a process of successively constrained choices. The first constrained choice—the setting of long-run developmental objectives for the region—being the most critical, and concerned with policies to influence the productivity of the region, the form and organisation of the region and consumer satisfaction relating to living and working conditions.

Figure 5, taken from Bieber[45] illustrates the systems approach in abstract. Wingo and Perloff indicate that this approach can be made

operational in the transport planning field by applying the following
sequence of constrained choices.

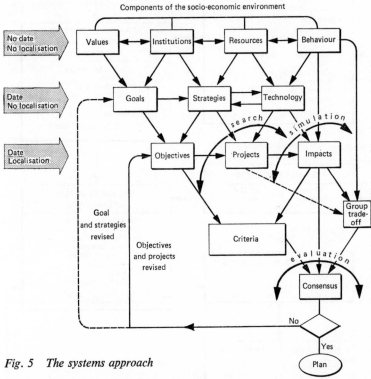

Fig. 5   The systems approach

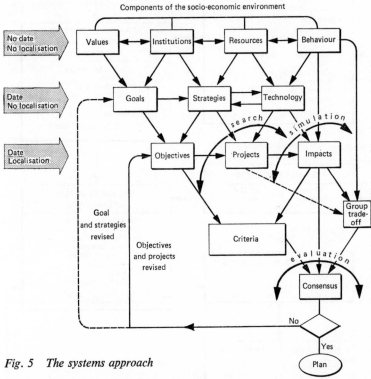

SOURCE Bieber A., Transportation planning and systems analysis, in Urban
Transport Planning Process, O.E.C.D. Paris 1971.

1. Specify the long-run developmental objectives for the region
e.g. make town *X* the regional capital, with a strong central area and
avoid low-density peripheral areas.

2. Identify the location and investment decisions which cumula-
tively move in the direction of the first level objectives e.g. to achieve
long-run developmental objectives in housing, investment would have
to be diverted from peripheral areas into the existing built-up area.

3. Specify the levels of accessibility needed to induce the locational
and investment changes required to achieve the long-run developmental objectives, e.g. ensure poor accessibility to the peripheral
areas, and good accessibility within the built-up area.

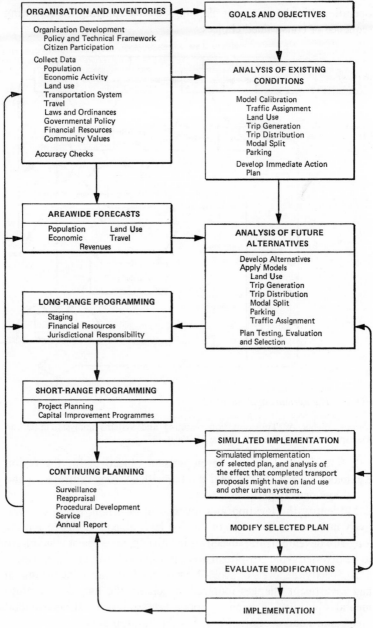

Fig. 6   Transport planning process incorporating the systems approach

4. Designate the levels of service implied by the accessibility conditions e.g. high-speed public transport within built-up area, with low-speed motor-vehicle access on dual-purpose streets from peripheral areas.

It can be seen that this approach is characterised by the desire to identify and define the objectives of the overall urban system, including the transport system. At the same time a rational evaluation and decision making procedure is essential to assist the assessment of whether the original objectives are met. This procedure is based on the use of criteria and standards which are related to the original objectives.

Figure 6, which extends the Bureau of Public Roads flow chart for the traditional transport planning process, illustrates how this approach might be implemented.

The advantages associated with the use of the systems approach are that it allows the implementation of transport proposals to be used positively as a determinant of urban form. It can be applied to assess the impact of transport proposals on both the short-term movement habits and the long-term locational behaviour of firms and individuals. At the same time it enables modifications to be made to the preferred urban structure in the light of the impact of the implementation of transport proposals. In short, it distinguishes between 'urban transport planning as an engineering exercise, on the one hand, and as the design of a framework for the interaction for a viable urban community on the other.'[46]

There are two major drawbacks with the approach. It is very difficult to develop true alternative structures and policies if the starting point of the exercise is one set of common objectives, whilst the complex inter-relationships involved in its application could well be self-defeating unless handled by experienced professionals.

The cyclic approach put forward by Boyce, Day and McDonald is concerned primarily with the development of true alternative sets of plans or policies. They argue that a revision is required of the traditional and basically linear progression from a common set of objectives to alternative sets of plans and policies to evaluation and selection. In substitution they propose that a cyclic planning process be adopted, with each cycle commencing with the formulation (or re-formulation) of design criteria, standards and proposed policies for each alternative to be tested. At the end of each cycle conclusions are drawn and decisions made in order to determine which aspects of the alternatives should be considered further, and only in exceptional circumstances is an alternative carried forward intact from one cycle to the next. Figure 7 illustrates the broad procedure, and at least three to four cycles are required to produce an effective final plan. As the cycles advance, so the plan-production and evaluation

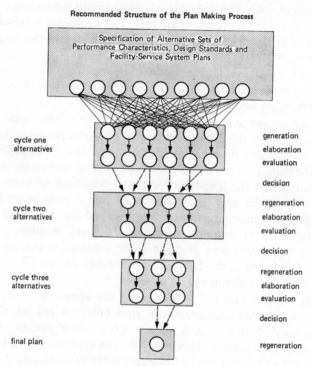

Recommended Structure of the Plan Making Process

Fig. 7   The cyclic approach to plan-making.

SOURCE Boyce, Day, & McDonald, Metropolitan Plan Making 1970

methodologies should develop. For example, in the early cycles broad tentative patterns of development are suitable with some *ad hoc* elaboration, whilst later cycles utilise allocation and simulation models.

200

The alternative plans considered should not be restricted to comprehensive, physical, end-state, twenty-year plans. Rather the whole range of alternatives should be explored, including 'both near and far time horizons, metropolitan and sub-metropolitan configurations, comprehensive and individual facility-service system schemes, as well as divergent assumption and staging'.[47]

Land use and transportation alternatives should be explored at the metropolitan scale only if there are proposals for major shifts in the relative location of population and employment groups, or if over a long term period (thirty-five to fifty years) there is a large increment of growth. This type of alternative should be prepared in a broad, generalised way. Other, more detailed alternatives need to be produced for the specific facility-service systems and for representative sub-metropolitan areas.

This approach has the advantage of ensuring that different goals and objectives can be derived for each alternative (in contrast to the traditional and systems approaches which rely on the formulation of one set of common goals). This in turn makes it easier to develop plans and policies which are true alternatives. The problems associated with operationalising this approach are severe, although it would seem that the systems approach could be incorporated as part of this cyclic approach.

Conclusions

To date, transport planning has been applied mainly in an attempt to solve the traffic functional elements of the transport problem—to eliminate bottlenecks, reduce delay and accidents, and improve accessibility. In practice, little conscious effort has been made to utilise this comparatively sophisticated process to help shape and guide the development of urban areas, despite the fact that the planning and implementation of transport proposals is probably the most powerful tool possessed by the land-use planner to influence change in the urban environment.

The failure on the part of the land-use planner to realise the full potential of transport planning almost certainly stems from the fact that transport planning developed largely in isolation from land-use planning. It was seen by many engineers as being a matter of research and design, prior to the physical construction of highway and

201

(rarely) other forms of transport network. Although the relationship between movement and land-use was recognised as fundamental to the process, land-use was seen merely as an 'input' control. That is, land-use data was used as an 'input' to the process as a means of obtaining an 'output' in the form of person movements and, ultimately, a design for a physical transport system. With the development of the 'systems approach' this conceptual weakness was recognised and efforts are now being made to secure the use of transport planning as an aid in the development of urban structure. However, it is doubtful whether the full potential of transport as 'the most effective single form-determining element in the man-made environment'[48] will be realised until such time as:

1. Transport planning is accepted as being an integral part of the land-use planning process and

2. land-use planners are fully conversant with the technicalities of the traffic estimation procedures and transport system design.

References

1 T. R. Stone, *Beyond the Automobile* (Prentice Hall, New Jersey, 1971).

2 J. A. Proudlove, 'Some comments on the West Midlands transport study', *Traffic Engineering and Control* (1968).

3 C. D. Buchanan, *Traffic in Towns* (HMSO, 1963).

4 R. L. Creighton, *Urban Transportation Planning* (University of Illinois Press, Chicago, 1970).

5 R. A. Gakenheimer, 'Urban Transportation: an Overview', from *Taming Megalopolis*, ed H. Wentworth Eldridge (Doubleday, NY, 1967).

6 From *Motorway Progress*, as at 31 October 1970 (British Road Federation, 1970).

7 J. M. Thomson, *Motorways in London* (Duckworth, 1969).

8 McCone, *Violence in the City: an End or a Beginning?* Report of the Governor's Commission on the Los Angeles riots (Los Angeles, 1966).

9 *Basic Road Statistics, 1972* (British Road Federation, 1972).

10 C. D. Buchanan, *op. cit.*

11 Committee on the Problem of Noise; Noise—Final report, Cmnd 2056 (HMSO, 1963).

12 R. Mitchell and C. Rapkin, *Urban Traffic—a Function of Land Use* (Columbia University Press, 1954).

13 R. L. Creighton, *op. cit.*

14 *Chicago Area Transportation Study. Final Report, vol. 1*, State of Illinois, County of Cook and City of Chicago (December 1959).

15 *London Traffic Survey, vol. 1* (The London County Council, 1964).

16 *SELNEC: A Highway Plan 1962*, prepared by the South-East Lancashire and North-East Cheshire Highway Engineering Committee (1962).

17 *London Traffic Survey* (The London County Council, 1964).

18 Ministry of Transport and Ministry of Housing and Local Government, circular 1/64, Buchanan report on traffic in towns (HMSO, 1964).

19 Freeman, Fox, Wilbur Smith and Assoc., *The West Midlands Transport Study* (1968).

20 R. Travers Morgan and Ptrs., *Travel in Belfast* (Belfast Corporation, 1968).

21 T. R. Davinroy, T. M. Ridley and H. J. Wootton, Predicting Future Travel, *Traffic Engineering and Control* (1963).

22 Melvin C. Branch, *The Corporate Planning Process* (American Management Assoc., NY, 1962).

23 W. Solesbury, and A. Townsend, 'Transportation Studies and British Planning Practice', *Town Planning Review* (1970).

24 For a full account of traffic estimation procedures see M. J. Bruton, *Introduction to Transportation Planning* (Hutchinson, 1970).

25 R. J. Whittle, Route Location in Oxford, *Journal of Instn. of Municipal Engineers* (1969).

26 Buchanan and Ptrs., *Traffic in Guildford* (1965).

27 *Chicago Area Transportation Study. Final Report, vol. 1* (1959).

28 *Modal Split* (Urban Planning Division, U.S. Dept. of Commerce, Bureau of Public Roads, Washington, 1966).

29 C. D. Buchanan, *op. cit.*

30 Buchanan and Ptrs., *Traffic in Canterbury* (1970).

31 D. W. F. Barrell, 'Cost-Benefit Analysis in Transportation Planning', *Oxford Working Papers in Planning Education and Research*, no. 10 (1972).

32 Solesbury and Townsend, *op. cit.*

33 *ibid.*

34 Bureau of Public Roads, *Urban Transportation Planning: General Information and Introduction to System 360* (Washington, June 1970).

35 D. Boyce, N. Day and C. McDonald, *Metropolitan Plan Making*, Regional Science Research Monograph 4 (Philadelphia, 1970).

36 *ibid.*

37 Ministries of Transport and Housing and Local Government, circular 1/64 (HMSO, 1964).

38 Highway Act 1962.
39 *The Urban Transport Planning Process*, Consultative Group on Transport Research (OECD, Paris, 1971). Available through HMSO.
40 L. Wingo and H. Perloff, 'The Washington Transportation Plan: Technics or Politics?' *Papers and Proceedings of the Regional Science Assoc.* (1961).
41 *ibid.*
42 Mitchell and Rapkin, *op. cit.*
43 Wingo and Perloff, *op. cit.*
44 *ibid.*
45 A. Bieber, 'Transportation Planning and Systems Analysis' in *The Urban Transport Planning Process* (OECD, Paris, 1971).
46 Wingo and Perloff, *op. cit.*
47 Boyce, Day and McDonald, *op. cit.*
48 Stone, *op. cit.*

8. Corporate Planning

John D. Stewart

Introduction

Corporate planning in local government determines the activities of a local authority in relation to the needs and problems of its area and of those who live and work within it. It is concerned with all the activities of the local authority, whether they involve physical development or social action, whether they involve capital or revenue expenditure, and whether they involve resources of land, personnel or finance.

Corporate planning has developed in local government as a response to problems identified in the management of local government and as a response to a set of ideas on how those problems should be met. It has developed in different ways in different authorities, as they have sought to apply those ideas to their own problems.

Corporate planning is difficult to describe. It cannot be described in the same way as some of the other forms of planning described in this book. There is no universal practice of corporate planning in local government. There is no statute requiring an authority to adopt corporate planning. There are many authorities where it has not yet been developed. There are neither clear procedures for corporate planning, nor is there any profession from which would-be corporate planners will be drawn. For all these reasons corporate planning cannot be described with the same degree of definition as many of the other forms of planning described in this book. It must be described in terms of its ideas and defined in terms of its characteristics, rather than in terms of its procedures.

To understand these ideas and these characteristics, one must understand the traditional view of management in local government to which the ideas of corporate planning are juxtaposed. The traditional viewpoint regards the local authority as a collection of separate services brought together more by historical accident or for administrative convenience rather than for anything they have in common. The prime task of the authority is to provide those services rather than to meet changing problems and needs. Because these services are provided by one organisation—the local authority—there is a certain minimum of co-ordination at the centre of the organisation, but it is co-ordination of the administration of the authority, rather than integration of its policies.

In the period between 1950 and 1967 this viewpoint on management in local government came under increasing attack, but it was an attack that challenged the traditional viewpoint from the standpoint of managerial efficiency. The assumption of this viewpoint was that because the services provided by the local authority were provided by the same organisation, there were economies to be achieved if only the local authority would organise itself so as to achieve them. This was the period of emphasis upon management services—and in particular upon organisation and methods and work study. These management techniques were seen as weapons in the armoury of the town clerk as chief executive officer in a fight against administrative inefficiency. This movement, although important, did not, however, challenge the traditional assumptions of management in local government—that a local authority was no more than a collection of separate services, brought together for convenience in one organisation and that a local authority exists to administer services, rather than to meet changing needs.

The Problems Faced by Corporate Planning

In the period from 1965 onwards these assumptions came under increasing challenge from the movement towards corporate planning. This movement arose because of growing problems in the management of local authorities.

The period up until 1965 followed a period of rapid growth in expenditure on local authority services. From this period on, the growth in local authority expenditure came under increasing scrutiny both nationally and locally. This was due in part to the prolonged period of national economic difficulty and in part also to an increasing recognition that local authority expenditure could not continue to grow indefinitely at a rate higher than the growth of expenditure generally. This implied hard choices for the local authority. Existing systems of resource allocation were not geared to the choices that had to be made. Dissatisfaction with existing systems of resource management was part of the driving force to corporate planning.

Town and country planning was also subject to pressure. There was growing dissatisfaction with the procedures of land-use planning as they had developed under the 1947 Act. This dissatisfaction drew strength from a feeling that many of the hopes that had surrounded that Act had not been realised. It centred upon the inflexibility of the system and, perhaps of critical importance to this chapter, its narrowness. Land-use planning cannot by itself resolve many problems. There was a growing awareness of the need for town and country planning to give recognition to social, economic and financial planning. The need for wider and more flexible forms of planning was recognised and was, to some extent, given expression in the 1968 Town and Country Planning Act. Dissatisfaction with existing systems of town and country planning was part of the driving force to corporate planning.

The problems of the cities came to loom large in the 1960s, highlighted perhaps in the first instance by public attitudes to immigration. This new perception of general urban problems was accompanied by growing disillusion with previous solutions to particular problems. This mood can perhaps be symbolised by two illustrations —the first a rejection of the early pattern of high-rise development as a solution to urban housing problems—the second a rejection of the urban motorway as a solution to urban transportation problems. In the complexity of urban life, solutions that appeared to solve one problem merely created others. The need for a new approach to the problems of urban management which could take better account of the complex interactions of city life became recognised—even though the exact nature of that approach was not readily identified. Renewed awareness of urban problems and of their complexity was part of the driving force to corporate planning.

This dissatisfaction was paralleled by dissatisfaction with traditional management styles in particular services. Certain local authority services were subject to major review and to major change. The main, although not the only example, was the social services. In other services a search for new approaches became stronger as pressure on resources became greater. The old reliance on greater expenditure as the solution to all problems became subject to challenge and the search for new alternatives grew. The capacity for that search was not always present. Dissatisfaction with prevailing styles of management in the local authority services was part of the driving force to corporate planning.

The period 1966 to 1972 was a period of exceptional political change in the composition of councils. In many borough councils large numbers of new members were brought on to the councils. In some councils powers changed for the first time since the war. These changes brought on to the councils, or into positions of power, councillors who were less attached to traditional systems of management and more inclined to challenge them. They had not been socialised into the system. The challenge of the councillor to the existing system was part of the driving force to corporate planning.

The importance of understanding the complex of factors influencing these developments is that it explains why the movement towards corporate planning cannot be described in simple terms. It cannot be described merely in financial terms. It cannot be described merely in management terms. It explains the difficulty of describing corporate planning in terms that will fit developments in corporate planning in all parts of the country. It was a movement that grew out of dissatisfaction. It was a challenge to traditional systems of management—but the particular combination of factors varied from authority to authority.

The Development of Corporate Planning

Corporate planning arose because of these problems, but it is more than a response to these problems. It is the application to these problems of a set of ideas.

Some of these ideas were first given expression in the report of the Maud Committee on management in local government published in 1967. This report was important. It stressed that:

In the wider context individual services, however disparate are provided for the community as a whole.[1]

It emphasised therefore, the corporate identity of the authority. It stressed too that the local authority had a task beyond the mere administration of services:

A local authority, in addition to providing a wide range of public services on a scale and to standards prescribed by Parliament or a Minister, must necessarily study the present physical and social environment of the area it serves, and assess its future needs and developments. In the light of this it must come to conclusions on what the objectives are to be and the means to be adopted to attain them. The problems cannot be taken in isolation; the objectives have to be reconciled with one another. Key decisions have to be taken on the means and plans to attain these objectives.[2]

These extracts and other passages in the report contain the essence of the ideas that were later to be given expression in the movement towards corporate planning. But the parts of the report which contained these ideas were curiously neglected by many of the authorities that studied the report. The report stood between two movements, the movement towards administrative efficiency and the movement towards corporate planning. It expressed something of the ideas underlying each. But precisely because it marked a turning point, the older ideas were recognised and the newer ideas were ignored. In fairness to local government the new ideas were not adequately described. The report talks of the need for a local authority 'to set objectives' or to set up 'effective control systems' but at no point describes what might be involved. With no easy reference point for these concepts, local authorities turned to the ideas with which they were familiar. The Maud Report was seen as a report about management structure and as such it had a deep impact on local government, although its main recommendation of a management board to take over the executive responsibilities of all other committees was rejected by most authorities. It led to a general reconsideration of management structure. Although the management board idea was rejected, policy committees were set up by the majority of the larger authorities to provide some degree of unity of direction to the authority. There was a radical reduction in the number of committees and to some extent in the number of departments. But many of these recommendations could be seen only as expressions of the movement to administrative efficiency. Even the policy committees which might aspire to a government role proved in many cases ineffective— indeed almost lacking a role.

The response to Maud was, however, the only response local government was equipped to give. It was a response in terms of management structure, i.e. the organisational framework set up to carry out the management task—rather than in terms of management process, that is, the task itself and the way it is carried out. The fundamental challenge of corporate planning is however to the management processes in local government and to the concept of the local authorities' task that underlies them. It is a challenge to a viewpoint on management in local government that sees it as the administration of a series of separate services. That challenge was not expressed in the immediate reactions to the Maud Report.

However, ideas about new approaches to policy-making developed during the period after the publication of the Maud Report in 1967. Between 1967 and 1972 there was growing discussion of the ideas of corporate planning. Some of these ideas were developed within local government. Others were introduced by management consultants. They were drawn from a variety of sources.

Ideas about new approaches to policy-making were not restricted to local government and not restricted to this country. The movement towards corporate planning in British local government has been paralleled by the impact of systems thinking upon large-scale organisation in many countries. In Britain the movement towards corporate planning in local government has been parallelled by a process in central government which started with the Plowden Report on public expenditure and has been developed in new systems of PESC (public expenditure survey committee) and PAR (programme analysis review) and in the work of CPRS (central policy review staff). This climate of ideas has influenced the approach to management in British local government.

By 1972 the degree of acceptance of corporate planning was marked by the Bains Report on management structures and processes for the new authorities. This report was based upon corporate planning and drew heavily upon the experience of the authorities which had been introducing systems of corporate planning over the previous years. It was, like the Maud Report, stronger on structure than process, but by this time there was more experience for local authorities to draw upon. The references to the need 'to set objectives' and 'to monitor performance' were now more readily understood.

The Ideas Underlying Corporate Planning

Corporate planning as it has developed in British local government can be regarded as a combination of two sets of ideas:

1. A model of policy-making applicable to a variety of organisations based on a national model of decision.

This can be described in the following terms:

(a) The organisation identifies certain needs, present and foreseen, in its environment.

(b) It sets goals and objectives in relation to those needs, i.e. the extent to which it will plan to meet those needs.

(c) It considers alternative ways of achieving those objectives.

(d) It evaluates those alternatives in terms of their use of resources and of their effects.

(e) Sets of decisions and individual decisions are made in the light of that evaluation.

(f) Those decisions are translated into managerial action.

(g) The result of the action taken is monitored and fed back to modify the continuing process; by altering the perception of needs, the objectives set, the alternatives considered, the evaluation, the decision made or the action taken.

Such a model in one form or another underlies most attempts to improve decision-making or policy-making, not merely in local government, but elsewhere. It underlies many approaches to management problems and management techniques.

2. A concept of the governmental role of the local authority. This is best expressed in the report of the Bains group on management structure and processes in the new authorities.

Local government is not, in our view, limited to the narrow provision of a series of services to the local community, though we do not intend in any way to suggest that these services are not important. It has within its purview the overall economic, cultural and physical well-being of that community and for this reason its decisions impinge with increasing frequency upon the individual life of its citizens. Because of this overall responsibility and because of the inter-relationship of problems in the environment within which it is set, the traditional departmental attitude within much of local government must give way to a wider-ranging corporate outlook.[3]

Corporate planning in local government expresses the combined impact of these sets of ideas on the management problems which have been its driving force.

Characteristics of Corporate Planning

Because corporate planning was the application of a set of ideas to a set of problems, it is best described by a set of characteristics, rather than in terms of procedures. These are the characteristics emphasised by corporate planning as opposed to traditional systems of management.

Planning rather than administration

The departments of the local authority centre upon the administration of a service. The day-to-day business of running the service can drive out consideration of whether the service is still required or whether it is required in the present form. It becomes only too easy for the provision of the service to become an end in itself. A libraries department is set up to provide libraries. A parks department is set up to provide parks.

An emphasis upon planning as opposed to administration is an emphasis upon the need to review the activities carried out by the various services in relation to changing needs and problems. Leisure and recreation needs are changing. Those needs are not necessarily met by the existing pattern of services provided by the local authority. The needs of young people are changing. Those needs are not necessarily met by the existing patterns of the youth service in local authorities. An organisation centring upon running services lacks the capacity to learn and to adapt to what it has learnt. It needs to identify changing needs and problems and the impact of its activities upon those problems. It needs to review those activities in the light of changes identified and changes anticipated. It needs to emphasise planning. Some of the implications of that emphasis are explored in the following characteristics.

Effectiveness rather than efficiency

Until recently movements towards management change in local government emphasised the need for increased efficiency. Local authorities have built up management services, but these have been based upon organisation and methods and work study. Each makes its main contribution to improving the efficiency with which the local authority carries out its task.

Efficiency is of importance to a local authority, but efficiency is of secondary importance to effectiveness in dealing with problems. The value of carrying out a policy efficiently is limited if that policy is not effective. There is no value in efficiently carrying out the wrong policy. Yet local authorities have not laid the same emphasis upon those techniques and approaches that will assist effectiveness rather than on those that assess efficiency. Local authorities have lacked data on the needs to be met by the services provided. There has been a tendency to measure the achievement of a service by the number of buildings provided or staff employed rather than by their impact. The provision of a health centre does not measure effectiveness. To measure effectiveness, one has to understand the impact of the health centre on both attendance and the quality of health care. Data is required by management that goes far beyond that which a management services unit is equipped to provide. An emphasis upon effectiveness should precede an emphasis upon efficiency.

Environmental understanding rather than organisational knowledge

Local authorities have long lacked adequate data on many problems in the environment. They have understood the environment only by reference to what lies inside their organisation. Many local authorities have lacked adequate data on housing needs and the extent of social needs. They have measured the extent of housing needs by the data held within the organisation—the waiting list rather than by surveys of actual needs. Recent surveys on the chronically sick and disabled have shown the inadequacy of existing data within the organisation. Corporate planning implies an emphasis on needs and problems in the environment.

Explicit rather than implicit policy

Local authority decision-making has traditionally centred upon the particular—a particular item in a capital programme or a particular item in an agenda. Presumably, underlying the particular item there is a policy. There is a reason why a particular department proposes one project rather than another—but it is not stated in the capital programme. It is left implicit.

A policy unstated is likely to be a policy unchallenged, and a policy unchallenged is likely to be a policy unchanged. The simple step of making the policies of an authority explicit is itself a dynamic step—even if it merely exposes the inadequacy of those policies. A move from implicit policy toward explicit policy is a decisive step in corporate planning.

Systematic policy review rather than ad hoc policy review

Of course not all local authority activities are simply continued. Of course policies are determined and policies are reviewed. But it is *ad hoc* policy-making started by a particular stimulus. It may be a government circular, a paper at a professional conference or a crisis in a service.

But there are many areas of activity in the authority where no policy review is initiated. In many local authorities there has never been a fundamental review of the leisure and recreation services, precisely because there is no stimulus. There is a need for a regular process of policy review which will, in time, encompass all the activities of the authority.

Corporate rather than separate

The characteristics outlined above relate to the need for an emphasis upon planning as opposed to the mere administration of the activities of the local authority. Those characteristics might be emphasised for each of the separate services of the local authority, but corporate planning also emphasises the corporate nature of an authority as opposed to one which consists of separate services. The case can be made out in terms of resources, but it can also be made out in terms of the task to be carried out.

Resources

The local authority deploys many resources. There are the physical resources of land, building and equipment. There is the resource of information. There are the precious resources of ideas, skills and knowledge held by those who work within the organisation.

There has been a tendency for resources to be treated as belonging to a department rather than to the authority. Property has been treated as belonging to a department. Different departments have held stocks of land for their own needs. Information has not always passed easily from one department to another. Perhaps more seriously, the resources possessed by the personnel of the local

authority have been restricted within departments. The departments in which the skills of the local authority have been placed have
become barriers to their wider use, rather than an effective base for
their use.

The management task

The fundamental issue is however the management task. The
management task of the local authority has been seen, as has already
been emphasised, as the provision of a series of separate services.
That view has been subject to attack, as awareness has grown of the
extent of the interaction between the activities of the local authorities, and even more the inter-relationship between the problems at
which those activities are directed.

A series of major government reports have plotted some of these
inter-relationships. The Buchanan Report emphasised the impact of
transportation on the living environment.[4] The Plowden Report
showed that the problem of educational deprivation could not be
separated from many other problems in the physical and social
environment to which the children were subject.[5] The Seebohm
Report argued that social problems were not separate problems but
were closely linked to many other problems.[6]

From these inter-relationships has grown a conception of a wider
management task, in which the local authority is regarded (in the
words of the Royal Commission on local government in England)[7]
as 'having an all-round responsibility for the safety, health and well-
being, both material and cultural, of people in different localities in
so far as these objectives can be achieved by local action and local
initiative, with a framework of national policies'. This leads to a
definition of the management task of the local authority not in
terms of the separate services but in terms of these wider responsibilities. Given this definition of the management task the various
services remain important, but as the means through which this
wider task (which can best be described as community or environmental management) is carried out. It is this central conception of
the management task of the local authority that gives corporate
planning its most distinctive characteristic.

Corporate planning is the combination of this wider management
task of the local authority, with an emphasis upon planning as

opposed to administration. The heightened need for planning arises because the task requires a general review of needs and problems of the area governed by the local authority.

Forms of Corporate Planning

This chapter has set out ideas or described characteristics. In an organisation for ideas to be effective and characteristics to be real, they have to be translated into procedures and supported by an appropriate organisational structure. In recent years different local authorities have approached the development of corporate planning in different ways. Different procedures have been built up. But these procedures have shared two features in common. They have attempted to build processes for the authority as a whole, rather than for particular departments. They have built up processes, which to a greater or lesser extent can be described as being based upon the model of the planning process set out above. They have expressed the ideas of corporate planning.

The main forms taken by the early developments in British local government followed PPBS (planning—programming—budgeting systems). PPBS can be described as a set of ideas or as a set of procedures. As a set of ideas, PPBS draws upon the same framework of ideas as those which gave rise to the characteristics of corporate planning. For the purpose of this chapter, corporate planning has been taken to represent the set of characteristics and the framework of ideas supporting those characteristics, while PPBS is a set of procedures to introduce those ideas.

PPBS was developed as a set of procedures in the federal government of the US and in both state and local government there. Early developments in British local government were influenced by these developments in America. They took place before the major re-appraisal of PPBS that has since taken place there.

PPBS in the form in which it was introduced was characterised by four main elements:

A programme structure which classifies the activities of the authority according to the objectives that they are designed to achieve. It requires therefore a statement of the objectives of the authority and a structuring of the activities of the authority in relation to those

216

objectives. In most authorities the activities were grouped under six to eight main objectives. Thus in Islington, activities were grouped under seven main objective heads:

> planning and development
> housing
> social services
> health, safety and protection
> leisure
> transportation
> general services

A programme plan which sets out the planned expenditure of the authority. It normally covers a three to five year period. It categorises expenditure not in terms of the traditional budgetary structure but in terms of the objectives of the authority as set out in the programme structure. It includes both capital and revenue expenditure. It also includes possible statements of the likely output from the expenditure.

A programme analysis which provides a systematic examination of current and proposed programmes of an authority and of alternatives to those programmes. It can take many forms. An exercise in cost benefit analysis could well be an example of programme analysis, but so could less sophisticated approaches. Programme analysis might involve an examination of a problem and of the contribution of existing programmes to that problem, the generation of alternative ways of meeting that problem, the assessment of the likely effect of those alternatives and the evaluation of those effects. Programme analysis in this sense can be and is undertaken over and apart from a PPBS system. The PPBS system provides a framework for identifying areas for analysis.

A programme review which is the procedure by which the results of programme analysis are fed into the policy-making system. It involves periodic review of activities within a given programme area (that set of activities contributing to a major objective of the authority constitutes a programme area), identifying major changes in the problems faced in that programme area, selecting issues for further programme analysis, applying the results of past analysis and setting out proposals for programme change.

A number of local authorities, including the Greater London Council, Islington, Greenwich and Liverpool, have carried out work on the development of PPBS systems. While these developments have met some of the aims of corporate planning, there are problems which suggest that PPBS, in the form which it has generally taken in this country, may not be entirely adequate to establish the ideas of corporate planning throughout local government. Four main sets of problems can be identified:

1. PPBS in the form in which it has developed in this country has the appearance of being an instrument of financial management. Yet as suggested above, the driving force for corporate planning came from many sources. PPBS, if it is merely to be an improved method of allocating financial resources, is not sufficiently comprehensive in its scope to support the ideas of corporate planning. The problem became critical because of the development of structure planning. In many authorities it almost seemed as though corporate planning (in the form of PPBS) and structure planning were developing as two separate forms of planning in the local authority. But this merely creates a new separatism in the policy planning of the authority.

2. In most applications of PPBS the basic starting point has been the programme structure. This has placed the main emphasis upon objectives. Yet it can be argued that this has obscured the need for authorities to build up their understanding of their environment. Few of the new PPBS systems are backed by any significant development in environmental analysis. Without that analysis, objectives can be merely abstractions or the reflection of past practice, rather than the setting of the authority's aims in relation to changing needs and problems.

3. In some authorities the programme structure became the framework for a new form of separatism, a separatism no less critical because it was a separatism based upon programme areas, i.e. sets of activities leading to the same objective. The ideas behind corporate planning stressed the interaction between the activities of the authority and those interactions included interaction between activities in different programme areas—between for example,

activities with the education and social welfare programme areas. Within a programme structure the corporate task of the authority could too easily be divided away into separate categories—different from the traditional categories, but still fundamentally separate.

4. To many authorities, PPBS did not seem to provide an appropriate line of development. It appeared to require a degree of commitment to a particular form of corporate planning when many local authorities were merely at the stage of exploration. They wanted break-in points to corporate planning rather than the immediate establishment of a comprehensive system. They wished, through a gradual approach, to develop processes adapted to their own perception of their needs—a perception that might change as they learnt through the development of the new approach.

For all these reasons new approaches developed which were in part based upon PPBS, but nevertheless represented modifications upon it. One authority has developed a distinctive approach to the relationship between the process of corporate planning and other processes of planning within the authority. Coventry has sought to build a central planning process from which the various plans produced by the authority will be derived and into which the input required for those plans will be fed. The key document is the local policy plan, which is described as:[8]

A comprehensive plan reviewed annually by the Council which sets out their policies over all those matters which are within the Council's control or which it can influence. It is not a plan defined by the requirements of statute and its contents are a matter for the Council to determine. Basically it should define the Council's policies for the whole of the City, state in broad terms how the Council seeks to achieve their objectives, and its priorities for doing so, and it must have regard not simply for what the Council wishes to do, but also for its ability, as restricted by the resources available to it, to carry out its plans.

Other authorities are developing different approaches. Few of these have developed total corporate planning systems. They represent attempts by these authorities to find break-in points to the development of new processes. They are all examples of gradual approaches, which will be modified and developed as experience is gained.

A number of local authorities have set up research and intelligence units for the authority in an attempt to improve the background environmental analysis on which any developed system of corporate planning must draw.

One authority—Stockport—saw the break-in point as the preparation of a position statement.[9]

In Stockport we have attempted to gather together in one series of documents a statement of the Council's present policies and the range of services provided. We have tried to link these with the clientele which those policies and services are intended to serve, and the needs and problems which they are to gratify. Wherever possible the statement has attempted to quantify not only the input (including finance and manpower) but also the output of those policies and services, i.e. what the Council expects to get for their investment. At the same time an attempt has been made to assess the likely future development of the service concerned.

The document is described as a position statement rather than a plan because it is meant to represent 'the position in which the Council finds itself in 1972'. This may not seem by itself an important step, but it makes policy explicit and that may well be the first step towards policy review.

Grimsby has pursued the approach of identifying certain selected areas of the authority's activities for analysis in depth—for example the needs of the aged or long-term housing policy. This may provide the basis for systematic policy review, developed and extended to other areas of the council's activities.

These are limited, but important steps—each taken without a necessary commitment to a particular form of corporate planning. The next step will be learnt from the steps already taken, as the authorities which introduced PPBS are themselves learning. The forms of corporate planning are changing as better methodologies are sought to give expression to the ideas and characteristics of corporate planning.

Organisational Structure for Corporate Planning

As the ideas of corporate planning have to be given form in new processes of management, so those new processes have to be given protection within the organisational structure.

A common approach to certain elements of organisational structure has been adopted by most of those authorities moving towards corporate planning. They have recognised that corporate planning requires support at member level and this has been secured through a central policy committee, charged with a major responsibility for the process of corporate planning. At chief officer level, the policy committee has been parallelled by a management team of chief officers led by a chief executive officer. This management team is based upon the principle of corporate responsibility, which means that a chief officer, while accepting a special responsibility for the department of which he is head, also has a responsibility for the affairs of the authority as a whole.

But corporate planning, if it is to develop, requires further support. In most of the authorities which have developed corporate planning, there is a unit with special responsibility for corporate planning. Such units are normally small, since it is dangerous if such units are built up to such a size as would mean that they would themselves undertake most of the corporate planning work. Unless much of the work is undertaken in the departments, corporate planning will be limited in its approach and isolated from those who have the responsibility for implementing the results of such planning. It is important that the departments are deeply involved in the process of corporate planning. This involvement is likely to be expressed through the development of departmental planning units and through inter-departmental groups designed to bring to bear on a wide range of problems, the different skills and experience present in the authority.

A few authorities have tried to avoid the creation of a central corporate planning unit, which depends on the inter-departmental groups and special departmental forward planning units. It is however unlikely that in the long run these will provide sufficient support. In the long run corporate planning will probably require the protection, suggested above, of a special unit.

The recommendations of the Bains Group on management structure in the new authorities reflect these developments.

Corporate Planning and Structure Planning

Corporate planning in a local authority has developed only recently. There are however other developed forms of planning in local government. Corporate planning does not remove the need for these other forms of planning. Rather it sets a framework within which they can operate more effectively. This can be illustrated by examining the relationship between corporate planning and physical planning. Physical planning operates within the system laid down by the 1968 Planning Act, which requires the production by local authorities of differing types of plan (structure plans, district plans, local plans, etc.). In this section the relationships between corporate planning and structure planning are examined, but the same issues arise in respect of other parts of the physical planning system.

Corporate planning is concerned with all the activities of the authority, whether they involve physical development or social action. Structure planning is concerned with physical development. Corporate planning includes, not merely those activities of the authority that involve capital expenditure, but also those that involve revenue expenditure. Indeed, included are those activities that involve little or no direct local authority expenditure because they use the licensing, inspection and approval functions of the authority or because they involve the use of the authority's influence on other bodies. The impact of corporate planning can be best realised when it is recognised that it covers these activities that are never mentioned in the structure plan and are only peripheral to the financial budget.

It will be argued that the structure plan is concerned with more than corporate planning because it is concerned with more than the activities of the authority, because it is concerned with private as well as public action. But this is to misunderstand the nature of corporate planning. Structure planning looks outward. But it is not unique in that. No service of the local authority can be adequately planned without understanding the community it serves. Education, social services, transportation, libraries have as much impact on the private sector as the public sector and can only be adequately planned if that impact is understood. If this is true of the individual services, it is even more true of corporate planning which is concerned with the cumulative impact of many activities on the environment. In this respect there is no difference between structure planning and corporate planning. They must both look outward to the environment with which they are concerned.

But there is a more important reason why structure planning should not be treated as wider in scope than corporate planning. The structure plan is itself part of the activities of the authority. If corporate planning covers the activities of the authority, then it covers structure planning. This may seem a trivial point, but it is fundamental. Unless accepted it means that structure planning is to be treated as separate from the main policy planning processes of the authority. But this could mean that a local authority pursued separate policies under corporate planning from the policies pursued under structure planning. If it is accepted that a local authority should look outward from the organisation to the environment, it is difficult to argue against the view that it should pursue the same purposes for its area in the allocation of land, the development of its services and in the use of its influence. Planning departments cannot claim a unique and special role because of the myths built around structure planning.

Perhaps a mere semantic issue has been allowed an importance it does not deserve. The way ahead lies in the building not of one plan —for there will always be many plans—but of one process, a corporate planning process from which many plans can emerge. It does not matter what it is called, provided it is conceived on a corporate basis. The danger of structure planning is that it will be conditioned by the physical traditions on which it is based. A structure planning process that was comprehensive in scope and drew on the corporate resources of the authority would embody the ideas of corporate planning and include all its characteristics. It would not then matter whether it was called corporate planning or structure planning. The aim is one planning process drawing upon all the resources of the authority to deal with the problems it faces. From the one process many plans can emerge.

Main Lines of Development

Corporate planning is in a stage of its development. The need for corporate planning is being recognised. It is likely that a large number of the new authorities will introduce forms of corporate planning. Those authorities will be acting under the impact of the Bains Report which urged the new authorities[10] to adopt a corporate approach to their affairs in order to ensure that their resources are most effectively deployed.

and emphasised that[11]

It is of the essence of the corporate approach to management which we are advocating that there should be a realistic attempt to plan ahead on an authority-wide basis, to formulate objectives, evaluate alternative methods of achieving those objectives and measure the effectiveness of ultimate performance against those objectives.

As already stressed, the Bains Report gave little guidance on how corporate planning was to be introduced. While many of the new authorities are likely to accept the need for corporate planning, it is also likely that they will be reluctant to set up, at the outset, comprehensive systems of corporate planning. They will be attracted by a learning approach that will lay a basis that can be developed as the new authority learns from its experience.

Three steps are suggested:

1. *Improved environmental analysis*
The systematic identification by the new local authority of gaps in its understanding of the environment in which it operates and a strategy for filling those gaps.

2. *Position statement*
An explicit statement of the policies inherited by the new authority and provision for the updating of this statement as decisions are made by the new authority.

3. *Annual policy reviews*
A requirement that each department or committee should prepare a major annual review of its policies, analysing achievement, describing changes in the problems faced, identifying key issues for analysis in depth and appraising the results of such analysis.

These are all steps that the new authority can take without a major commitment. Yet they provide the local authority with an explicit statement of its policies and a process of policy review against a background of a developing understanding of the environment. An authority that took these steps would have gone far to building corporate planning and a base for future development.

The value of pursuing a gradual approach—provided the learning approach is not an excuse for inaction—is that forces are at work which are likely to modify the nature of corporate planning. Corporate planning in some authorities has been built at the centre of the local authority, focusing on the activities of the authority and as an officer-structured system.

These features are not inherent in corporate planning. It is rather that corporate planning has inherited certain of the characteristics of the local authorities in which it has been developed. The traditional structure of the local authority, it could be argued, has tended to depoliticise the process of community and environmental management, concentrating the attention of councillors upon the details of administration rather than the conflicts of policy. The role of the local authority in the government of its area has been underemphasised, as opposed to its role in the administration of services. The traditional process has been highly centralised within the departmental hierarchy.

It is because some developments in corporate planning have inherited traditions of a centralised, apolitical, administrative process, that further change is required. These changes would centre on the need for new dimensions in the management of the local authority. They require an emphasis upon

the wider role of the local authority in its concern for its area— the assertive authority;

the political nature of the local authority—the political authority;

the need for a recognition of the localities within the city—the responsive authority.

This will require a development on three dimensions:

The community dimension, in which the local authority will give a lead in the development of community planning between public authorities—a need that becomes yet more urgent in a situation where the responsibility for the main urban problems is divided between county, district, area health authorities and regional water authorities. If to date, the emphasis has been upon corporate planning within an authority, a new emphasis to community planning between authorities will have to be given after 1 April 1974. This can only adequately be built upon a basis of corporate planning within an authority. In this, both county and district have a role to play. At times it may have to be an assertive role, highlighting problems created by other public agencies, by use of its representatives on outside bodies, by use of the equivalent of a government green paper exploring major policy issues and the equivalent of committees of enquiries. The local authority must be prepared to assert itself, but it must also be willing to co-operate. New forms of joint committees, joint working and joint use of resources are required between the public authorities engaged in community and environmental management.

The political dimension, to which the local authority should be more effectively structured. This perhaps requires three changes, of which the move to explicit policy-making is one, provided that the policies are stated in terms that expose political choice rather than hide it. It also requires new roles for the councillor. Too often the councillor is imprisoned by the agenda of the committees on which he serves. Roles in which he can explore policy issues in depth before they are formalised into committee papers, or investigate their impact after they have been implemented, need to be developed. Above all he needs independent support by information, research and analysis services. At present he depends upon one source of information—the chief officer and his department. Without alternative sources he has no basis for challenge. The political dimension needs its own support.

The areal dimension would recognise that corporate planning, to be effective, cannot be built at the centre. This assumes a uniformity within the area of the local authority that does not exist. There are issues appropriate to the whole of the county or the whole of the district, but not all issues require to be handled at that level. Maybe both within the political and the management process, recognition is required for localities within the authority. The area committee within the district and the county, composed of the councillors elected for a given area would recognise politically a dimension long neglected. Area decentralisation of administration could parallel this political decentralisation within the limits set by authority-wide policies.

The dimensions explored above are important; more important

than the specific proposals put forward for recognising those dimensions in the management processes of the local authority. Their importance is that unless these dimensions are recognised, it is likely that corporate planning will be limited in its impact because it will be built on traditional styles of local government management. It is perhaps because change is required on many dimensions, that many authorities will adopt a learning approach to corporate planning. As they learn, so will corporate planning change.

References

1 Committee on the Management of Local Government, vol. 1, para. 98 (HMSO, 1967).
2 *ibid.* p. 44.
3 The New Local Authorities, Management and Structure, para. 2.10 to 2.11 (HMSO, 1972).
4 Traffic in Towns (HMSO, 1963).
5 Children in their Primary Schools (HMSO, 1967).
6 Report of the Committee on Local Authority and Allied Personal Social Services (HMSO, 1968).
7 Royal Commission Report on Local Government in England 1966 to 1969, vol. 1, para. 253.
8 City of Coventry, *Summary of Management Handbook*, para. 5.3a (February 1972).
9 Stockport County Borough, *Position Statement 1972*, foreword, pp. iii to iv.
10 The New Local Authorities, Management and Structure, p. xv (HMSO, 1972).
11 *ibid.* para. 7.24.

9. Conclusions

Michael J. Bruton

The techniques and procedures of town planning as 'a process, involving a recurring cycle of operations, for preparing and controlling the implementation of plans for changing systems of land use and settlement of varying scale'[1] have been altered dramatically by the provisions of the Town and Country Planning Acts of 1968 and 1971. These acts developed in response to the review by the Planning Advisory Group of the planning system operated under the 1947 Town and Country Planning Act.[2] This group confirmed that the inordinate delays experienced under the 1947 Act system were a symptom of the general inability of this system to cope with current physical planning problems. They found that the 1947 style development plans:

1. Were basically land-use allocation maps which provided little scope for influencing either the form of development or the quality of the physical environment produced.

2. Were unsuited for dealing with large-scale and long-term policy matters and could not cope with issues at the regional and subregional scale.

3. Failed to provide an adequately detailed framework for dealing with issues at the local level.

4. Were inflexible and incapable of readily adapting to changing conditions and circumstances.

5. Were produced through an extraordinarily cumbersome process which made them and subsequent developments subject to inordinate delays.

In reviewing this system the group aimed to improve the technical quality of development plans, strengthen their policy content, simplify planning administration and achieve a level of responsibility commensurate with the type of planning action proposed (i.e. local matters should be settled locally, whereas matters of fundamental policy should be approved at ministerial level). Their proposals, which were introduced through the Town and Country Planning Act 1968, replaced the old style development plans by a range of plans, each having a specific form and purpose, namely:

Structure plans—statements of policy on strategic issues for as far ahead as can be reasonably foreseen, and concerned with the physical system of the area and the way in which it interacts with the social and economic systems.

Local plans—for detailed proposals developed within the context of the structure plan and taking the form of a district plan (where the issues in a local planning matter need to be set out and resolved in a comprehensive way), a subject plan (where specific problems can be tackled outside of a time-table or the constraints of a physical plan) or an action area plan (where the local authority can deal with those issues of development, redevelopment and renewal which it intends to implement within a comparatively short space of time).

At the same time as the physical planning process was being reviewed and changed, there was intense activity in other related fields. In transport, local authorities were attempting to meet the requirements of circular 1/64,[3] which advocated using land-use transportation studies to achieve a co-ordinated approach to land-use and transport studies. Initially this was seen as being solely a matter of using land-use as an 'input' control, to derive estimates of future traffic flows and patterns of movement. With time the full potential of transport planning to shape and modify the structure of urban areas was realised (if not practised) and the inter-relationship between land-use planning and transport planning began to take on a new significance. Unfortunately, the developments in transport planning occurred in parallel with, but almost entirely divorced from, the developments in land-use planning. The 1968 Town and Country Planning Act now requires that the inter-relationship between traffic and land-use be analysed as part of the emergent planning process, and the problems resolved in a comprehensive and co-ordinated way. Although local authorities are working to this end, and most accept that transport planning and policy must be considered in conjunction with land-use planning, few accept the fact that transport planning and policy is an integral

229

aspect of the land-use planning process. There are many indications that the dichotomy between land-use planning and transport planning will continue in the immediate future. That is despite the requirements of the Transport Act 1968, which set up the passenger transport authorities for the conurbations, and the Local Government Act 1972, which requires the new metropolitan and county councils to develop policies which will promote the provision of a co-ordinated and efficient system of public passenger transport. During the same period developments in the economic and social planning fields were also occurring—again in parallel with but outside the field of physical planning. In the 1960s the government embarked on a programme of indicative economic planning, with the objective of increasing the rate of economic growth, rather than securing the optimal allocation of national resources. As part of this programme it set up the National Economic Development Council to establish the essential conditions for realising potential economic growth, and, through the regional economic planning councils and boards, attempted to give an indication of the implications of differential economic growth for the various regions. These regional economic planning councils and boards have contact with the planning system of local authorities, but the relationship is limited and advisory. Now, although economic planning within the government is a reality at the national and regional levels, the degree of interaction between economic factors and the physical planning process at the regional, sub-regional and local levels is minimal. Economic policies ultimately require physical expression, whilst land use policies make demands on economic resources, yet the two processes are kept separate and there is no statute requiring economic planning to be adopted. If realistic economic objectives and constraints are not considered as part of the physical planning process, then the chances of securing certain fundamental physical planning objectives are considerably reduced. Although the 1968 Town and Country Planning Act requires that structure plans be concerned with the social, economic, and physical systems of an area, this concern is limited to the extent to which these systems can be controlled or influenced in a physical way. In the absence of a defined process of economic planning the task of physical planners is made that much more difficult.

Similarly, the absence of a defined and formalised process of social planning makes it difficult to establish a clear relationship between it and physical planning. This difficulty is further complicated by the fact that those who practise different aspects of what could be considered to be social planning have a variety of definitions of social planning. To some it is a means of eliminating the many inequalities associated with social stratification. To others it is a means of improving the quality of municipal social services.

However, the setting up of the new departments of social services in local authorities, under the Local Authorities (Social Services) Act 1970, is a first step towards formalising some aspects of social planning. These new departments will be concerned with social welfare functions, and are intended to provide a community-based and family-orientated service concerned with more than the rescue of social casualties. Similarly the proposed reorganisation of the National Health Service setting up area health authorities to plan, organise and administer comprehensive health services to meet the needs of their areas will formalise other aspects of social planning. Physical planning can adjust to this limited but formalised structure for aspects of social planning. But social planning involves more than a concern with municipal social services—in essence it should be concerned with the processes of change and development within the whole community, enveloping physical, economic, political and cultural components. Until this more comprehensive view of social planning is accepted and formalised, the relationship between social planning and physical planning will be an uneasy one.

The net result of these developments and changes has been one of confusion and uncertainty for both professional town planners and for the public at large. The public has in recent years given voice to its disillusionment with the end product of planning activities, especially road proposals. It can identify and understand physical planning; it wants to be involved in the decision-making process and to be convinced of the validity of the proposals being put forward. However it is often unaware of the inter-relationships which exist between physical, social and economic planning, and the problems of defining and formalising the roles of social and economic planning.

Practising town planners are uncertain as to their position in relation to social, economic and transport planning and in relation to the role of the public in the whole process. They are aware of the inter-relationships between physical, social and economic planning; they are aware that social and economic and transport planning are evolving in such a way that these inter-relationships are often ignored; they find it difficult to practise town planning in the absence of clear-cut and formalised social and economic policies. In these circumstances it is understandable but unacceptable for some town planners to attempt to interpret and develop social and economic policies of their own to provide what in their eyes constitutes a more satis-factory framework within which they can practise. Such a step in-variably results in misunderstanding, misinterpretation, wrong policies and wrong decisions. It also antagonises those who are practising certain aspects of social and economic planning and makes co-ordination and co-operation that much more difficult.

Against the background of the development of the new concept of structure and physical planning, the evolution of the transport planning process, and the development of aspects of social and economic planning, the administrators within local authorities are developing a process which enables them to deal more effectively with the problems of their areas, whether these involve physical development or social action, capital or revenue expenditure and the resources of land, or personnel. This process, now known as corporate planning, aims to co-ordinate the many types of planning practised by local authorities, and to ensure that they work towards the achievement of compatible objectives in a complementary way. However, local authorities are not required by law to adopt cor-porate planning, and there is no ready-made profession from which corporate planners can be drawn at short notice. Yet the develop-ment of corporate planning is highly significant for town planning because it allows a framework of policy and constraint to be developed within which physical planning can operate. Corporate planning is concerned with all the activities of the local authority, whether they involve physical or social action. It is orientated towards the availability of resources and priorities in their use. Thus it can be used to provide a framework within which social, economic, transport, health, housing, education, recreation and other client-based policies can be developed in a realistic and complementary way. It can determine priorities in the implementation of these policies, and it allows the inter-relationship between these policies and physical planning to be more readily determined.

There are no set procedures in corporate planning, and different local authorities are feeling their way towards a process which best fits their particular problems and circumstances. The approaches adopted to date range from, at one extreme, a centralised planning approach (which provides the stimulus for the derivation of the various plans produced by the authority) through an 'explicit statement and review of policy' approach, to 'no approach to corporate planning'. However, in those authorities where the corporate approach is taking shape, there is already a better understanding of the contribution of physical planning to the total planning function of the authority. At the same time the complexity of the interrelationships between the various forms of planning, and the extent of our imperfect understanding of it, are better appreciated.

In some quarters, possibly because of the non-statutory basis of corporate planning and the statutory basis of structure planning, it is argued that the structure plan and its related development planning, can and should become the main policy instrument of the local authority. Indeed in the short term this is likely to be the case, as corporate planning procedures may take some time to become established in many local authorities. However, the adoption of this approach in the long term would be to misunderstand the concept of both corporate planning, which is concerned with all the activities of a local authority, and structure planning, which is concerned with one major aspect of the local authorities' activities—namely physical development. Corporate planning provides a framework within which physical and other forms of planning can operate more effectively. To practise physical planning without this framework is to make a difficult task even more difficult. Within the framework provided by corporate planning there is every reason to hope that physical planning will be able to make a more positive contribution to securing the solution or amelioration of many of the social problems which motivated the founders of the town planning movement, and the early practitioners.

References

1 *Progress Report on Membership Policy—Revised Scheme for the Final Examination* (Town Planning Institute, May 1967).
2 Report of the Planning Advisory Group on the Production of Development Plans (HMSO, 1964).
3 Ministry of Transport and Ministry of Housing and Local Government, circular 1/64, Buchanan report on traffic in towns (HMSO, 1964).